Writing the research paper

A handbook

Anthony C. Winkler

Jo Ray McCuen

GLENDALE COLLEGE

D0048012

HBJ Harcourt Brace Jovanovich, Inc.

NEW YORK   SAN DIEGO   CHICAGO   SAN FRANCISCO   ATLANTA

ISBN: 0-15-598290-7

Library of Congress Catalog Card Number: 78-73967

Printed in the United States of America

Figure Credits

Page 27, Figure 4-1: Reprinted with the permission of the R. R. Bowker Company, 1180 Ave. of the Americas, New York, N.Y., 10036. Copyright © 1977 by Xerox Corporation.

Page 29, Figure 4-2: (From p. 791) *Book Review Digest,* copyright © 1976, 1977 by The H. W. Wilson Company. Material reproduced by permission of the publisher.

Page 31, Figure 4-3: From the *New York Times Index,* 1976, Vol. 64, copyright © 1976, 1977 by The New York Times Co. Reprinted by permission.

Page 32, Figure 4-4: (From p. 914) *Readers' Guide to Periodical Literature,* copyright © 1976, 1977 by The H. W. Wilson Company. Material reprinted by permission of the publisher.

Page 33, Figure 4-5: (From p. 449) *Social Sciences Index,* copyright © 1975, 1976 by The H. W. Wilson Company. Material reprinted by permission of the publisher.

Page 35, Figure 4-6: From *Webster's New Collegiate Dictionary,* copyright © 1977 by G. & C. Merriam Co., publishers of the Merriam-Webster Dictionaries. Reprinted by permission.

Page 36, Figure 4-7: From *Roget's International Thesaurus,* 4th edition, revised by Robert L. Chapman, copyright © 1977 by the Thomas Y. Crowell Company. All rights reserved.

Page 39, Figure 4-8: From the *International Who's Who 1976–1977,* Europa Publications Ltd., London.

Page 42, Figure 4-9: (From p. 13) *Biography Index,* copyright © 1977 by The H. W. Wilson Company. Material reproduced by permission of the publisher.

Preface

This project began with a simple assumption: that research paper texts, like dictionaries, are never read, but merely consulted. Moreover, they are consulted only for specific information about the process of preparing a research paper: how to narrow a topic; where to find information about government publications; how to mark an editorial interpolation in a manuscript.

In intent and design, therefore, *Writing the Research Paper: A Handbook* unabashedly resembles a dictionary. No one part of this book is dependent for continuity upon another. Instead, the process of writing a research paper is atomized and presented in minuscule steps that are carefully explained and catalogued under separate, indexed heads. Students may thus use as much of the book as they need, or as little.

The student is not assumed to have previous research experience. Every aspect of research paper writing is explained to him or her. The student gets advice on finding and narrowing the topic. General and specialized references are annotated to show their usefulness. Preparation of both the literary and the nonliterary paper is given in detail, and an example of each included in the text. The more sophisticated researcher, for whom some parts of the book will be superfluous, will nevertheless find many entries that are indispensable.

Finally, *Writing the Research Paper: A Handbook* is based on the most recent (1977) edition of the *MLA Handbook*. MLA now favors endnotes over footnotes, a departure from tradition that, we suspect, many instructors will resist. Leaving the final choice up to the individual instructor, we thoroughly explain the format of both endnotes and footnotes and demonstrate each in separate papers. The general paper, *Rasputin's Other Side,* uses endnotes; the literary paper, *Shakespeare's Cosmology,* uses footnotes.

Thanks go to William J. Strange, Marshall E. Nunn, Vitalia E. Aguero, Lillian V. Webb, and Aglae I. Webster for their help in locating sources and annotating the bibliography; and to John McCuen and Cathy Winkler for their advice and assistance in preparing the manuscript.

ANTHONY C. WINKLER

JO RAY McCUEN

Contents

nine Documentation 165

one

Basic information about the research paper

1a

Definition of the research paper

The research paper is a typewritten paper in which students present their views and research findings on a chosen topic. Variously known as the "term paper" or the "library paper," the research paper is usually between five and fifteen pages long, with most teachers specifying a minimum length. No matter what the paper is called, the student's task is essentially the same: to read on a particular topic, gather information about it, and report the findings in a paper.

1b

Format of the research paper

The research paper cannot be written according to a random formula, but must conform to a specific format, such as the one devised by the Modern Language Association, a society of language scholars. The format governs the entire paper from the placing of the title to the width of the margins, and to the notation used in acknowledging material drawn from other sources. By writing the paper the student learns how to do library research and becomes familiar with the format a majority of language scholars have agreed to use in their papers. For instance, a student might come across the following paragraph in a paper about bilingually handicapped children:

> In a study of bilingual Chinese children in Hawaii and monolingual children in the United States, "it was found that in either language the bilingual group was below the average of monolinguals of the same age."[4] Only "the superior bilingual child," who is more adept at concept formation and has a greater mental flexibility, is capable of performing as well or better than the monolingual child.[5]

The superscript number 4 tells the reader that the quoted material was taken from a source identified after this number at the end of the paper. Turning to the end of the paper, the student finds the following entry:

[4] Catherine Landreth, *Early Childhood Behavior and Learning* (New York: Alfred A. Knopf, Inc., 1969), p. 194.

This entry—known as an endnote—contains the information necessary for any reader to track down the quotation to its original source. Author, title, place of publication, publisher, year of publication, and page number are recorded in a specific and conventional order. The endnote after the superscript number 5, on the other hand, merely reads:

[5] Landreth, p. 194.

2

This is a subsequent reference; publication information has already been given in the initial reference.

In sum, the format of scholarly writing is simply an agreed-upon way of doing things—much like etiquette, table manners, or rules of the road. This sort of standardization is as time-saving to scholars as standardization of pipe fittings is to plumbers. Once familiar with the conventions of research writing, readers can spend their time pondering the wisdom of an author rather than puzzling over his peculiar format.

1c
Reasons for the research paper

One obvious reason has already been mentioned in passing, namely that the experience familiarizes the student with the conventions of scholarly writing. The student learns the conventions of the footnote, the bibliography, the ethics of research, and the rudiments of scholarly writing.

A second reason is that students become familiar with the library through the "learn by doing" method. Even the simplest library is an intricate storehouse of information, bristling with indexes, encyclopedias, abstracts, and gazetteers. How to ferret out from this maze of sources a single piece of needed information is a skill that students learn by doing actual research. The ability to use a library is a priceless skill, because sooner or later everyone needs to find out about something: a mother needs to know how to stop her child from biting his fingernails; a physician, how to treat a rare illness; a lawyer, how to successfully argue an unusual case. Everyone can profit from knowing how to do research.

Third, writing the research paper teaches an appreciation for the intricacies and difficulties of research. We are all prone to whine about why "they" can't find a cure for the common cold, or why "they" can't devise a simple income-tax form, or why "they"—meaning by "they" the innumerable specialists and authorities who affect our lives—can't do one thing or another. The experience of doing actual research tends to squash this sort of pointless griping. Discovering for themselves the complexity of apparently simple and straightforward subjects, students learn to appreciate the labors of the researcher and the scholar, and to regard the results of their work more kindly.

There are other benefits besides. Writing the research paper is a complicated and trying exercise in logic, imagination, and common sense. As students chip away at the mass of data and information available on their chosen topics, they learn

- how to think
- how to organize

- how to discriminate between worthless and useful opinions
- how to summarize the gist of wordy material
- how to budget their time
- how to conceive of a research project from the start, manage it through its intermediary stages, and finally assemble the information uncovered into a useful, coherent paper.

1d

Steps involved in writing a research paper

Generally, there are seven distinct steps.

- A topic must be selected that is complex enough to be researched from a variety of sources, but narrow enough to be covered in ten or so pages.
- Exploratory reading and research must be done on the chosen topic.
- The information gathered must be recorded on note cards and assembled into a coherent sequence.
- A thesis statement must be drafted, setting forth the idea the student wishes to argue, prove, disprove, or support.
- The paper must be outlined in its major stages.
- The paper must be written and the thesis argued, proved, or supported, with the information uncovered by research. Borrowed ideas, data, and opinions must be acknowledged in footnotes.
- A bibliography must be prepared listing all the books, articles, films, and other sources from which information, data, and opinion were taken.

Ordinarily, writing the research paper takes in all these stages, although not necessarily in this exact order.

1e

The report paper and the thesis paper

The two kinds of papers usually assigned in colleges are the report paper and the thesis paper. The report paper summarizes and reports a writer's findings on a particular subject. The writer neither judges nor evaluates the findings, but merely catalogs them in a sensible sequence. For instance, a paper that listed the opinions of statesmen during the debate over the Panama Canal treaty would be a report paper. Likewise, a paper that chronologically narrated the final days of Hitler would also be a report paper.

Unlike the report paper, the thesis paper takes a definite stand on an issue. A thesis is a proposition or point of view that a writer or speaker is willing to argue against or defend. A paper that argued for ratification of the Panama Canal treaty would therefore be a thesis paper. So would a paper that attempted to prove that Hitler's political philosophy was influenced by the writings of the philosopher Nietzsche. Here are a few more examples of topics as they might conceivably be treated in report papers and thesis papers:

Report paper: A summary of the theories of hypnosis.
Thesis paper: Hypnosis is simply another form of Pavlovian conditioning.

Report paper: The steps involved in passage of federal legislation.
Thesis paper: Lobbyists have a disproportionate amount of influence on federal legislation.

Teachers are more likely to assign a thesis paper than a report paper, for obvious reasons. Writing the thesis paper requires the student to exercise judgment, evaluate evidence, and construct a logical argument, whereas writing the report paper does not.

two

Choosing a topic

2a

How to choose a topic

Because topic selection is almost entirely a matter of common sense, it can be astoundingly difficult. Students often err by choosing a topic that is either too vast or too trivial. Ordinarily, vastness comes first. Ambitious students writing a first research paper tend to opt for mammoth and spectacular topics such as "Wars in the World," "The Reasons Why the North Won the American Civil War," or "The Division of Labor between the Sexes throughout History." But after vainly trying to make sense out of the millions of words that have been penned on these mysteries, students usually despair and rethink the topic. What is required, they reason, is something less weighty. From "Wars in the World" and "Division of Labor between the Sexes," they flee to "Badges Worn by Cub Scouts" or "High-Altitude Baking." But a trivial, insignificant topic is just as perplexing to write about. Trivia is frustrating to research; often, the trivial topic yields only one or two research sources—not enough to build a paper on; always, such a topic will bore both student and teacher, making the paper just as maddening to read as it is to write.

Ideally, students should choose a topic that interests them, that is complex enough to generate several research sources, and that will neither bore nor stultify. This is more difficult than it sounds. We offer the following advice.

- Don't just grab on to "any old topic." A casually chosen topic will eventually have you tearing your hair and will most likely result in a bad paper.
- Pick a subject that you're curious about, or that you're either an expert on or are genuinely interested in. For example, if you have always been intrigued by the character of Rasputin, the "mad monk" of Russia, you can learn more about him by using him as the topic of your paper. Similarly, an interest in the career of Elvis Presley might lead to a paper analyzing and evaluating his music.
- If you are utterly at a loss for a subject, have positively no interest in anything at all, and cannot for the life of you imagine what you could write ten whole pages on, then go to the library and browse. Pore over books, magazines, card catalogs. No matter how tormented with emptiness you may be, you are bound to find something that will fascinate you. It may be something stupendously huge, but never mind. Once you've got an area of interest, you can generally narrow it down to a specific and exciting topic (see **2c** below).

2b
Topics to avoid

Some topics present unusual difficulties; others are simply a waste of time. Here is a summary of topics to avoid.

2b-1 Topics that are too big

We have mentioned this already. We will only add that the research paper, though it may be the longest writing assignment you will receive during the semester, is still scarcely longer than a short magazine article. Obviously, you can neither review the evolution of man nor completely fathom the mysteries of creation in ten pages. Don't even try. Regrettably, we cannot even give you a good rule of thumb for avoiding impossibly broad topics. Use your common sense. Check the card catalog. If you find that numerous books have been written about your topic, then it is probably too big. The signs that you may have bitten off more than you can chew usually come only after you're already deeply mired in the research. Reference sources that multiple like flies; a bibliography that grows like a cancer; opinions, data, and information that come pouring in from hundreds of sources—these signs all indicate a topic that is too big. The solution is to narrow the topic without darting to the sanctuary of the trivial. Here are some examples of hopelessly big topics: "The Influence of Greek Mythology on Poetry"; "The Rise and Fall of Chinese Dynasties"; "The Framing of the U.S. Constitution."

2b-2 Topics that are too controversial

Controversy can often muddy up a topic, drowning the student in perplexing contradictions. Facts become impossible to separate from opinions; experts pick at each other; the air is thick with claims and counterclaims. In the midst of all this row, the student's own bias is likely to emerge, slanting the paper in favor of one side over another. If the teacher is of an entirely different opinion, the paper will simply antagonize him or her. Controversial topics aren't worth the trouble they can cause. Some students handle controversial topics well and manage to pick their way through masses of dissenting opinions, but the great majority do not and therefore should avoid such topics. Here are a few examples of controversial topics: "Why College Test Scores Have Fallen Dramatically"; "Reasons Why Lovers Should Live Together out of Wedlock"; "Prayers Should Be Banned from the Public Schools."

2b-3 Topics that can be traced to a single source

Research papers must be documented with a variety of opinions drawn from different authorities and sources. One reason for assigning the research paper in the first place is to expose the students to the opinions of different authorities, to a variety of books and articles, and to other reference sources. Consequently, if the topic is so skimpy that all data on it can be culled from a single source, the purpose of the paper is defeated. Choose only topics that are broad enough to be researched from multiple sources. The following topics can be traced to a single source and are therefore unsuitable for a term paper: "How to Macrame a Wall Hanger"; "Basket Weaving among the Zulus"; "The Meaning of the Stations of the Cross in Catholic Ritual"; "Where to Find Second-Hand Parts for Bentley Automobiles."

2b-4 Topics that are too technical

A student may have an astonishing expertise in one technical subject, and may be tempted to display this dazzling knowledge in a research paper. Resist the temptation. Technical subjects often require a technical jargon that the teacher might not understand and might even dismiss as an elaborate "snow job." The skills that a research paper should instill in the student are better displayed in a paper on a general subject. Stick to some subject broad enough to be understood by any decently educated reader. The following are examples of overly technical topics: "The Use of Geometry in the Perspective of Paolo Uccelo"; "Heisenberg's Principle of Indeterminacy as It Applies to Subparticle Research"; "Utilitarianism versus Positivism in Legal Rights Cases Involving Minorities."

2b-5 Topics that are too trivial

We've already struck a glancing blow against trivial topics, and will now have done with the entire subject. Obviously, your own common sense and judgment must steer you away from such topics, but here are some that teachers would reject as too trivial: "The Use of Orthopedic Braces for Dachshunds Prone to Backaches"; "The Cult of Van Painting in America"; "The History of the Tennis Ball"; "How to Get Dates When You're Divorced."

2c
Narrowing the topic

Big, monster-sized topics are easy enough to think of, probably because big issues such as feminism, civil rights, and human aggression, are constantly bandied about in the press and in casual talk. But it is a serious mistake to try to corral one of these monsters in a ten-page paper. First, it is difficult to make sense out of the millions of words in the library on such issues. Deluged with innumerable sources, most of which he simply hasn't got the time to go through, the student ends up choosing a few random sources out of hundreds, with the attendant risk of making a bad, unrepresentative choice. Second, apart from being more difficult to research, the big topic is also more difficult to write about: one never knows quite where to begin, and one never knows how to end without seeming silly. Third, omissions and oversights are nowhere more crudely obvious than in a small paper on a big topic.

The first step, then, once a general subject area is found, is to narrow it down to a suitably small topic. There is no easy or set way of doing this. One must simply be guided by the available sources and information; again, common sense must come into play. No python knows the exact dimensions of its mouth, but any python instinctively knows that it cannot swallow an elephant. Experiment with your topic: pursue one train of thought and see where it leads, and whether or not it yields an arguable thesis. Pare down and whittle away until you've got something manageable. Bear in mind that ten pages amount to a very modest length—some books have longer prefaces. Here are a few examples of the narrowing that you'll have to do:

BROAD TOPIC	FIRST NARROWING	FURTHER NARROWING
Mythology	*Beowulf*	Courtesy codes in *Beowulf*
Migrant workers	California migrant workers	Major California labor laws and their impact on Mexican migrant workers
Theater	Theater of the Absurd	Theater-of-the-Absurd elements in *Who's Afraid of Virginia Woolf?*
Jack Kennedy	Jack Kennedy's cabinet	The contribution of Averell Harriman as U.S. Ambassador to Russia
Russia	The Bolshevik Revolution of 1917	The role of Grigory Efimovich Rasputin in pre-revolutionary Russia
Indians	Famous Indian fighters	Major Rogers' Rangers during the Indian wars

The first attempt at narrowing a topic is usually easier than the second, which must yield a specific topic. Use trial and error until you've got a topic you're comfortable with. Further narrowing, if necessary, will suggest itself once you're into the actual research.

three

The library

3a
Layout of the library

Most of the research for your paper will be done at a library. Basic architectural design varies from one library to another, but certain facilities are standard. All well-organized libraries include the following:

3a-1 Card catalog

The card catalog is an alphabetical index of all books in the library. It consists of 3×5 cards that are stored in little drawers, usually near the main entrance of the library. The card catalog lists all books under at least three headings: author, subject, and title. A book that straddles two or more subjects will be listed separately under each subject. If an editor, translator, or illustrator is involved, the book will also be listed under the name of each, in addition to being listed under the name of the author. A jointly authored book is also likely to be listed under the name of each author.

Basic research generally begins with a search of the card catalog, which literally puts a wealth of information at a researcher's fingertips. On pages 15 and 16 are examples of three index cards that list the same book separately.

In combing the card catalog for books and sources on a topic, don't overlook the possibility of finding useful material under separate but related headings. For example, if you are looking for sources on "Pablo Picasso," you should also look under such headings as "Modern Art," "French Art," "Abstract Art," and "Cubism."

3a-2 Stacks

"Stacks" is the name given to the shelves on which the books and periodicals are stored in the library. The stacks may be either *open* or *closed*. If the stacks are open, readers may roam at will among the shelves and handle the books; if the stacks are closed, readers are denied direct access to the shelves, and must obtain books from clerks by listing the title of the book, its author, and its call number on a request slip. Closed stacks are more common at larger libraries; in smaller libraries the stacks are usually open. While slightly inconvenient to a reader, closed stacks reduce the chance of pilferage, misfiling, and defacement of books. Open stacks, on the other hand, allow a reader to browse at leisure.

3a-3 Reference room

Encyclopedias, indexes, gazetteers, and other works that are ordinarily consulted for information, rather than read from cover to cover, are stored in a reference room. Usually large and unwieldy, these volumes

Figure 3-1 Author card (also called "Main entry")

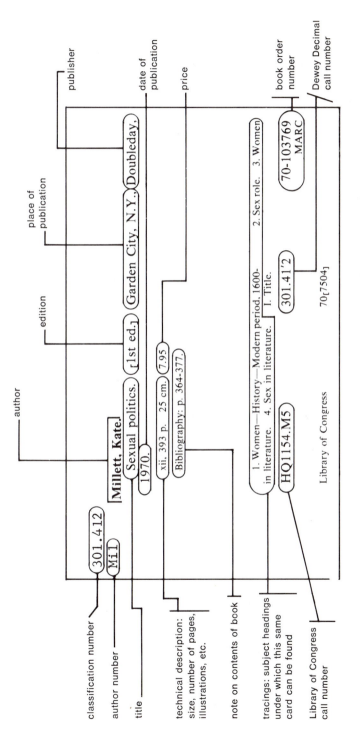

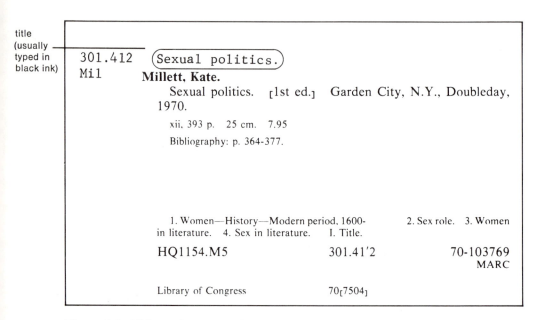

title
(usually
typed in
black ink)

301.412
Mil

Sexual politics.

Millett, Kate.
Sexual politics.   [1st ed.]   Garden City, N.Y., Doubleday,
1970.

xii, 393 p.   25 cm.   7.95

Bibliography: p. 364-377.

1. Women—History—Modern period, 1600-   2. Sex role.   3. Women
in literature.   4. Sex in literature.   I. Title.

HQ1154.M5   301.41'2   70-103769
                                                            MARC

Library of Congress   70[7504]

Figure 3-2   Title card

Figure 3-3   Subject card

subject
heading
(usually
typed in
red ink)

301.412
Mil

WOMEN--HISTORY

Millett, Kate.
Sexual politics.   [1st ed.]   Garden City, N.Y., Doubleday,
1970.

xii, 393 p.   25 cm.   7.95

Bibliography: p. 364-377.

1. Women—History—Modern period, 1600-   2. Sex role.   3. Women
in literature.   4. Sex in literature.   I. Title.

HQ1154.M5   301.41'2   70-103769
                                                            MARC

Library of Congress   70[7504]

16

are generally confined to use within the reference room; they cannot be checked out and taken home.

3a-4 Main desk

The main desk functions as an information center as well as a checkout counter for books. Librarians and clerks stationed here are trained to help the perplexed researcher find material or track down difficult sources. Library personnel can be of invaluable assistance to the hapless beginner; if you are confused and lost, don't be afraid to ask them for help.

3a-5 Reserve desk

Reserve books are kept at the reserve desk. Books on reserve are available for use only in the library and only for a limited time— generally for an hour or two. Teachers will often place on reserve any book or magazine essential to their lectures or courses. When the demand for a book exceeds the supply, the book will often be placed in the reserve collection, which in many libraries is listed in a separate reserve catalog.

3a-6 Audiovisual room

Cassettes, tapes, picture slides, filmstrips, and other nonbook media are stored in an audiovisual room and generally indexed by whatever conventional filing system the library uses (see Dewey Decimal System and Library of Congress System below). The audiovisual librarian will help you locate this kind of material. Often the audiovisual supply room adjoins an equipment area where students can listen to tapes or watch a film. Some libraries, replete with extensive new audiovisual hardware, now call themselves media centers rather than libraries.

3a-7 Microform room

Microfiche and microfilm are stored in a microform room. Microfilm is material photographically stored on filmstrips; microfiche is material photographically mounted on frames. For centuries, back issues of journals, magazines, and newspapers were piled up in dusty heaps in the dark, cobwebbed stock rooms of libraries. But with the advent of cameras that can reduce entire pages to a tiny filmstrip, periodical material is now economically stored in this microscopic form and read with magnifying equipment.

3a-8 Newspaper racks

The newspaper racks are long wooden clamps that hold and store newspapers. Many libraries subscribe to major national and foreign newspapers. Often the newspaper racks are surrounded by comfortable chairs in which a reader can sit for a leisurely assessment of world events. Typical newspapers found in these racks include the *New York Times, Washington Post, Los Angeles Times, Christian Science Monitor, Wall Street Journal, London Times, Manchester Guardian, Hindustan Times,* and *Die Zeit.*

3a-9 Xerox room

Xerox machines are available in most libraries for photocopying. The charge for this service ranges anywhere from a nickel to a quarter.

3a-10 Typing room

Typewriters are available in many libraries either at a reasonable rental or without charge. The machines are usually kept in a designated typing room, which is often soundproof.

3a-11 Carrels

Carrels are small enclosed desks provided with bookshelves, and are especially designed to provide students with a quiet, insulated enclosure for reading or research. The carrel section of a library is set aside for students intent on serious scholarship. Some libraries even impose fines on students caught capering in this area. Carrels can generally be reserved by advanced students for either a semester or an entire school year; the remaining carrels are distributed among lower-division students on a first-come, first-served basis.

3b
Organization of the library

Even the great libraries of antiquity, such as the one in Nineveh in the sixth century B.C., or in Alexandria in the third century B.C., searched constantly for more efficient systems of organizing their collections. Clay tablets were grouped by subject and stored on shelves; papyrus rolls were stacked in labeled jars. The Chinese, whose library tradition dates back to the sixth century B.C., grouped their writings under four primary headings: classics, history, philosophy, and belles lettres. And by 1605 the English philosopher Sir Francis Bacon had independently devised a system of classifying all knowledge into three similar categories of

18

history, poetry, and philosophy, which were then further subdivided to yield specific subjects.

Knowledge has grown so enormously and classification systems have become so complex, that today librarians are trained extensively in classifying books. The two major classification systems now used by libraries are the Dewey Decimal System and the Library of Congress System.

3b-1 The Dewey Decimal System

Devised in 1873 by Melvil Dewey and first put to use in the library of Amherst College, the Dewey Decimal System divides all knowledge (fiction and biography excepted) into ten general categories:

000–099	General Works
100–199	Philosophy and Psychology
200–299	Religion
300–399	Social Sciences
400–499	Language
500–599	Pure Science
600–699	Technology (Applied Sciences)
700–799	The Arts
800–899	Literature
900–999	History

Each of these ten general categories is subdivided into ten smaller divisions. For example, the category of Literature (800–899) is further divided into:

800–809	General Works (about Literature)
810–819	American Literature
820–829	English Literature
830–839	German Literature
840–849	French Literature
850–859	Italian Literature
860–869	Spanish Literature
870–879	Latin Literature
880–889	Greek and Classical Literature
890–899	Literature of Other Languages

The specific category of English Literature is further divided into narrower groups:

820	English Literature (General)
821	Poetry
822	Drama
823	Fiction
824	Essays
825	Speeches

826	Letters
827	Satire and Humor
828	Miscellany
829	Minor Related Literature

An endless number of more specific headings are easily created through the addition of decimal places. For instance, from the category of English Literature—820—the more specific heading of Elizabethan Literature is devised: 822.3. The addition of another decimal place creates an even more specific category for the works of Shakespeare: 822.33.

The obvious advantage of the Dewey Decimal System is the ease with which it yields specific categories to accommodate the rapid proliferation of books. Probably for this reason, the system is currently used in more libraries throughout the world than all other systems combined.

3b-2   The Cutter/Sanborn Author Marks

The Dewey Decimal System is generally used in conjunction with the Cutter/Sanborn Author Marks, devised originally by Charles Ammi Cutter and later merged with a similar system independently invented by Kate Sanborn. The Cutter/Sanborn Author Marks distinguish between books filed under an identical Dewey number. In the early days of the Dewey system, books with the same Dewey number were simply shelved alphabetically by author. But as more and more books were published, alphabetical shelving became impossibly difficult, leading eventually to the invention of the Author Marks.

The Author Marks eliminate alphabetical shelving by assigning a number to every conceivable consonant/vowel or vowel/consonant combination that can be used to spell the beginning of an author's surname. These numbers are published in a table that alphabetically lists the various combinations and assigns each a number. For instance, the "G" section of the Cutter/Sanborn Table lists the following combinations and numbers:

Garf	231
Gari	232
Garl	233
Garn	234
Garnet	235
Garni	236

To assign, for example, an Author Mark to the book, *Double Taxation: A Treatise on the Subject of Double Taxation Relief,* by Charles Edward Garland, a librarian (1) looks up the combination of letters in the Cutter/Sanford Table closest to the spelling of the author's surname—in this case, "Garl," with the number 233; (2) places the first letter of the author's surname before the number; and (3) places after the number the first letter or letters of the first important word in the title, giving an Author Mark of G233d. The call number of the book is its Dewey Decimal number plus its Author Mark:

336.294
G233d

Similarly, the book *Religion and the Moral Life,* by Arthur Campbell Garnett, has a Dewey Decimal number of 170 and an Author Mark of G235r, giving the following call number:

170
G235r

Under this dual system, a book is shelved first by sequence of its Dewey Decimal number, and then by sequence of its Author Mark. To find any title, a student must therefore first locate the Dewey Decimal category on the shelf, and then identify an individual book by its Author Mark.

Fiction and biography are classified in a special way under the Dewey Decimal System. Fiction is marked with the letter "F" and shelved alphabetically by author. For example, F-Pas is the classification of a novel by Boris Pasternak; B-C56 is one of the several biographies about Sir Winston Churchill. If the library has an especially large fiction or biography collection, these books might also be classified under Author Marks.

3b-3 The Library of Congress System

The Library of Congress System is named for the library that invented it. Founded in 1800, the Library of Congress at first simply shelved its books by size. Its earliest catalog, issued in 1802, showed the United States as the owner of 964 books and 9 maps. By 1812 the nation's collection had increased to 3,076 books and 53 maps. By 1897, when the library finally acquired a building of its own, the collection had grown to half a million items and was increasing at the staggering rate of 100,000 per year. The library had acquired such a vast and expansive collection that a new system was necessary for classifying it. Published in 1904, the Library of Congress Classification System has since grown immensely in popularity and is now widely used, especially by larger libraries.

The system represents the main branches of knowledge with twenty-one letters of the alphabet. These branches are further divided by the addition of letters and Arabic numerals up to 9999, allowing for a nearly infinite number of combinations. The system is therefore especially useful for libraries possessing enormous collections. Here is a list of the general categories:

A	General Works—Polygraphy
B	Philosophy—Religion
C	History—Auxiliary Sciences
D	History and Topography (except America)
E–F	America
G	Geography—Anthropology
H	Social Sciences
J	Political Science
K	Law
L	Education
M	Music
N	Fine Arts
P	Language and Literature
Q	Science
R	Medicine
S	Agriculture—Plant and Animal Industry
T	Technology
U	Military Science
V	Naval Science
Z	Bibliography and Library Science

These general categories are narrowed by the addition of letters. Numerous minute subdivisions are possible. The Language and Literature category, designated by "P," is further subdivided thus:

P	Philology and Linguistics: General
PA	Greek and Latin Philology and Literature
PB	Celtic Languages and Literature
PC	Romance Languages (Italian, French, Spanish, and Portuguese)
PD	Germanic (Teutonic) Languages

The addition of numerals makes possible even more minute subdivisions within each letter category. From the general category "P"—Language and Literature—is derived the more specific category of Literary History and Collections, designated by "PN." The call number PN 6511 indicates works dealing with Oriental Proverbs; PN 1993.5 U65, on the other hand, is the call number for a book about the history of motion pictures in Hollywood.

The classification under this system proceeds from the general to the specific, with the longer numbers being assigned to the more specialized books. Like the Dewey Decimal System, the Library of Congress System also uses an author number to differentiate books shelved within a specific category. To locate a book with a Library of Congress classification, the student must first find the subject category on the shelf, and then track down the individual title by its author number.

Figure 3-4 Cross-reference sample catalog cards for nonbook materials

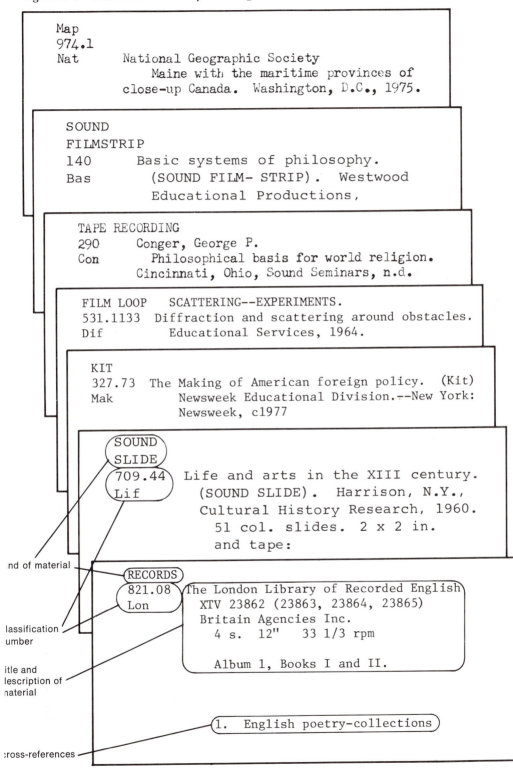

Map
974.1
Nat   National Geographic Society
              Maine with the maritime provinces of
         close-up Canada. Washington, D.C., 1975.

SOUND
FILMSTRIP
140   Basic systems of philosophy.
Bas   (SOUND FILM- STRIP). Westwood
             Educational Productions,

TAPE RECORDING
290   Conger, George P.
Con   Philosophical basis for world religion.
         Cincinnati, Ohio, Sound Seminars, n.d.

FILM LOOP   SCATTERING--EXPERIMENTS.
531.1133 Diffraction and scattering around obstacles.
Dif   Educational Services, 1964.

KIT
327.73 The Making of American foreign policy. (Kit)
Mak   Newsweek Educational Division.--New York:
             Newsweek, c1977

SOUND
SLIDE
709.44 Life and arts in the XIII century.
Lif   (SOUND SLIDE). Harrison, N.Y.,
         Cultural History Research, 1960.
             51 col. slides. 2 x 2 in.
             and tape:

kind of material

RECORDS
821.08 The London Library of Recorded English
Lon   XTV 23862 (23863, 23864, 23865)
         Britain Agencies Inc.
             4 s. 12"   33 1/3 rpm

             Album 1, Books I and II.

classification
number

title and
description of
material

1. English poetry-collections

cross-references

3b-4 Classification of periodicals

Periodicals and newspapers are classified differently from books. Current issues are usually shelved alphabetically by title and are accessible to the public. Back issues, either bound in book form or reproduced on microfilm, are stored elsewhere—usually in a special section of the library to which the public may or may not be admitted, depending on whether the stacks are open or closed.

3b-5 Classification of nonbooks

Nonbook materials—films, microfilms, recordings, news clippings, sheet music, reproductions of masterpieces, transparencies, slides, programmed books, and other audiovisual material—may be listed either in the general catalog or as a special collection. No hard-and-fast rule exists for classifying this kind of material; ask your librarian how it is cataloged. (See Figure 3-4, p. 23.)

four

Finding background sources

4a An annotated list of general references

4b An annotated list of specialized references

■ You've decided on a narrowed topic. The next step is to research the sources available on it. Typical sources include books, magazine or newspaper articles, essays, speeches, documents of various kinds, and any other useful material stored in nonbook form. Someone who is an acknowledged authority on a topic, or has had some unique experience with it, might also be used as a source. For instance, a paper about the antiwar movement in Los Angeles during the 1960s might include eyewitness accounts from actual participants. Research papers, however, are assembled and documented primarily from printed material—the form in which the prevailing body of opinion on most topics generally exists.

The preliminary research should give you an overview of your topic, provide you with some notion about available sources, and produce a tentative bibliography. If your topic is too ambitious, you'll find out now: sources will seem to leap at you from every chink in the library. On the other hand, if your topic is too trivial, you'll soon find yourself poring over stacks and stacks of references and coming up with pitifully few sources.

Since you're merely getting a feel for the topic, note-taking at this point is unnecessary. Browse through the various books, essays, speeches, and articles you find on the topic. Jot down the titles of sources that seem to have useful information; ignore all others. Don't linger interminably over any single book or article; move on from one source to the next, skimming to get an idea of the information each contains.

4a
An annotated list of general references

In the library, information on a topic is likely to be scattered throughout numerous books, magazines, journals, and newspapers, most of which are indexed by general references. Some of these references alphabetically index by author and subject the contents of magazines, journals, and newspapers; other similarly index the titles and contents by available books. The experienced researcher, therefore, usually begins a search for information by consulting the general references.

This section will systematically list the common general references and give a brief description of what they do. General references index information available on a variety of subjects; specialized references, which we will cover later, index information on specific subjects.

4a-1 Books that list other books

The best efforts of ambitious bibliographers cannot produce an exhaustive list of all books in print. Nevertheless, many important references catalog the publication of books. The following are the prime sources for information about existing books.

Paperbound Books in Print. New York: Bowker, 1960–present. Monthly record of paperback books. Contains a cumulative index. Listed here are all paperbacks in print.

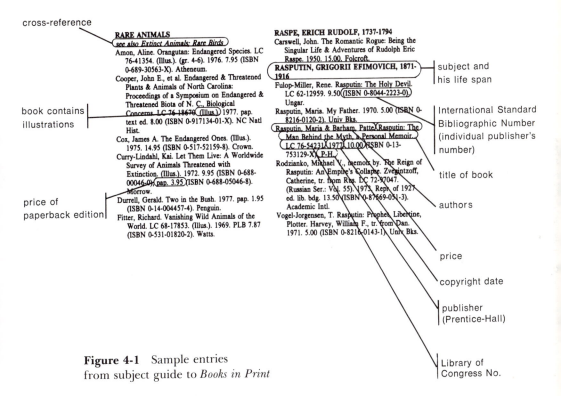

cross-reference

RARE ANIMALS
(see also Extinct Animals: Rare Birds)
Amon, Aline. Orangutan: Endangered Species. LC 76-41354. (Illus.). (gr. 4-6). 1976. 7.95 (ISBN 0-689-30563-X). Atheneum.
Cooper, John E., et al. Endangered & Threatened Plants & Animals of North Carolina: Proceedings of a Symposium on Endangered & Threatened Biota of N. C., Biological text ed. 8.00 (ISBN 0-917134-01-X). NC Natl Hist.

book contains illustrations — Concerns. LC 76-18670. (Illus.). 1977. pap.

Cox, James A. The Endangered Ones. (Illus.). 1975. 14.95 (ISBN 0-517-52159-8). Crown.
Curry-Lindahl, Kai. Let Them Live: A Worldwide Survey of Animals Threatened with Extinction. (Illus.). 1972. 9.95 (ISBN 0-688-00046-0). pap. 3.95 (ISBN 0-688-05046-8). Morrow.

price of paperback edition — Durrell, Gerald. Two in the Bush. 1977. pap. 1.95 (ISBN 0-14-004457-4). Penguin.
Fitter, Richard. Vanishing Wild Animals of the World. LC 68-17853. (Illus.). 1969. PLB 7.87 (ISBN 0-531-01820-2). Watts.

RASPE, ERICH RUDOLF, 1737-1794
Carswell, John. The Romantic Rogue: Being the Singular Life & Adventures of Rudolph Eric Raspe. 1950. 15.00. Folcroft.

RASPUTIN, GRIGORII EFIMOVICH, 1871-1916 — subject and his life span
Fulop-Miller, Rene. Rasputin: The Holy Devil. LC 62-12959. 9.50 (ISBN 0-8044-2223-0). Ungar.
Rasputin, Maria. My Father. 1970. 5.00 (ISBN 0-8216-0120-2). Univ Bks.
Rasputin, Maria & Barham, Patte. Rasputin: The Man Behind the Myth, a Personal Memoir. LC 76-54231. 1977. 10.00. (ISBN 0-13-753129-X). P-H.
Rodzianko, Michael V., memoirs by. The Reign of Rasputin: An Empire's Collapse. Zveginetzoff, Catherine, tr. from Rus. LC 72-97047. (Russian Ser.: Vol. 55). 1973. Repr. of 1927 ed. lib. bdg. 13.50 (ISBN 0-87569-051-3). Academic Intl.
Vogel-Jorgensen, T. Rasputin: Prophet, Libertine, Plotter. Harvey, William F., tr. from Dan. 1971. 5.00 (ISBN 0-8216-0143-1). Univ Bks.

International Standard Bibliographic Number (individual publisher's number)

title of book

authors

price

copyright date

publisher (Prentice-Hall)

Library of Congress No.

Figure 4-1 Sample entries from subject guide to *Books in Print*

Publishers' Trade List Annual. New York: Bowker, 1873–present. Includes publishers' catalogs, alphabetically arranged. Two important indexes accompany this book: *Books in Print: An Author-Title-Series Index* and *Subject Guide to Books in Print: A Subject Index.* Both indexes are published annually. They are useful for checking if a book is still on the market. (See Fig. 4-1.)

Publishers Weekly. Bowker, 1872–present. Weekly record of all books published in the United States. Semiannual issues announce books scheduled for publication.

The catalogs of the following three famous national libraries come closer to achieving bibliographical universality than do any other listings:

Bibliothèque Nationale. *Catalogue général des livres imprimés.* Paris: Imprimerie Nationale, 1900–present.

British Museum, Department of Printed Books. *General Catalogue of Printed Books.* 263 vols. London: British Museum, 1959–66.

U.S. Library of Congress. *A Catalog of Books Represented by Library of Congress Printed Cards Issued to July 31, 1942.* 167 vols. Ann Arbor, Mich.: Edwards, 1942–46. Supplemented by catalogs covering 1942–54, and superseded by *The National Union Catalog: a Cumulative Author List Representing Library of Congress Printed Cards and Titles Reported by Other American Libraries,* 1952–present, and *National Union Catalog, Pre-1956 Imprints.* London: Mansell, 1968–present, to be completed in 610 volumes. Locates books in hundreds of American libraries.

For information on the existence of incunabula—books published before 1500—see the following:

British Museum Library. *Catalogue of Books Printed in the XVth Century Now in the British Museum.* 9 vols. London: British Museum, 1908–62. Valuable for its listing of incunabula.

Gesamtkatalog der Wiegendrücke. 40 vols. Leipzig: Hiersemann, 1925. Lists copies of incunabula found all over the world.

Goff, Frederick R. *Incunabula in American Libraries; a Third Census of Fifteenth-Century Books Recorded in North American Collections.* New York: Bibliographical Society of America, 1964. Locates close to 50,000 copies of incunabula in America.

Lower-division students, although not likely to do research based on incunabula, should know that catalogs exist for them.

4a-2 Books about book reviews

Book reviews evaluate books, acquainting readers and libraries about them. The most useful guides to book reviews are:

Book Review Digest. New York: Wilson, 1905–present. Lists reviews from all major American and English periodicals. Published monthly except for February and July, with annual cumulations. (See Fig. 4-2.)

Book Review Index. Detroit: Gale Research Co., 1965–68, 1972–present. Lists reviews appearing in all periodicals of general circulation.

4a-3 Books about periodicals and newspapers

Since its beginning in the eighteenth century, periodical literature—whether published weekly, monthly, seasonally, in serial form, or simply

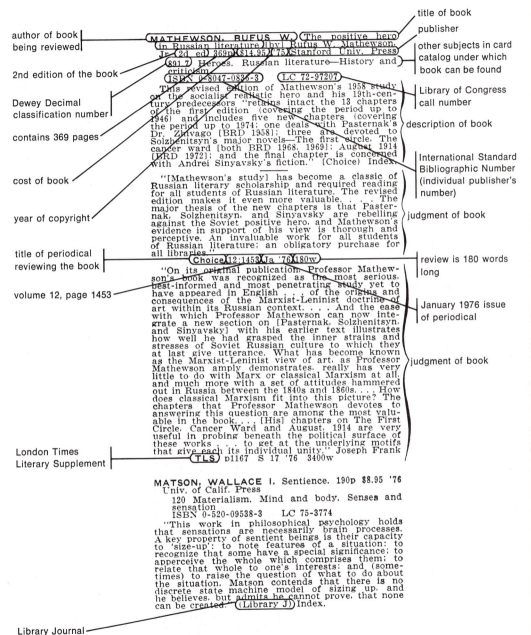

Figure 4-2 Entries from *Book Review Digest*

on a random basis—has become increasingly important for scholarly research, especially in any field where up-to-date knowledge is important. Millions of articles are published annually in periodicals, making a complete indexing of them nearly impossible. However, the following books about periodicals are especially useful:

a. Periodical directories

These list the names, addresses, and titles of magazines. Among the most useful are the following:

Ayer's Directory of Newspapers and Periodicals. Philadelphia: N. W. Ayers and Sons, 1880–present. An annual list of newspapers and periodicals currently published in the United States. The directory is organized by states and cities, and contains indexes.

Editor and Publisher International Year Book. New York: Editor and Publisher, 1920–present. Provides information on newspapers, advertising agencies, syndicates, and other aspects of journalism in the United States, Canada, and foreign countries.

Standard Periodical Directory. New York: Oxbridge, 1964–present. Issued annually, this directory is an exhaustive list of periodicals published in the United States and Canada; arranged by subjects.

Ulrich's International Periodicals Directory. 15th ed. 2 vols. New York: Bowker, 1973. Published biennially. Lists 55,000 foreign and domestic periodicals in the fields of science, technology, medicine, arts, humanities, social sciences, and business. Includes a title and a subject index.

b. Union lists of periodicals and newspapers

Union lists catalog and record the collection of periodical and newspaper titles available in various libraries. The following are among the most prominent union lists:

American Newspapers, 1821–1936; A Union List of Files Available in the United States and Canada. New York: Wilson, 1937. Catalogs files of newspapers in nearly 6,000 libraries and private locations.

Brigham, Clarence S. *History and Bibliography of American Newspapers, 1690–1820.* 2 vols. Worcester, Mass.: American Antiquarian Society, 1947. The best list for anyone trying to find articles in old newspapers.

British Union-Catalogue of Periodicals: A Record of the Periodicals of the World, from the Seventeenth Century to the Present Day, in British Libraries. 4 vols. London: Butterworth, 1955–58. The most distinguished union list for England.

Union List of Serials in Libraries of the United States and Canada. 3rd ed. 5 vols. New York: Wilson, 1966. First published in 1927, this list does an extraordinarily thorough job of locating files of periodicals in nearly a thousand libraries. It is supplemented by:

U.S. Library of Congress. *New Serial Titles.* Washington, D.C.: Library of Congress, 1954–present. Keeps track of periodicals published after 1949.

c. Indexes of periodicals and newspapers

An index lists topics of magazine and newspaper articles alphabetically, giving each article's title and page number. William Poole, working with a group of dedicated librarians, compiled the first American index in 1802. His index is still in use, along with the following:

Index to the Times, 1906–present. London: The Times, 1907–present. A thorough bimonthly index to the *London Times.*

Newspaper Index. Wooster, Ohio: Newspaper Indexing Center, Bell & Howell, 1972–present. Indexes articles in the *Chicago Tribune, Los Angeles Times, New Orleans Times-Picayune,* and *Washington Post.* Includes subject and author indexes.

New York Times Index. New York: The Times, 1913–present. A semi-monthly and annual index to the daily issues of the *New York Times.* (See Fig. 4-3.)

general subject

AIRLINES Note: Material on accidents and safety is carried under subhead Accidents and Safety regardless of whether domestic or internatl services are involved. Geog subheads are used for domestic services and employe-mgt relations only

cross-references follow

See also
Airplanes (for new models, purchases, leasing and servicing)
Airports
Helicopters
Postal Service
Transportation (for relations with other transport means)
co names
commodity names (for shipments)
  Alfred Strassler Jr querying whether Customs agents can prohibit Amer citizens from disembarking at alternate airport lacking proper Customs facilities; Customs Bur Regional Comr Fred R Boyett replies, Ja 4,X,p5
  Travel Information Bur to offer booklet covering more than 20,000 charter flights being offered to gen public in '77 (S), Ja 4,X,p20

subheading of general subject

Accidents and Safety Note: All delays, whether or not due to accidents, are included here
  DC-10 airliner with 364 Turkish pilgrims en route from Mecca to Istanbul lands short of runway at Istanbul airport, injuring 2 persons (S), Ja 3,42:6
  Informed Soviet sources rept crash of Soviet airplane on Jan 3 at Vnukovo Airport near Moscow; craft with 56 passengers aboard was on flight from Moscow to Brest; reptdly exploded on take-off (S), Ja 5,20:4
  PATCO pres John Leyden urges US ban on Concorde SST; warns plane 'can only raise threats to the safety of Amer airways' (S), Ja 12,30:1; Concorde mfrs dispute Leyden's contentions (S), Ja 12,30:2
  Transportation Sec William T Coleman says Govt inquiry finds no evidence to substantiate charge by Jacksonville, Fla, air traffic controller that mil jets have been intercepting commercial airliners in practice maneuvers (S) Ja 24,54:1
  Destruction of DC-10 jetliner at Kennedy Internatl Airport in '75 after striking gulls during takeoff, as well as other instances of hazardous damage from similar collisions, forces decision to reinforce key parts of engines by Gen Elec; crash recalled (M), Ja 27,62:1

short article (M = medium, L = long)

summary of article under subheading "Accidents and Safety"

January 24, page 54, column 1 (refers to issue of New York Times)

Figure 4-3 Entries from *New York Times Index*

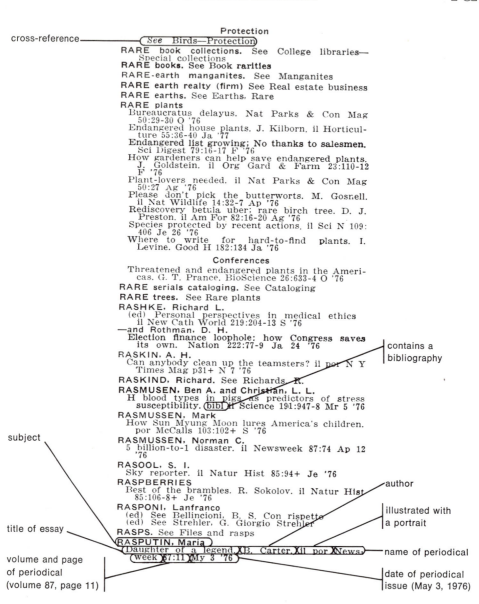

Figure 4-4 Facsimile of page from *Readers' Guide to Periodical Literature*

Poole's Index to Periodical Literature, 1802–1907. 7 vols. Boston: Houghton Mifflin & Co., 1882–1907. This pioneer work indexes close to 600,000 articles in American and English periodicals. Contains a subject index only.

Readers' Guide to Periodical Literature, 1900–present. New York: Wilson, 1905–present. Published semimonthly (monthly in July and August)

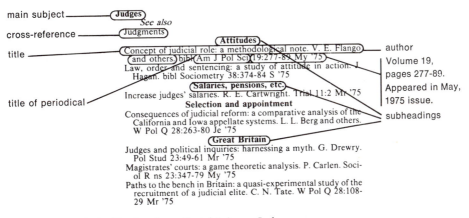

Figure 4-5   Entries from *Social Sciences Index*

with quarterly and annual cumulations, this is by far the most popular periodical index, and has been widely used to research sources for thousands of freshman and graduate papers. Contains an author, subject, and title index to about 160 notable magazines in numerous fields. (See Fig. 4-4.)

Social Sciences and Humanities Index.   New York: Wilson, 1965–present. Replaced *International Index.* New York: Wilson, 1907–1965. Since 1974, published separately as *Social Sciences Index* and *Humanities Index.* An excellent guide to essays in scholarly journals such as the *New England Quarterly* or *Political Science Quarterly.* Includes a subject and author index. (See Fig. 4-5.)

4a-4   Books about general knowledge: encyclopedias

The encyclopedia is the czar of general knowledge books, and a good place to begin research on almost any topic. While they seldom treat a topic in minute detail, encyclopedias are usually factual and current. Among the best are:

Collier's Encyclopedia.   24 vols. New York: Crowell-Collier, 1969. Emphasizes modern subjects, but also contains information that supplements high school and college courses. Aims at covering every major area of language in simplified terms. Includes an index volume.

Columbia Encyclopedia.   3rd ed.   New York: Columbia University Press, 1963. Of all the one-volume encyclopedias, by far the best. Its 75,000 articles are short, concise, but far-ranging. Excellent for desk use.

Encyclopaedia Britannica.   15th ed. 30 vols. Chicago: Encyclopaedia Britannica, 1974. The latest and most up-to-date of the multivolume general encyclopedias. Published originally in England, it retains a British flavor. It is the oldest and most distinguished of the encyclopedias, emphasizing both old and new areas of knowledge. The newest edition comes with elaborate index volumes that synopsize information on various topics.

Encyclopedia Americana. 30 vols. New York: Americana Corporation, 1969. A scholarly encyclopedia consisting mainly of short entries, with complex subjects treated in longer articles. Excellent coverage of science and technology. Includes an index volume.

Encyclopedia International. 20 vols. New York: Grolier, 1964–present. A recent encyclopedia, containing 36,000 articles, many illustrated in color. Contains up-to-date information. Includes an index.

The Lincoln Library of Essential Information. Columbus, Ohio: Frontier Press, 1968–present. Available in one or two volumes. Revised with every printing to remain current. Divided into twelve areas of knowledge that are subdivided into sections. Contains numerous charts, graphs, and tables. Includes an index.

4a-5 Books about words: dictionaries

Dictionaries were originally invented to list the translated meanings of words from one language to another. Sumerian clay tablets listed Sumerian words beside their Semitic-Assyrian equivalents. By the seventeenth century, "dictionary" had come to mean a book that explained the etymology, pronunciation, meaning, and correct usage of words. Nathan Bailey's *Universal Etymological English Dictionary,* published in 1721, was the first comprehensive dictionary in English.

Modern dictionaries provide information about the meaning, derivation, spelling, and syllabication of words, and about linguistic study, synonyms, antonyms, rhymes, slang, colloquialisms, dialect, and usage. Unabridged dictionaries contain complete information about words; abridged dictionaries condense their information so as to be more portable.

a. General dictionaries

The American Heritage Dictionary of the English Language. Boston: American Heritage Co., Inc. and Houghton Mifflin, 1969. The distinguishing feature of this dictionary is that it was written in conjunction with a usage panel and a long list of consultants in specialized areas. It is greatly praised for its excellent photography and illustrations.

Oxford English Dictionary. 13 vols. Oxford: Clarendon Press, 1888–1933. A monumental work that presents the historical development of each word in the English language since 1150, illustrating correct usage with varied quotations. An updated version has been in the works since 1972.

Random House Dictionary of the English Language. New York: Random House, 1966. Contains approximately 260,000 entries. Emphasizes current usage. Lists the latest technical terms as well as slang. Includes proper names, names of places, and titles of literary works.

Webster's Third New International Dictionary of the English Language. 3rd ed. Springfield, Mass.: G.&C. Merriam Co., 1961. At one time a controversial dictionary because it accepted usage considered colloquial or nongrammatical by purists. However, today it is the standard dictionary of most academic institutions. Some scholars still prefer the second edition. *Webster's Seventh New Collegiate Dictionary* is a derivative of this dictionary which tries to meet the needs of college students and nonspecialist readers; it is available in paperback (see Fig. 4-6).

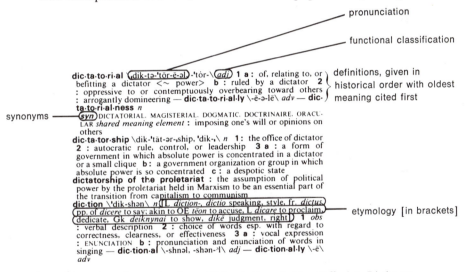

Figure 4-6 Sample entries from *Webster's Seventh New Collegiate Dictionary*

b. Specialized dictionaries

Craigie, William A., and James R. Hulbert. *Dictionary of American English on Historical Principles.* 4 vols. Chicago: University of Chicago Press, 1936–44. A valuable work for anyone interested in how English developed during Colonial times. Indicates which words originated in America and which in other English-speaking countries. Excludes dialect and slang.

Partridge, Eric. *A Dictionary of Slang and Unconventional English: Colloquialisms and Catch-Phrases, Solecisms and Catachreses, Nicknames, Vulgar-*

980. VIRTUE

(moral goodness)

synonyms for <u>virtue</u>

.1 NOUNS virtue, virtuousness, goodness, righteousness, rectitude, right conduct, the straight and narrow; probity 974; morality, moral rectitude *or* virtue, morale; saintliness, saintlikeness, angelicalness; godliness 1028.2.

.2 "the health of the soul" [Joseph Joubert], "the fount whence honour springs" [Marlowe], "the adherence in action to the nature of things" [Emerson], "victorious resistance to one's vital desire to do this, that *or* the other" [James Branch Cabell], "to do unwitnessed what we should be capable of doing before all the world" [La Rochefoucauld].

quotation by Marlowe

.3 purity, immaculacy, chastity 988; guiltlessness, innocence 984.

.4 uncorruptness, uncorruptedness, incorruptness, unsinfulness, sinlessness; unwickedness, uniniquitousness; undegenerateness, undepravedness, undissoluteness, undebauchedness.

.5 cardinal virtues, natural virtues; prudence, justice, temperance, fortitude; theological virtues *or* supernatural virtues; faith, hope, charity *or* love.

verbs associated with <u>virtue</u>

.6 VERBS be good, do no evil; keep in the right path, walk the straight path, follow the straight and narrow, keep on the straight and narrow way *or* path; fight the good fight.

adjectives associated with <u>virtue</u>

.7 ADJS virtuous, good, moral; upright, honest 974.13–20; righteous, just, straight, right-minded; angelic, seraphic; saintly, saintlike; godly 1028.9.

.8 chaste, immaculate, pure 988.4; guiltless, innocent 984.6.

.9 uncorrupt, uncorrupted, incorrupt, incorrupted; unsinful, sinless; unwicked, uniniquitous, unerring, unfallen; undegenerate, undepraved, undemoralized, undissolute, undebauched.

981. VICE ——— antonym of virtue

(moral badness)

.1 NOUNS vice, viciousness; criminality, wrongdoing 982; immorality, unmorality, evil; amorality 957.4; unvirtuousness, ungoodness; unrighteousness, ungodliness, unsaintliness, unangelicalness; uncleanness, impurity, unchastity 989; waywardness, wantonness, prodigality; delinquency, moral delinquency; peccability; backsliding, recidivism; evil nature, carnality 987.2.

synonyms for vice

.2 vice, weakness, weakness of the flesh, flaw, moral flaw, frailty, infirmity; failing, failure; weak point, weak side, foible; bad habit, besetting sin; fault, imperfection 678.

.3 iniquity, evil, bad, wrong, error, obliquity, villainy, knavery, reprobacy, peccancy, abomination, atrocity, shame, disgrace, scandal, infamy; sin 982.2.

.4 wickedness, badness, naughtiness, evilness, viciousness, sinfulness, iniquitousness; baseness, rankness, vileness, foulness, arrantness, nefariousness, heinousness, villainousness, flagitiousness; fiendishness, hellishness; devilishness, devilry, deviltry.

.5 turpitude, moral turpitude; corruption, corruptedness, corruptness, rottenness, moral pollution *or* pollutedness; decadence *or* decadency, debasement, degradation, demoralization, abjection; degen-

Figure 4-7 Entry from *Roget's International Thesaurus*

isms, and Such Americanisms as Have Been Naturalized. 7th ed. New York: Macmillan, 1970. Published as two volumes in one book, this is a comprehensive treatment of both old and current slang.

Wentworth, Harold, and Stuart B. Flexner. *Dictionary of American Slang.* New York: Crowell, 1967. A comprehensive listing of current American slang, including taboo words and expressions.

c. Dictionaries of synonyms and antonyms

Dictionaries of synonyms and antonyms list the equivalents and opposites of words. Among the best-known are the following:

Hayakawa, S. I., comp. *Funk & Wagnalls Modern Guide to Synonyms and Related Words.* New York: Funk & Wagnalls Company, 1968. Contains over one thousand essays discussing, defining, comparing, and contrasting synonyms and related words.

March, Francis A. *March's Thesaurus Dictionary.* Garden City, N.Y.: Hanover House, 1968. The unique contribution of this book is its listing of words in paired opposites. For example, it lists synonyms for the word *betterment* side by side with synonyms for the word *deterioration.*

Roget's International Thesaurus. 3rd ed. New York: Crowell, 1962. This is the modern edition of a work first published in 1852. It is the most popular of all thesauruses. (See Fig. 4-7.)

Sturges, Allen F. *Synonyms and Antonyms.* New York: Harper, 1938. Includes colloquial, vulgar, technical, and specialized terms.

Webster's New Dictionary of Synonyms: A Dictionary of Discriminated Synonyms, with Antonyms and Analogous and Contrasted Words. 2nd ed. Springfield, Mass.: G.&C. Merriam Co., 1968. Illustrates usage with quotations from old as well as new authors.

4a-6 Books about places

Reference books on places come in two forms: atlases and gazetteers.

a. Atlases

An atlas is a bound collection of maps, sometimes amplified by charts, tables, and plates, that provide information about the people, culture, and economy of the countries covered. Among the most comprehensive and useful atlases are the following:

Bartholomew, John. *The Advanced Atlas of Modern Geography.* 3rd ed. New York: McGraw-Hill, 1956. Contains 160 pages of maps covering the entire world. Includes an extensive index.

Encyclopaedia Britannica World Atlas. Chicago: Encyclopaedia Britannica, 1963. Forms part of the Index volume of the encyclopedia. Contains 102 pages of modern maps, followed by 6 pages of maps depicting historical regions such as Alexander's empire, the Roman Empire, and the barbarian invasion routes. Includes an index to maps.

The National Atlas of the United States of America. Arlington, Va.: U.S. Department of the Interior, 1970. The official atlas of the United States, and therefore authoritative as well as comprehensive. The index refers to 41,000 names of places; the maps identify physical, economic, social, and historical features.

National Geographic Atlas of the World. 3rd ed. Washington, D.C.: National Geographic Society, 1970. Maps are arranged according to region and are accompanied by brief gazetteer information.

The Pictorial Atlas of the World. New York: Chartwell Books Inc., 1976–77. Superb photographs of towns and landscapes accompany over 70 maps. Includes an informative text on each country.

Times Atlas of the World. 5 vols. London: Times Publishing Co., 1955–60. One of the most comprehensive and authoritative atlases in print. It has been supplemented by *The Times Atlas of the World: Comprehensive*

Edition. 2nd ed. Boston: Houghton Mifflin, 1971. This edition reflects some recent changes in place names and political boundaries. It includes maps of the world's food, mineral, and energy supplies.

b. Gazetteers

A gazetteer is a geographical dictionary or index that gives basic information about the most important regions, cities, and natural features of the countries of the world. The pronunciation and even syllabication of names are often included with this information. A gazetteer is consulted when a researcher wants information about the legal or political status of a country, its location, and its most important features. The best general gazetteers are:

Columbia-Lippincott Gazetteer of the World. New York: Columbia University Press, 1962. This is the most comprehensive gazetteer in the English language. Provides basic information about 130,000 places.

Macmillan World Gazetteer and Geographical Dictionary. New York: Macmillan, 1957. Emphasizing British interests, this dictionary contains 164 pages of geographical names and facts.

The Times Index Gazetteer of the World. Boston: Houghton Mifflin, 1966. Based on the *Times Atlas of the World,* this work has an index of almost 350,000 locations. Gives longitude and latitude coordinates.

Webster's New Geographical Dictionary. Springfield, Mass.: G.&C. Merriam Co., 1972. Locates and identifies about 47,000 countries, regions, cities, and geographical features. Based on 1970 census figures.

4a-7 Books about people

Biographical reference books are classifiable under four primary headings: (a) general biography about deceased persons, (b) general biography about living persons, (c) national biography about deceased persons, and (d) national biography about living persons.

a. General biography about deceased persons

Chamber's Biographical Dictionary: The Great of All Nations and All Times. Rev. ed. New York: St. Martin's, 1969. Gives close to 10,000 sketches of famous people of the past.

The McGraw-Hill Encyclopedia of World Biography. 12 vols. New York: McGraw-Hill, 1973. Geared to high school and college students, this work is a compilation of 5,000 biographies of individuals famous throughout history. Each entry includes a bibliography. An index is also provided.

New Century Cyclopedia of Names. Rev. ed. 3 vols. New York: Appleton-Century-Crofts, 1954. Identifies all kinds of important proper names, including the names of persons, places, events, and characters from literature and opera.

Slocum, Robert B. *Biographical Dictionaries and Related Works.* Detroit: Gale Research Co., 1967. (*Supplement,* 1972.) This work lists all major biographical works—over 8,000 titles. An excellent place to begin finding biographies. International in scope.

Webster's Biographical Dictionary. Springfield, Mass.: G.&C. Merriam Co., 1971. A dictionary of the names of noteworthy persons, with pronunciations and concise biographies. Covers heads of state and other high officials.

b. General biography about living persons

Current Biography. New York: H. W. Wilson, 1940–present. Editions come out monthly and annually. Contains sketches, written in popular style, of prominent persons featured in national and international news. The annual edition includes an index. Excellent photographs of the subjects accompany the text.

Hayakawa, Samuel Ichiye, PH.D.; American university professor; b. 18 July 1906, Vancouver, B.C., Canada; s. of Ichiro Hayakawa and Tora Isono; m. Margedant Peters 1937; two s. one d.; ed. public schools in Calgary, Vancouver, and Winnipeg, Univ. of Manitoba and McGill Univ., Montreal.
Formerly taught at Univs. of Wisconsin and Chicago and Illinois Inst. of Technology, Chicago; Prof. of English, San Francisco State Coll. 55-, Pres. 69-73; Claude Bernard Prof., Inst. of Experimental Medicine and Surgery, Univ. of Montreal 59; Alfred P. Sloan Visiting Prof., Menninger School of Psychiatry, Topeka, Kan. 61; has held many other summer and visiting professorships in American univs. and colls. and lectured in several European countries; Hon. D.Litt. (Grinnell Coll.); Hon. LL.D. (The Citadel).
Leisure interests: African art, Chinese ceramics.
Publs. include: *Oliver Wendell Holmes* 39, *Language in Action* 41, *Language in Thought and Action* 49, *Symbol, Status and Personality* 63, *A Modern Guide to Synonyms* 68, and contributions to numerous other volumes.
P.O. Box 100, Mill Valley, Calif. 94941, U.S.A.

summary of main facts in Hayakawa's life up to the time he was elected to the U.S. Senate.

Figure 4-8 Entries from *International Who's Who*

International Who's Who. London: Europe Publications, Ltd., 1935–present. Issued annually. Provides sketches of important people all over the world. (See Fig. 4-8.)

World Biography. 5th ed. Farmingdale, N.Y.: Institute for Research in Biography, 1954. Contains brief sketches of close to 50,000 people from countries all over the world.

c. National biography of deceased persons (American and British)

Appleton's Cyclopaedia of American Biography. 7 vols. New York: Appleton-Century-Crofts, 1887–1900. Contains full-length articles, often illustrated with portraits and autographs of the biographee. Includes people from Mexico and South America.

Dictionary of American Biography. 21 vols. New York: Scribner, 1928–37. A 1944–73 supplement in 3 vols. This is considered the most scholarly of all American biographical dictionaries. An abbreviated edition is available: *Concise Dictionary of American Biography*. New York: Scribner, 1964; this provides in one volume all the essential facts contained in the larger work.

Dictionary of National Biography. 22 vols. London: Smith, Elder, 1908–09. Supplements 1–7. 7 vols. London: Smith, Elder, 1912–71. Condensed edition: *The Concise Dictionary of National Biography from the Beginnings to 1950*. 2 vols. London: Oxford University Press, 1948–61. The large edition provides rounded-out sketches of notable inhabitants (now deceased) of Great Britain and the colonies from the earliest historical period to contemporary times. The small edition contains abstracts of the large edition.

James, Edward T., and Janet W., eds. *Notable American Women, 1607–1950*. 3 vols. Cambridge, Mass: Belknap Press of Harvard University, 1972. One of the best scholarly biographies to focus on the work of prominent women in America.

d. National biography about living persons (American and British)

National Cyclopaedia of American Biography. 59 vols. New York: James T. White & Co., 1892–present. A monumental work that presents a complete political, social, commercial, and industrial history in the form of sketches of individuals, deceased and living, who helped shape America.

Who's Who. London: Black, 1849–present. This was the first "Who's Who" to be printed. Contains excellent biographical sketches of prominent people living in Great Britain and its Commonwealth.

Who's Who in America. Chicago: Marquis, 1899–present. Editions come out biennially. Identifies people of special prominence in all lines of work. Supplemented by *Who's Who in the East, Who's Who in the Midwest, Who's Who in the South and Southwest,* and *Who's Who in the West*—all issued by the Marquis Company.

Who's Who of American Women. Chicago: Marquis, 1958–present. A dictionary identifying American women who have made a name for themselves in various fields.

Many countries and professions now publish "Who's Who" rosters. Examples are:

> *Prominent Personalities in the USSR*
> *Who's Who in Australia*
> *Who's Who in China*
> *Who's Who in France*
> *Who's Who in Germany*
> *Who's Who in Italy*
> *Who's Who in the U.A.R. and the Near East*

> *Who's Who in American Art*
> *Who's Who in American Politics*
> *Who's Who in Engineering*
> *Who's Who in Finance and Industry*
> *Who's Who in Government*
> *Who's Who in Music*
> *Who's Who in Soviet Social Sciences, Humanities, Art and Government*

Ask your librarian about other areas in which a "Who's Who" roster is published. There are too many to include here.

e. Biography index

One general and most useful index to biographical material in books and magazines needs to be mentioned.

Biography Index. New York: Wilson, 1974–present. Issued quarterly with annual and triennial cumulations. This work is a guide to articles and books written about all kinds of persons, living and dead. (See Fig. 4-9.)

4a-8 Books about government publications

The work of government bureaucracy is reflected in government publications—in speeches, annual reports, transcripts of hearings, statistical charts, regulations, and research results. Government publications—issued at public expense by thousands of federal, state, and local agencies—are available to the general public. The United States Government Printing Office (GPO), an independent body of the legislative branch of government, is the chief government printer. Distribution of materials is supervised by the Superintendent of Public Documents, from whom government publications may be ordered. The most important references that list government publications are:

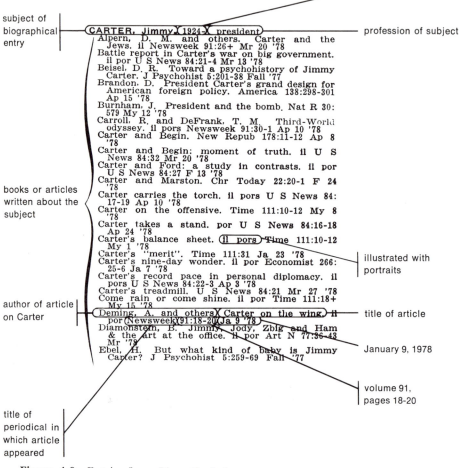

Figure 4-9　Entries from *Biography Index*

Ames, John G. *Comprehensive Index to the Publications of the United States Government, 1881–1893.* 2 vols. Washington, D.C.: GPO, 1905. This work will help a researcher locate government information by subject or title. Covers a decade of post-Civil War times.

Poore, Benjamin P. *A Descriptive Catalogue of the Government Publications of the United States, September 5, 1774–March 4, 1881.* Washington, D.C.: GPO, 1885. A 1,392-page compilation, invaluable to the student of early U.S. history.

U.S. Superintendent of Documents. *Catalog of the Public Documents of Congress and of All Departments of the Government of the United States for the Period March 4, 1893–December 31, 1940.* 25 vols. Washington, D.C.:

GPO, 1896–1945. A comprehensive summary of materials published before 1945.

U.S. Superintendent of Documents. *Checklist of United States Public Documents, 1789–1909.* 3rd ed. Washington, D.C.: GPO, 1911. Covers 120 years of government printing.

U.S. Superintendent of Documents. *Monthly Catalog of United States Government Publications.* Washington, D.C.: GPO, 1895–present. A monthly catalog, arranged by departments, that provides up-to-date listings of publications from all governmental agencies. Includes subject indexes.

U.S. Superintendent of Documents. *Price Lists.* Washington, D.C.: GPO, 1898–present. Gives the price of government publications; listed by subjects.

Several guides exist that orient the novice to the vast number of government publications. Among the best are the following:

Boyd, Anne Morris, and Rae E. Rips. *United States Government Publications.* 3rd ed. New York: Wilson, 1950. A useful work to help a researcher find and interpret government publications.

Jackson, Ellen. *Subject Guide to Major United States Government Publications.* Chicago: American Library Association, 1968. Useful for pointing out the most important publications of the Government Printing Office from its beginning to the present.

Leidy, W. Philip. *A Popular Guide to Government Publications.* 3rd ed. New York: Columbia University Press, 1968. An excellent guide to the most popular government publications issued between 1961 and 1966. Arranged by subject. Has limited use.

Mechanic, Sylvia, comp. *Annotated List of Selected United States Government Publications Available to Depository Libraries.* New York: Wilson, 1971. Lists about 500 items of general contemporary interest. Includes a subject and title index.

Pohle, Linda C. *A Guide to Popular Government Publications for Libraries and Home Reference.* Littleton, Colo.: Libraries Unlimited, 1972. Emphasizes publications printed between 1967 and 1971. Titles are arranged alphabetically by subject.

Schmeckebier, Laurence F., and Roy B. Eastin. *Government Publications and Their Use.* 2nd rev. ed. Washington, D.C.: Brookings Institution, 1969. As the Foreword states, this work is designed "to provide an understanding of government publishing practices past and present, to indicate sources of information concerning the existence of publications, and to describe how copies may be obtained."

U.S. Library of Congress. *Monthly Checklist of State Publications*. Washington, D.C.: GPO, 1910–present. Keeps track of all state government publications received by the Library of Congress.

Foreign countries have their own government printing offices, catalogs, and indexes.

4a-9 Books about nonbooks

In recent years nonbooks have become a necessary and distinctive part of library collections. Material stored on microform, film, and sound recordings is often valuable to researchers.

a. Indexes of microforms

Microforms are miniaturized photographic records of printed or graphic material. The technique of microform originated in the 1930s, when the first printed page was miniaturized on a roll of film. Miniaturizing technology has become so sophisticated that today 1,200 pages of print can be reduced and stored on a card two inches square, which is then read with magnifying equipment. The two principal kinds of microform are (1) microfilm: material recorded on rolls of film; and (2) microfiche: material recorded on cards.

The use of microforms has resulted in an astonishing saving of library space. Libraries now typically store periodicals, rare manuscripts, and specialized research materials in microform. Here are some useful guides to this material:

Bell and Howell Micro Photo Division. *Microforms*. Wooster, Ohio: Bell and Howell, 1977. This is a new catalog that lists all material now available on Bell and Howell microforms. Of particular interest are the collections of newspapers on microfilm, the periodicals on microfiche, and the list of special microform collections such as "The Mission of Apollo II," "LBJ Clip File," and "The Kent State University Disorders."

Dissertation Abstracts International. Ann Arbor, Mich.: Xerox University Microfilms, 1969–present. Issued monthly, this index lists and provides copies of dissertations produced in all major American universities.

Guide to Microforms in Print. Washington, D.C.: Microcard Editions Books, 1974–present. The first principal and general listing of microforms in an annual publication.

Microfilm Reference Volume. Santa Monica, Calif.: UpData Publications, 1974. Lists chiefly titles of serial publications issued by thirty publishers. Contains an index.

Microforms and Professional Books. Englewood, Colo.: Information Handling Services, Library and Education Division, 1977. This is the first edition of a catalog containing a subject, title, and author index to a wealth of valuable material available in microform. Included are numerous important journals.

Readex Microprint Publications, 1972–73. New York: Readex Microprint Corp., 1972. 65 pages listing 1,500,000 titles available on microfiche. Needs to be updated.

Serials in Microform, 1973–78. Ann Arbor, Mich.: Xerox University Microfilms, 1973–78. Lists hundreds of documents, newspapers, and other serial literature alphabetically by title. Also contains a subject index.

U.S. Library of Congress, Union Catalog Division. *Newspapers on Microfilm.* 6th ed. Washington, D.C.: Library of Congress, 1967. Locates the files of about 21,000 titles of American and foreign newspapers.

b. Guides to films

Films available for educational purposes range from abbreviated versions of *A Man for All Seasons* and *Hamlet* to films on specialized subjects such as linguistics or abnormal psychology. The cataloging of films is imprecise because of the many uncataloged private collections owned by school districts or universities. Nevertheless, the following guides to films are useful:

The College Film Library Collection. 2 vols. Williamsport, Pa.: Bro-Dart Publishing Company, 1977. Contains a selected annotated list of 16mm films, and some selected feature films, currently available for rental by colleges.

Educational Film Guide. New York: Wilson, 1936–62. Records 6,000 titles. Not up-to-date, therefore mostly of historical interest.

Educators Guide to Free Films. Randolph, Wis.: Educators Progress Service, 1941–present. Describes films currently available and gives suggestions on how to use them. Indexed by title, subject, source, and curriculum area.

Feature Films on 8mm and 16mm. New York: Bowker, 1977. A directory of 15,000 feature films available for rental, sale, or lease in the United States. Listings by title; comes with a geographic index to film distributors.

Film Evaluation Guide. New York: Educational Film Library Association, 1946–65. With supplements covering 1965–71. Gives essential facts about more than 5,600 films carefully reviewed by over 100 committees of audiovisual experts all over the United States. Recommends the academic level and courses for which the films may be used.

Guide to Military Loan Films. Alexandria, Va.: Serina Press, 1969. Contains synopses of over 1,430 motion pictures available on loan for public nonprofit exhibition, free of charge, from the U.S. Army, U.S. Air Force, U.S. Navy, U.S. Marine Corps, and the Corps of Engineers. Includes a consolidated alphabetical listing of all films appearing in the guide, an index, and sources for borrowing the film.

Guide to State-Loan Films. Alexandria, Va.: Serina Press, 1969. Contains synopses of 540 films produced or available under the auspices of 60 official state agencies in 43 states and the District of Columbia. Films available on loan free of charge.

Library of Congress Catalog: Motion Pictures and Filmstrips. Washington, D.C.: Library of Congress, 1948–present. A comprehensive list by authors and subjects of all kinds of educational films.

National Audiovisual Center. *U.S. Government Films.* Washington, D.C.: National Archives and Records Service, 1969 to present. Lists all motion pictures and filmstrips for rent and sale by the National Audiovisual Center.

National Information Center for Educational Media. *Index to 16mm Educational Films.* 4 vols. New York: McGraw-Hill, 1977. Lists films recorded since 1958 in the Master Data Bank at the University of Southern California

Universities and colleges throughout the United States are among the finest sources for films, but to date no central cataloging of this material exists. Many universities, however, have extensive and up-to-date descriptive catalogs of their own collections, from which films are often available on loan. Catalogs are available from the following:

Boston University
Indiana University
Mountain Plains Educational Media (a consortium of the Universities
 of Colorado, Nevada, Wyoming, and Utah)
Pennsylvania State University (issues a series of pamphlets organized
 by subject areas)
University of Arizona
University of California at Berkeley
University of Iowa and Iowa State University, operating as a
 consortium
University of Kansas
University of Michigan
University of Southern California

c. Guides to sound recordings

Recordings of music and speeches on disc or tapes are part of the collections of many libraries. The best sources for up-to-date information about recorded music are:

Harrison Catalog of Stereophonic Tapes. New York: M.&N. Harrison, 1955–present. Issued bimonthly, this catalog has an extensive listing of music on cassettes, eight-track cartridges, and open reel tapes.

Library of Congress Catalog: Music and Phono-Records. Washington D.C.: Library of Congress, 1953–present. This is a listing of permanently valuable musical recordings received by the Library of Congress.

Malone, Bill C. *Country Music, U.S.A.: A Fifty Year History.* Austin, Tex.: University of Texas Press, 1968. Provides what the title says.

Records in Review. New York: Scribner, 1955–present. Reviews numerous current music recordings, arranged alphabetically by composer.

Rust, Brian. *Jazz Records, A–Z, 1897–1931.* 2nd. ed. Hatch End, Middlesex, England, 1962. Supplemented by:

————. *Jazz Records, A–Z, 1932–1945.* Hatch End, Middlesex, England, 1965. Good guide for someone interested in the origins and development of American jazz.

Schwann Records and Tape Guide. Boston: W. Schwann, 1949–present. Issued monthly, this guide lists over 45,000 items of recorded music.

U.S. Library of Congress. *Folk Music: A Catalog of Folk Songs, Ballads, Dances, Instrumental Pieces, and Folk Tales of the United States and Latin America on Phonograph Records.* Washington, D.C.: Library of Congress, 1958. Excellent collection for anyone doing research on the history of folk music in the Americas.

The best sources for up-to-date information about recorded speeches, readings, etc., are:

Roach, Helen. *Spoken Records.* 3rd ed. Metuchen, N.J.: Scarecrow Press, 1970. Lists such varied material as recorded plays, poems, documentaries, and authors reading from their own work.

U.S. Library of Congress. *Literary Recordings: A Checklist of the Archive of Recorded Poetry and Literature in the Library of Congress.* Washington D.C.: Library of Congress, 1966. Consists of 190 pages listing a variety of spoken material important in the field of literature.

d. Guides to oral history recordings

Oral history, as captured in recorded interviews, can be invaluable to historical research. Various guides exist to oral history; among the best are the following:

Columbia University Oral History Research Office. *The Oral History Collection of Columbia University.* New York: The Office, 1973. Describes the taped interviews contained in this vast collection.

Meckler, Alan, and Ruth McMullin. *Oral History Collections.* New York: Bowker, 1974. Contains general information on important oral history collections.

Oral History Association. *Oral History in the United States: A Directory.* New York: The Association, 1971. Contains descriptions of 230 collections, arranged according to states and giving the names of the institutions holding each collection.

4b

An annotated list of specialized references

A specialized reference indexes and classifies information about a specific subject. Depending on the complexity of your topic, you may or may not have to consult a specialized reference. Numerous such references exist, covering virtually all subjects. A complete listing of all the specialized references on popular subjects such as history and literature, for instance, would easily fill an entire book.

Specialized references are listed here in alphabetical order by subject, and are restricted to those most likely to be useful in student research.

4b-1   Art

American Art Directory. New York: Bowker, 1899–present. Gives information about museums and other art organizations in the United States and Canada.

The American Library Compendium and Index of World Art. New York: American Archives of World Art, 1961. Contains general information on international art.

Art Index. New York: Wilson, 1929–present. Provides an index to archaeology, architecture, history of art, fine arts, industrial design, interior decorating, landscape design, photography, and other subjects connected with art.

Canaday, John. *Lives of the Painters.* 4 vols. New York: Norton, 1969. Contains sketches of the lives of most great painters.

Chamberlin, Mary W. *Guide to Art Reference Books.* Chicago: American Library Association, 1959. An annotated bibliography for the arts.

Chase, George H., and Chandler R. Post. *A History of Sculpture.* New York: Harper, 1925. An old but informative book on the development of sculpture.

Clapp, Jane. *Sculpture Index.* 2 vols. Metuchen, N.J.: Scarecrow Press, 1970.

———. *Art Reproductions.* Metuchen, N.J.: Scarecrow Press, 1961. Contains excellent reproductions of famous paintings from major schools of art.

Encyclopedia of World Art. 15 vols. New York: McGraw-Hill, 1959–68. Contains scholarly articles on architecture, sculpture, painting, and other arts, accompanied by good photographic reproductions of art works.

Gardner, Helen. *Art Through the Ages.* 5th ed. New York: Harcourt, 1970. A survey of Western art from its beginnings to contemporary times, accompanied by colored plates.

Gaunt, William. *Everyman's Dictionary of Pictorial Art.* 2 vols. New York: Dutton, 1962. Contains brief background information on major artists, explains the various periods of art, and comments on famous paintings and the galleries that contain them.

Haftmann, Werner. *Painting in the Twentieth Century.* Rev. ed. 2 vols. New York: Praeger, 1965. Recognized as one of the standard works on modern art.

Harper's Encyclopedia of Art. 2 vols. in 1. New York: Harper, 1937. Reprinted as *New Standard Encyclopedia of Art.* New York: Garden City Publishing Co., 1939. Gives a broad overview of all aspects of art.

Janson, Horst W., and Dora Jane. *History of Art.* Rev. ed. Englewood Cliffs, N.J.: Prentice-Hall and Abrams, 1969. Gives a history of all the major art forms from the dawn of history to contemporary times.

Larousse Encyclopedia of Byzantine and Medieval Art. New York: Prometheus Press, 1963. Provides background information and pictures of important works from the Byzantine and Medieval periods.

Larousse Encyclopedia of Modern Art, from 1800 to the Present Day. New York: Putnam, 1965. Similar coverage of modern art.

Larousse Encyclopedia of Prehistoric and Ancient Art. New York: Prometheus Press, 1962. Similar coverage of prehistoric and ancient art.

Larousse Encyclopedia of Renaissance and Baroque Art. New York: Prometheus Press, 1964. Similar coverage of Renaissance and Baroque art.

Myers, Bernard S., ed. *Encyclopedia of Painting: Painters and Painting of the World from Prehistoric Times to the Present Day.* New York: Crown, 1955. A monumental work, containing brief articles on painters—their styles, schools, and techniques—with excellent illustrations. Contains sections on Chinese, Japanese, and Persian art.

———, *McGraw-Hill Dictionary of Art.* 5 vols. New York: McGraw-Hill, 1969. A comprehensive guide to art styles, periods, galleries, and techniques. Contains 2,300 illustrations. Provides good bibliographies.

Osborne, Harold, ed. *The Oxford Companion to Art.* Oxford: Clarendon Press, 1970. An excellent source for the student who wants to become familiar with the fundamentals of art and art history.

The Pelican History of Art. Baltimore: Penguin Books, 1953–present. In progress, to be completed in 50 vols. When completed, this expansive work will cover all aspects of art—ancient, medieval, and modern. Includes architecture.

The Praeger Encyclopedia of Art. 5 vols. New York: Praeger, 1971. A good encyclopedia with entries on individual artists, schools, and movements. Contains close to 5,000 illustrations, some in color.

ART JOURNALS

> *Art Bulletin*
> *Art Forum*
> *Art Journal*
> *Arts*
> *Arts and Activities*
> *Arts Yearbook*
> *Schools of Arts Magazine*

4b-2   Dance

Balanchine, George. *Balanchine's New Complete Stories of the Great Ballets.* Garden City, N.Y.: Doubleday, 1968. Gives good summaries of plots and explanations relating to classical and modern ballets.

Beaumont, Cyril W. *Complete Book of Ballets.* 3 vols. New York: Putnam, 1938. Supplements, 1942–55. Contains summaries and commentaries on the most important nineteenth- and twentieth-century ballets.

Chujoy, Anatole, and P. W. Manchestor. *The Dance Encyclopedia.* Rev. ed. New York: Simon and Schuster, 1967. Contains essays dealing with dance form, biography, and dance terminology.

Gadan, Francis, and R. Maillard, eds. *Dictionary of Modern Ballet.* New York: Tudor, 1959. A guide to terms and titles associated with modern ballet.

Magriel, Paul David. *A Bibliography of Dancing.* New York: H. W. Wilson, 1936. With additional supplements updating the lists. A good source for reading material on almost any aspect of dance.

Martin, John J. *Book of the Dance.* New York: Tudor, 1963. Provides extensive information on the history of dance, major dancers, and ballet.

DANCE JOURNALS

> *Dance Magazine*
> *Dance Observer*
> *Dance Perspectives*
> *Dance Scope*

4b-3 Ecology

Air Pollution Abstracts. Research Triangle Park, N.C.: Air Pollution Technical Information Center of the Environmental Protection Agency, 1970–present. Issued quarterly, these abstracts from periodicals, books, and reports cover the entire field of air pollution and air standards.

Bond, Richard G., and Conrad P. Straub. *Handbook of Environmental Control.* 2 vols. Cleveland: CRC Press, 1972. The first volume focuses on air pollution, the second on solid waste.

Clepper, Henry. *Leaders of American Conservation.* New York: Ronald Press, 1971. A good source for basic information about people in the United States who have made a name for themselves in conservation of wildlife and natural resources. Contains 360 biographies.

The Earth and Man: A Rand McNally World Atlas. Chicago: Rand McNally, 1972. Contains over 400 pages of maps, charts, and commentary on ecology.

Environment Information Access. New York: Environment Information Center, 1971–present. Issued monthly, this handbook is a guide to information from periodicals, reports, government hearings, and conferences dealing with environmental problems or facts.

Fisher, James, et al. *Wildlife in Danger.* New York: Viking, 1969. Provides information on endangered species among mammals, birds, reptiles, amphibians, fish, and plants. Numerous illustrations accompany the text.

Pollution Abstracts. La Jolla, Calif.: Oceanic Library and Information Center, 1970–present. Contains abstracts of articles on every kind of pollution: air, fresh water, salt water, land, and noise. Includes full essays on how to overcome pollution.

Winton, Harry N. M. *Man and the Environment: A Bibliography of Selected Publications of the United Nations System, 1946–1971.* New York: Bowker, 1972. An annotated bibliography of over a thousand United Nations publications that deal with man, his environment, and his resources. Includes author, title, and subject indexes.

ECOLOGY JOURNALS

> *Journal of Animal Ecology*
> *Journal of Ecology*
> *Journal of Wildlife Management*
> *National Wildlife*

4b-4   Education

Blishen, Edward. *Encyclopedia of Education.* New York: Philosophical Library, 1970. A guide to information on all aspects of education: philosophy, history, administration, teaching, and important educational legislation.

Burke, Arvid H., and Mary A. Burke. *Documentation in Education.* New York: Teachers College, 1967. A good source of important titles in the field of education.

Current Index to Journals in Education. New York: CCM Information Corp., 1969–present. Issued monthly, with semiannual and annual cumulations. An excellent guide to educational literature, arranged by subject as well as by author. Covers over 200 journals dealing with educational matters.

Education Abstracts. 16 vols. Fulton, Mo.: Education Clearing House, 1936–present. Contains abstracts of most of the important essays in the field of education.

Education Index. New York: Wilson, 1929–present. Issued monthly except July and August, with annual cumulations. Indexes articles from some 240 educational periodicals, conferences, yearbooks, bulletins, and monographs.

Good, Garter V., ed. *Dictionary of Education.* New York: McGraw-Hill, 1959. Gives definitions of educational terms, including related words from psychology, sociology, and philosophy. Needs updating.

Handbook of Private Schools. Boston: Porter Sargent, 1915–present. Issued annually, this handbook lists all private schools by locations. Describes the type of school and mentions any distinguishing characteristics.

International Yearbook of Education. Paris: UNESCO, 1948–present. Published annually, this book provides information about educational systems in countries throughout the world. An excellent source of what other nations are doing in the field of education. Also published by UNESCO: *World Survey of Education*. 4 vols. Paris: UNESCO, 1955–66.

Richmond, W. Kenneth. *The Literature of Education: A Critical Bibliography, 1945–1970*. London: Methuen, 1972. Critically evaluates the educational literature published over a period of twenty-five years in the following areas: philosophy, theory, curriculum, psychology, history, sociology, administration, comparative studies, economics, and technology.

Teacher's Encyclopedia. Englewood Cliffs, N.J.: Prentice-Hall, 1966. A sourcebook assembled with the teacher in mind. Contains articles by specialists on all kinds of learning problems and situations. Includes excellent bibliographies and a subject index.

Who's Who in American Education. New York: Who's Who in American Education, 1928–present. Provides biographical sketches of men and women who have made notable contributions to the field of education. Issued annually.

EDUCATION JOURNALS

American School Board Journal
Change
Childhood Education
Chronicle of Higher Education
Educational Forum
Elementary School Journal
Harvard Educational Review
Journal of Educational Research
Journal of Experimental Education
Journal of Higher Education
Journal of Secondary Education
Junior College Journal
NEA Journal
Review of Educational Research

4b-5 Ethnic studies

a. Afro-American

Baskin, Wade, and Richard N. Runes. *Dictionary of Black Culture*. New York: Philosophical Library, 1973. A guide to notable black persons, black literature, historical events concerning blacks, and controversial issues related to black interests.

Bergman, Peter M. *The Chronological History of the Negro in America.* New York: Harper, 1969. A year-by-year account of blacks from their arrival in America to modern times. Contains an index.

Black List. New York: Panther House, 1971. "The Concise Reference Guide to Publications and Broadcasting Media of Black America, Africa, and the Caribbean."

Davis, John P., ed. *The American Negro Reference Book.* Englewood Cliffs, N.J.: Prentice-Hall, 1966. A guide to general information on the life and history of blacks in America. Contains an index.

Index to Periodical Articles by and about Negroes. Boston: G. K. Hall, 1950–present. Formerly entitled *Index to Selected Periodicals,* this guide indexes articles on Negro life that have appeared in a dozen or so different periodicals.

International Library of Negro Life and History. New York: Publishers Co., Inc., 1967–68. A collection of materials treating in detail the cultural and historical background of American Negroes.

McPherson, James M., et al. *Blacks in America: A Research Bibliography.* Garden City, N.Y.: Doubleday, 1971. Contains 100 bibliographical essays dealing with various aspects of the Afro-American experience from 1500 to contemporary times.

Ploski, Harry A., and Ernest Kaiser. *The Negro Almanac.* 2nd ed. New York: Bellwether, 1971. Over a thousand pages of information on a wide range of historical and cultural events in the life of American blacks. Also covers black organizations.

Sloan, Irving J., ed. *Blacks in America, 1492–1970: A Chronology and Fact Book.* Dobbs Ferry, N.Y.: Oceana, 1971. In addition to providing an excellent chronological summary of American black history, this volume supplies data on publications and associations related to blacks. Includes an extensive bibliography of books and audiovisual materials on the subject.

Welsch, Erwin K. *The Negro in the United States: A Research Guide.* Bloomington: Indiana University Press, 1965. Excellent source for research in black history. Analyzes books and periodicals dealing with black history, civil rights issues, and the black contribution to the arts.

AFRO-AMERICAN JOURNALS

> *Black Scholar*
> *Black World*
> *Ebony*
> *Journal of Black Studies*
> *Negro Heritage*
> *Negro History Bulletin*

b. Chicano

Barrios, Ernie, ed. *Bibliografía de Aztlán.* San Diego, Calif.: Centro de Estudios Chicanos Publications, San Diego State College, 1971. A thoroughly annotated bibliography of books on contemporary Chicano history, philosophy, literature, education, and sociology. Provides extensive lists of Chicano journals and periodicals along with an author and subject index. Militant editorial point of view.

Jordan, Lois B. *Mexican Americans: Resources to Build Cultural Understanding.* Littleton, Colo.: Libraries Unlimited, Inc., 1973. A selective annotated bibliography of materials—books, films, filmstrips, recordings, slides, and other audiovisual helps—that provide information on the historical background, cultural heritage, and contemporary political problems of Mexican Americans.

Trejo, Arnulfo D. *Bibliografía Chicano: A Guide to Information Sources.* Detroit: Gale Research Company, 1975. A scholarly and annotated selective bibliography of works on the Chicano movement. The bibliography is divided into the following headings: general reference works, humanities, social sciences, history, and applied sciences. Ranges from 1848 to the present.

Woods, Richard D. *Reference Materials on Mexican Americans.* Metuchen, N.J.: Scarecrow Press, 1976. An annotated bibliography arranged alphabetically by author. The reference works included have a multiethnic perspective, with one section dealing entirely with Chicanos. Subjects emphasized are: migrant education, poverty in the United States, industrial relations, and legal defenses. Includes guides to periodicals.

CHICANO JOURNALS

> *Aztlán*
> *La Gente*
> *El Grito*
> *Journal of Mexican American History*
> *El Malcriado*
> *Mundo Hispánico*

c. American Indian

Dennis, Henry C. *The American Indian, 1492–1970: A Chronology and Fact Book.* Dobbs Ferry, N.Y.: Oceana, 1971. Surveys the history of American Indians. Contains biographies of famous Indians, a bibliography of books, audiovisual materials relating to Indian life, and an index.

Hodge, Frederick W. *Handbook of American Indians North of Mexico.* 2 vols. Washington, D.C.: GPO, 1907–08; rpt. St. Clair Shores, Mich.:

Scholarly Press, 1968. An old but informative source of facts about Indian tribes, settlements, confederacies, and institutions. Provides information about famous Indians, Indian customs and crafts, and Indian history.

Index to Literature on the American Indian. San Francisco: Indian Historian Press, 1972–present. Annual index to literature dealing with Indians of North, South, and Central America.

Klein, Bernard, and Daniel Icolari, eds. *Reference Encyclopedia of the American Indian*. New York: Klein, 1967. A handy guide for information about agencies, associations, museums, and libraries specializing in Indian affairs. Lists tribal councils and gives brief biographical sketches of notable Indians.

Swanton, John R. *The Indian Tribes of North America*. Washington, D.C.: GPO, 1952. An excellent source for research on the Indian tribes of Central and North America and the West Indies.

Wauchope, Robert. *Handbook of Middle American Indians*. 12 vols. Austin: University of Texas Press, 1964–present.

AMERICAN INDIAN JOURNALS

> *American Indian Crafts and Culture*
> *Americans Before Columbus*
> *Blue Cloud Quarterly*
> *Indian Historian*
> *The Sentinel*
> *Smoke Signals*

4b-6   History

a. World history

Annual Register of World Events: A Review of the Year. New York: St. Martin's, 1758–present. Annual guidebook of world events. Includes texts of important documents and speeches. Issues cover two hundred years of world history.

Baldwin, Hanson W., ed. *The Great Battles of History Series*. 12 vols. Philadelphia: Lippincott, 1962–present. An excellent source-book for students interested in the details of militia and warfare.

Cambridge Ancient History. 3rd ed. 17 vols. New York: Macmillan, 1970–present. Provides a chronological regional assessment of history. Includes illustrations.

Cambridge Mediaeval History. 8 vols. New York: Macmillan, 1911–36.

Focuses on historical events in Western Europe from the end of the Roman Empire through the Middle Ages. 3rd ed. in progress.

Coulter, Edith M., and Melanie Gerstenfeld. *Historical Bibliographies: A Systematic and Annotated Guide.* Berkeley: University of California Press, 1935. A compendium of sources in all areas of historiography.

Historical Abstracts: Bibliography of the World's Periodical Literature, 1775 to Present. Santa Barbara, Calif.: American Bibliographical Center, Clio Press, 1955–present. Issued quarterly, this guide focuses on articles about world history published in over 2,200 periodicals. Contains annual and five-year author and subject indexes.

Keller, Helen R. *Dictionary of Dates.* 2nd ed. 2 vols. New York, 1934; rpt. New York: Hafner, 1971. A listing of dates of world events. Chronological arrangement under names of countries. Covers from ancient times to 1930.

Larousse Encyclopedia of Ancient and Medieval History. New York: Harper, 1963. (See next entry.)

Larousse Encyclopedia of Modern History: From 1500 to the Present Day. New York: Harper, 1964. Both Larousse encyclopedias are known for their scholarly and expansive treatment of historical events. Excellent source of basic historical information.

Nevins, Allan, and Howard Ehrmann, eds. *The University of Michigan History of the Modern World.* Ann Arbor, Mich.: University of Michigan, 1958–present. Provides dates and summaries of all important events of the modern epoch.

Williams, Neville. *Chronology of the Modern World: 1763 to the Present Time.* New York: McKay, 1967. Dates and explicates events of world-wide significance, including facts of historical significance in art and science. Contains an index.

WORLD HISTORY JOURNALS

> *History*
> *History Today*
> *Journal of Modern History*
> *Journal of the History of Ideas*
> *Past and Present*
> *Renaissance News*
> *Speculum*

b. *American history*

Adams, James Truslow, et al. *Album of American History.* Rev. ed. 7 vols. New York: Scribners, 1945–61. A pictorial history of the United States from Colonial times to the present.

————. *The Dictionary of American History.* 7 vols. New York: Scribners, 1942–61. Abridged edition: *Concise Dictionary of American History.* New York: Scribners, 1962. Consists of brief essays by renowned historians on such subjects as politics, economics, sociology, industry, and cultural history in the United States.

The Annals of America. 21 vols. Chicago: Encyclopaedia Britannica, 1968–71. A collection of 2,202 original source readings drawn from American history, chronologically assembled. Contains an index to proper names.

Commager, Henry S. *Documents of American History.* 8th ed. New York: Appleton, 1968. A collection of the most famous documents relating to American history from 1492 to contemporary times.

Johnson, Thomas H. *The Oxford Companion to American History.* Oxford: Oxford University Press, 1966. Contains nearly 5,000 brief summaries of significant events, places, and people in American history.

Pageant of America: A Political History of the United States. 15 vols. New Haven, Conn.: Yale University Press, 1925–29. A pictorial history of people and events that affected the development of America. Includes coverage of political history, the military, sports, arts, literature, and education. Photographs and illustrations are accompanied by historical commentary.

Writings on American History. Washington, D.C.: GPO, 1918–present. An excellent bibliography of books and articles on United States history. Issued annually.

AMERICAN HISTORY JOURNALS

> *American Historical Review*
> *Journal of American History*
> *Journal of Southern History*

4b-7 Literature

a. General

Adelman, Irving, and Rita Dworkin. *The Contemporary Novel: A Checklist of Critical Literature on the British and American Novel since 1945.* Metuchen, N.J.: Scarecrow Press, 1972. An excellent source of critical opinions on modern fiction. Cites critical reviews on 187 authors from 400 journals and 600 books.

Arms, George, and Joseph M. Kuntz. *Poetry Explication.* Denver: Swallow, 1962. A checklist of interpretations, written since 1925, of poems by past and present British and American authors.

Baker, Ernest A., and James Packman. *Guide to the Best Fiction, English and American.* 3rd ed. New York: Barnes & Noble, 1967. Treats several thousand masterpieces, giving brief summaries of each work. The index is particularly useful because it is a guide to authors, titles, subjects, historical names, allusions, places, and characters.

Bartlett, John. *Familiar Quotations.* 14th ed. Boston: Little, Brown, 1968. A collection of quotable passages from ancient and modern literature. Includes an index to authors and key words.

Cassell's Encyclopaedia of World Literature. New York: Crowell, 1965. Provides general information about world literature. Includes 10,000 biographies of authors.

Columbia Dictionary of Modern European Literature. New York: Columbia University Press, 1947. Contains articles about literary works written since 1870 in thirty-one European countries. The emphasis is biographical.

Encyclopedia of World Literature in the Twentieth Century. 3 vols. New York: Ungar, 1967–71. Consists of articles treating authors, literary movements, genres, and national literatures.

Essay and General Literature Index. New York: Wilson, 1934–present. Continuation of *A.L.A. Index to General Literature.* Contains an author and subject index to collections of essays and anthologies of every kind published since 1900.

Granger's Index to Poetry. 5th ed. New York: Columbia University Press, 1962. *Supplement*, 1967. Provides an extensive index to almost 600 anthologies of poetry. Indexes to titles, first lines, authors, and subjects make the material easy to trace.

Great Books of the Western World. Chicago: Encyclopaedia Britannica, 1952. This set of 54 volumes is often found in private libraries because it is considered a classic of its kind. Includes close to 500 works by the world's great authors from Homer to Dickens.

Hackett, Alice P. *Seventy Years of Best Sellers, 1895–1965.* New York: Bowker, 1967. An intelligent analysis of 600 books that have each sold over 750,000 copies. Includes a title and author index.

Haydn, Hiram, and Edmund Fuller. *Thesaurus of Book Digests.* New York: Crown, 1949. Synopses of the world's greatest writings from the ancient classics to contemporary literature.

Holman, C. Hugh. *A Handbook to Literature.* 3rd ed. Indianapolis, Ind.: Odyssey, 1972. An excellent source of knowledge about literary terms, periods, schools, and general concepts.

Hornstein, Lillian H., ed. *Reader's Companion to World Literature*. New York: New American Library, 1958. Contains articles on world masterpieces, biographies of authors, definition of literary terms, and other important general information.

Magill, Frank. *Cyclopedia of Literary Characters*. New York: Harper, 1963. An excellent source of information about major and minor characters from novels, plays, epics, and other notable literary works. Covers world literature.

Magill, Frank N. *Magill's Quotations in Context*. New York: Harper, 1966. Clarifies the background against which famous quotations appear. Covers all of Western literature. Supplemented by *Magill's Quotations in Context: Second Series*. New York: Harper, 1969. Adds 1,500 quotations.

————, ed. *Masterplots*. 6 vols. New York: Salem Press, 1960. Provides summaries of plots for literary masterpieces. A good source to consult, for example, if you want to know what actually happened in a novel such as *Vanity Fair*.

MLA International Bibliography of Books and Articles on the Modern Languages and Literature. 1921–present. New York: New York University Press, 1964–present. The most scholarly index to literary criticism in international publications. Issued annually.

Moulton, Charles Wells. *Library of Literary Criticism of English and American Authors*. 8 vols. New York, 1901–05; rpt. New York: Peter Smith, 1935–40. An old but honored work still consulted because of its collection of incisive critiques.

The Penguin Companion to American Literature.
The Penguin Companion to Classical, Oriental and African Literature.
The Penguin Companion to English Literature.
The Penguin Companion to European Literature.
New York: McGraw-Hill, 1969–71. 4 vols. Arranged alphabetically by authors, these works supply some excellent brief critical biographies of authors and their works.

Thompson, Stith. *Motif-Index to Folk Literature*. Rev. and enl. ed. 6 vols. Bloomington, Ind.: Indiana University Press, 1955–58. A classification of narrative elements in folk tales, ballads, myths, fables, and medieval romances.

b. American

American Literature Abstracts. San Jose, Calif.: Department of English, California State University, San Jose, 1967–present. Issued semiannually, these abstracts of articles and book reviews represent current scholarship in American literature.

Blanck, Jacob. *Bibliography of American Literature.* 5 vols. New Haven, Conn.: Yale University Press, 1955–69. Contains bibliographies of more than 300 American authors who died before 1930. Lists such information as first editions, important reprints, biographical works, and critical works related to the authors.

Cambridge History of American Literature. 4 vols. New York: Putnam, 1917–21. Reissued, New York: Macmillan, 1954. 3 vols. A scholarly work of extraordinary significance. Interprets American literature from its beginnings in the Colonial and Revolutionary periods until it revealed a national consciousness. Includes accounts of early travelers and observers in addition to the standard masterpieces. Updated by: Spiller, Robert E., et al. *Literary History of the United States.* 3rd ed. 2 vols. New York: Macmillan, 1963.

Coan, Otis W., and R. G. Lillard. *America in Fiction.* 5th ed. Palo Alto, Calif.: Pacific Books, 1967. An annotated bibliography of novels that give insight into aspects of life in the United States, Canada, and Mexico.

Dickinson, A. T., Jr. *American Historical Fiction.* 3rd ed. Metuchen, N. J.: Scarecrow Press, 1971. Provides brief descriptions, chronologically arranged, of fiction from the Colonial period to 1970.

Hart, James D. *The Oxford Companion to American Literature.* 4th ed. Oxford: Oxford University Press, 1965. Provides information on an expansive scale about all aspects of American literature. Includes social as well as literary history from 1000 to 1964, biographies, bibliographies, summaries of masterpieces, and comments on literary movements.

Jones, Howard Mumford, and Richard M. Ludwig. *Guide to American Literature and Its Backgrounds since 1890.* 3rd ed. Cambridge, Mass.: Harvard University Press, 1964. Provides an excellent list of important background books dealing with all aspects of American literature.

Richards, Robert F., ed. *Concise Dictionary of American Literature.* 3rd ed. New York: Ungar, 1964. Lists and defines hundreds of terms associated with American literature.

c. British

Baker, Ernest A. *History of the English Novel.* 10 vols. New York, 1924–30; rpt. New York: Barnes & Noble, 1960. Vol. 11, *Yesterday and After,* by Lionel Stevenson, was published in 1967. These volumes are constantly referred to by students of the English novel because they provide so much important information, in chronological form, about how the novel developed and what each novelist contributed to the genre.

Baugh, Albert C. *A Literary History of England.* New York: Appleton, 1967. Excellent scholarship and readability has made this work a standard source of English literature. Provides a biographical, historical, and critical account of all major works, beginning with the Old English period and culminating with the twentieth century. Contains 1,673 pages, including a detailed index.

Cambridge Bibliography of English Literature. 5 vols. Cambridge, Eng.: Cambridge University Press, 1941–57. The most comprehensive bibliography of English literature. New edition in progress.

Cambridge History of English Literature. 15 vols. Cambridge, Eng.: Cambridge University Press, 1919–30. Considered the most authoritative history of English literature. The volumes represent a collaboration by specialists, and cover all aspects of English literary history from its beginnings to the twentieth century. The work is updated by: Sampson, George. *Concise Cambridge History of English Literature.* 3rd ed. Cambridge, Eng.: Cambridge University Press, 1970.

McSpadden, J. Walker. *Shakespearean Synopses.* New York: Crowell, 1959. A handy reference for getting acquainted with the bare plots of all of Shakespeare's plays.

Martin, Michael R., and Richard C. Harrier. *The Concise Encyclopedic Guide to Shakespeare.* New York: Horizon Press, 1971. Provides plot synopses, identification of characters, facts about the Elizabethan theater, and biographical information about Shakespeare.

Myers, Robin. *A Dictionary of Literature in the English Language from Chaucer to 1940.* 2 vols. Oxford: Pergamon, 1970. Biographical and bibliographical guide to thousands of authors and their works.

Oxford Companion to English Literature. 4th ed. Oxford: Clarendon Press, 1967. Alphabetical arrangement of terms. Contains brief entries on all manner of literary matters, such as authors, characters, titles, genres, allusions, and the like.

Oxford History of English Literature. 12 vols. Oxford: Oxford University Press, 1945–present. A comprehensive, scholarly presentation covering the entire field of English literature. No other work of this kind can compete with the scope of these volumes.

LITERATURE JOURNALS

Abstracts of English Studies
American Literature
American Quarterly
American Scholar
ELH

English Studies
PMLA
Review of English Studies
Shakespeare Quarterly
Victorian Studies

4b-8 Music

American Society of Composers, Authors and Publishers. *The ASCAP Biographical Dictionary of Composers, Authors, and Publishers.* 2nd ed. New York: Crowell, 1952. Provides brief sketches of prominent composers.

Apel, Willi. *Harvard Dictionary of Music.* 2nd ed. Cambridge, Mass.: Harvard University Press, 1969. One of the most popular references consulted on such matters as music terminology, history, and theory.

Baker, Theodore. *Biographical Dictionary of Musicians.* 5th ed. New York: Schirmer, 1958. *Supplement*, 1965. *Supplement*, 1971. Provides brief sketches of musicians all over the world, ancient and modern.

Duckles, Vincent H. *Music Reference and Research Materials.* 2nd ed. New York: Free Press of Glencoe, 1967. An annotated bibliography of works dealing with all phases of music.

Ewen, David. *Encyclopedia of Concert Music.* New York: Hill & Wang, 1959. Provides information on 1,500 music masterpieces along with brief biographies of musicians.

Grove, Sir George. *Grove's Dictionary of Music and Musicians.* 5th ed. 10 vols. New York: Macmillan, 1954–61. New York: St. Martin's, 1954–61. A comprehensive reference source on all aspects of music since 1450.

New Oxford History of Music. London: Oxford University Press, 1954–present. Still in progress, this ambitious work proposes to cover the history of music from ancient to modern times.

Records in Review. Great Barrington, Mass.: Wyeth Press, 1955–present. Issued annually. Provides a compilation of reviews appearing in *High Fidelity* magazine.

Thompson, Oscar. *Plots of the Operas.* 9th ed. New York: Dodd, Mead, 1940. Gives excellent summaries of the story lines of all famous operas.

Westrup, Jack A., and F. C. Harrison. *The New College Encyclopedia of Music.* New York: Norton, 1960. Geared to the college student, this reference provides brief articles on composers, performers, compositions, and musical terms.

MUSIC JOURNALS

Educational Music Magazine
Journal of Renaissance and Baroque Music
Modern Music
Music and Letters
Music Journal
Musical Quarterly
Opera News

4b-9 Mythology/Classics

Brewer, E. Cobham. *Brewer's Dictionary of Phrase and Fable.* New York: Harper, 1972. A new edition of an old standard reference source. Contains entries on a variety of material related to myths and fables.

Bullfinch's Mythology. 2nd rev. ed. New York: Thomas Y. Crowell Co., 1950. Provides summaries and comments on the "age of fables, age of chivalry, and legends of Charlemagne."

Encyclopedia of Classical Mythology. Englewood Cliffs, N.J.: Prentice-Hall, 1965. Provides detailed background material on Greek and Roman mythology.

Evans, Bergen. *Dictionary of Mythology, Mainly Classical.* Lincoln, Neb.: Centennial Press, 1970. Describes mythological characters and briefly summarizes their stories.

Frazer, James. *The Golden Bough.* 3rd ed. 13 vols. New York: St. Martin's, 1958. Considered a standard reference work on mythology and its relationship to magic and religion. Traces many myths to their historical beginning.

Gayley, Charles M. *Classic Myths in English Literature and in Art.* New York: Wiley, 1939. A standard guide to mythology found in English literature and art.

Gray, Louis H. *The Mythology of All Races.* Boston: Marshall Jones, 1916–32. 13 vols. An old but still useful work. Surveys the myths of different races. Includes numerous illustrations.

Grimal, Pierre, ed. *Larousse World Mythology.* 26th ed. New York: G. P. Putnam's, 1965. Analyzes myths from all major world religions. An excellent reference source for students of art, literature, history, and religion.

Jung, Carl G. *The Archetypes and the Collective Unconscious.* Vol. IX, Part I, of *The Collected Works of Carl Jung.* 2nd ed. Trans. R. F. C. Hull. Princeton, N.J.: Princeton University Press, 1969. Provides a psychological interpretation of mythology.

New Century Classical Handbook. New York: Prentice-Hall, 1962. A compilation based on recent archeological findings. Well illustrated.

MYTHOLOGY/CLASSICS JOURNALS

> *Arion*
> *Classical Bulletin*
> *Classical Journal*
> *Classical Quarterly*
> *Classical Review*
> *Mythic Society Quarterly*

4b-10   Philosophy

Baldwin, James M. *Dictionary of Philosophy and Psychology.* 2nd ed. New York, 1901–05; rpt. Gloucester, Mass.: Peter Smith, 1960. A time-honored work, defining thousands of philosophical and psychological terms. Does not, however, cover contemporary philosophy or psychology.

Bibliography of Philosophy, 1933–1936. 4 vols. New York: Journal of Philosophy, 1934–37. A thorough accumulation of reference sources for any student doing research in philosophy.

Clark, Gordon H. *Thales to Dewey: A History of Philosophy.* Boston: Houghton Mifflin, 1957. A good overview of the development of philosophy.

The Encyclopedia of Philosophy. 8 vols. New York: Macmillan, 1967. Treats numerous philosophical topics at length, with an emphasis on individual philosophers. Includes bibliographies and thorough cross-referencing. Vol. VIII is an index.

Magill, Frank H. *Masterpieces of World Philosophy in Summary Form.* New York: Harper, 1961. Provides an excellent overview of Western philosophy by summarizing all major philosophic works in chronological order.

Miller, Hugh. *An Historical Introduction to Modern Philosophy.* New York: Macmillan, 1947. An excellent source for background material on philosophies of the nineteenth and twentieth centuries.

Philosopher's Index: An International Index to Philosophical Periodicals. Bowling Green, Ohio: Bowling Green University, 1967–present. Issued quarterly with annual cumulations, this index covers over 175 major American and British philosophical periodicals. Includes abstracts of articles and a book review index.

Russell, Bertrand. *A History of Western Philosophy.* New York: Simon and

Schuster, 1945. A highly readable reference source, written by one of the most notable twentieth-century philosophers.

Urmson, James O. *The Concise Encyclopaedia of Western Philosophy*. New York: Hawthorn Books, 1960. A 431-page volume that explains technical terms, identifies individual philosophers, and clarifies all the major philosophies of the Western world.

PHILOSOPHY JOURNALS

> *Ethics*
> *Journal of Philosophy*
> *Journal of the History of Ideas*
> *Personalist*
> *Philosophical Review*

4b-11   Psychology

Annual Review of Psychology. Stanford, Calif.: Annual Reviews, Inc., 1950–present. Reviews current literature in psychology.

Deutsch, Albert. *Encyclopedia of Mental Health*. 6 vols. New York: Franklin Watts, 1963. Contains well-developed articles on all general aspects of mental health.

Drever, James. *A Dictionary of Psychology*. Rev. ed. Baltimore: Penguin Books, 1964. Provides brief but concise definitions of psychological terms and concepts.

Eysenck, H. J., ed. *Encyclopedia of Psychology*. 3 vols. Contains some 5,000 articles on all aspects of psychology and human behavior.

Harvard List of Books in Psychology. 4th ed. Cambridge, Mass.: Harvard University Press, 1971. An annotated guide to books in the field of psychology, alphabetized by subject. Includes an author index.

Psychological Abstracts. Washington, D.C.: American Psychological Association, 1927–present. Issued monthly. Provides abstracts in English of international literature in the field of psychology. Alphabetized by subject with an author-subject index.

PSYCHOLOGY JOURNALS

> *American Journal of Psychology*
> *American Psychologist*
> *Annual Review of Psychology*
> *Behavioral Science*
> *Contemporary Psychology*
> *Journal of Applied Psychology*
> *Journal of Clinical Psychology*

Journal of Educational Psychology
Journal of General Psychology
Journal of Psychology
Psychological Record
Psychological Review

4b-12   Religion

Adams, Charles J., ed. *A Reader's Guide to the Great Religions.* New York: Free Press, 1965. A bibliographic index to works on the major religions of the world. Suggests what works to read and why.

Attwater, Donald, ed. *The Catholic Encyclopaedic Dictionary.* New York: Macmillan, 1958. Explains terms associated with the theology, liturgy, and history of the Catholic Church. Includes biographies of saints.

Ballou, Robert O. *The Bible of the World.* New York: Viking, 1939. Contains important excerpts from the sacred writings of the eight major living religions.

Berry, Gerald L. *Religions of the World.* Rev. ed. New York: Barnes & Noble, 1956. Gives basic information on all the world's principal religions. Considerable information packed into a mere 136 pages.

Catholic Encyclopedia. 17 vols. New York: Gilmary Society, 1902–22. A monumental scholarly work, providing a wealth of information about the medieval age, its history, philosophy, and art, and Catholic beliefs.

Cross, F. L., ed. *Oxford Dictionary of the Christian Church.* New York: Oxford University Press, 1957. Focuses on the historical development, doctrines, and lives of important Christian churchmen.

Encyclopaedia Judaica. 16 vols. New York: Macmillan, 1972. Offers comprehensive information on all aspects of Judaism in the twentieth century.

Jewish Encyclopedia. 12 vols. New York: KTAV Publishing House, 1964. Provides information on the history, religion, literature, and culture of the Jewish religion. Includes many biographical entries.

Magill, Frank N., ed. *Masterpieces of Catholic Literature in Summary Form.* New York: Harper & Row, 1965. Useful summaries of essays that review a wide selection of Roman Catholic literature, from the beginning of Christianity to the present.

————. *Masterpieces of Christian Literature in Summary Form.* New York: Harper & Row, 1963. A collection of essays with a Protestant point of view.

Mead, Frank S. *The Encyclopedia of Religious Quotations.* New York: Revell,

1965. Contains more than 10,000 quotations taken from religious literary masterpieces.

Religious and Theological Abstracts. Youngtown, Ohio: Theological Publishers, 1958–present. Issued quarterly. Abstracts of essays on religion taken from selected religious periodicals throughout the world. Edited from a nonsectarian point of view. Includes Jewish, Christian, and Moslem publications.

Sacred Books of the East. 50 vols. Oxford : Clarendon Press, 1885–1910. An old but admirable piece of scholarship. Consists of English translations of all the important religious texts of major Oriental religions.

RELIGIOUS JOURNALS

> *Catholic Digest*
> *Christian Century*
> *Christianity and Crisis*
> *Christianity for Today*
> *Ecumenical Review*
> *Encounter*
> *History of Religions*
> *International Review of Missions*
> *Journal of Religion*
> *Religious and Theological Abstracts*

4b-13 Science

American Men and Women of Science. 12th ed. 8 vols. New York: Bowker, 1971–73. Gives biographical sketches of noted contributors to the physical, biological, social, and behavioral sciences.

Annual Review of Information Science and Technology. New York: Interscience and Wiley, 1966–present. An annual review of developments in science and technology.

Asimov, Isaac. *Asimov's Biographical Encyclopedia of Science and Technology.* Rev. ed. Garden City, N.Y.: Doubleday, 1972. Contains articles on the "lives and achievements of 1,195 great scientists from ancient times to the present, chronologically arranged."

Collocott, T. C., ed. *Dictionary of Science and Technology.* New York: Barnes & Noble, 1972. Succeeds Chambers' *Technical Dictionary* (3rd ed., 1958). Provides explanations for at least 60,000 terms in 100 subject areas. Includes numerous important tables and charts.

Dictionary of Scientific Biography. New York: Scribners, 1970. Still in progress, this mammoth work is to be completed in twelve volumes.

It will cover the lives and contributions of major scientists throughout history.

Government Reports Announcements. Springfield, Va.: National Technical Information Service, U.S. Dept. of Commerce, 1938–present. Issued semimonthly. Provides abstracts of reports sponsored by government agencies in all areas of science and technology. See also *Government Reports Index,* issued semimonthly with annual cumulations.

Grogan, Denis J. *Science and Technology: An Introduction to the Literature.* Hamden, Conn.: Archon, 1970. Gives summaries of important literature written in the field of science and technology.

Herner, Saul. *A Brief Guide to Sources of Scientific and Technical Information.* Washington, D.C.: Information Resources Press, 1969. An annotated listing of important reference sources in science and technology.

Jenkins, Frances B. *Science Reference Sources.* 5th ed. Cambridge, Mass.: M.I.T. Press, 1969. A standard guide to reference sources in all areas of science and technology.

McGraw-Hill Encyclopedia of Science and Technology. 3rd ed. 15 vols. New York: McGraw-Hill, 1971. Contains more than 7,000 articles covering all natural sciences and including technologies such as engineering, agriculture, forestry, and food production.

McGraw-Hill Modern Men of Science. New York: McGraw-Hill, 1967. Supplements the *McGraw-Hill Encyclopedia of Science and Technology.* Gives essential biographical information on major contributors to science during the twentieth century.

Van Nostrand's Scientific Encyclopedia. 14th ed. Princeton, N.J.: Van Nostrand, 1968. Gives comprehensive coverage to basic as well as applied science. Especially good for such modern fields as planetary exploration, rocketry, and space travel. Contains many illustrations.

SCIENCE AND TECHNOLOGY JOURNALS

Advancement of Science
Science
Science Abstracts
Scientific American
Scientific Monthly

4b-14 Social sciences

Encyclopaedia of the Social Sciences. 8 vols. New York: Macmillan, 1937. A scholarly and accurate source of general information on economics, law, anthropology, sociology, penology, social work, and political science.

Gould, Julius, and William L. Kolb. *A Dictionary of the Social Sciences.* New York: Free Press of Glencoe, 1964. Sponsored by UNESCO, this is the most outstanding single-volume dictionary of the social sciences.

Hoselitz, Berthold F. *A Reader's Guide to the Social Sciences.* Rev. ed. New York: Free Press, 1970. Consists of bibliographic essays written by experts in such areas as sociology, anthropology, psychology, political science, economics, and geography. Does an excellent job of tracing the development of the social sciences in the last 200 years.

International Encyclopedia of the Social Sciences. 17 vols. New York: Macmillan, 1968. Complements *Encyclopaedia of the Social Sciences* by emphasizing the social sciences of the 1960s. Stresses the analytical and comparative aspects of each topic. Includes biographical articles and bibliographies.

Public Affairs Information Service Bulletin. New York: Public Affairs Information Service, 1905–present. Issued weekly, cumulated five times a year and annually. Serves as a guide to current books, government publications, and periodical articles in the social sciences.

Social Sciences and Humanities Index. See p. 33.

Stevens, Rolland E. *Reference Books in the Social Sciences and Humanities.* 3rd ed. Champaign, Ill.: Illinois Union Bookstore, 1971. This is an annotated guide to more than 500 bibliographies, periodical indexes, dictionaries, encyclopedias, and other reference works in the social sciences and humanities. Organized by subject.

White, Carl M., et al. *Sources of Information in the Social Sciences: A Guide to the Literature.* 3rd ed. Chicago: American Library Association, 1973. Compiled by specialists in the field, this is an annotated guide to the literature of the social sciences in general and to each of its subdivisions. Discusses the history and methodology of each discipline. Includes bibliographies.

Zadrozny, John T. *Dictionary of Social Science.* Washington, D.C.: Public Affairs Press, 1959. Defines and gives actual usages of the most important terms in the social sciences.

JOURNALS OF SOCIAL SCIENCE

(The journals listed below cover only sociology, political science, and economics.)

Human Organization
International Social Science Journal
Journal of Politics
Social Education
Social Science

Social Science Review
Sociological Abstracts
Quarterly Journal of Economics

4b-15 Women

Backscheider, Paula R., and Felicity A. Backscheider. *An Annotated Bibliography of 20th Century Critical Studies of Women and Literature, 1660–1800.* New York: Garland Publications, 1977. An excellent reference guide to writings by and about women. Covers 1660–1800.

Barrer, Myra E., ed. *Women's Organizations and Leaders: 1977–78 Directory.* Washington, D.C.: Today Publications and News Service, 1977. Lists important women's organizations and prominent individuals in the feminist cause. Covers the United States, Canal Zone, Guam, Puerto Rico, and the Virgin Islands. Includes subject, geographical, and alphabetical indexes. Updated annually.

Beard, Mary Ritter. *Women As a Force in History: A Study in Traditions and Realities.* New York: Octagon Books, 1976. An analysis of women as a subject sex within the historical realities of law, religion, the military, politics, morality, and philosophy.

Brownlee, W. Elliot, and Mary M. Brownlee. *Women in the American Economy: A Documentary History, 1675–1929.* New Haven: Yale University Press, 1976. A concise history of female employment in the U.S. task force. Includes numerous bibliographical references.

Chamberlin, Hope. *A Minority of Members: Women in the U.S. Congress.* New York: Praeger, 1973. Provides definitive biographies of eighty-five Congresswomen, using their own words or writings. Includes illustrations.

Hole, Judith, and Ellen Levine. *Rebirth of Feminism.* New York: Quadrangle Books, 1971. A history and analysis of the origins, issues, and activities of the new women's movement. Includes a bibliography.

Hughes, Marija M. *The Sexual Barrier: Legal and Economic Aspects of Employment.* San Francisco: the Author, 1970–present. Updated annually. Provides a bibliographic guide to various printed materials on the laws and conditions that govern the employment of women. Includes an author index.

Ireland, Norma O. *Index to Women of the World from Ancient to Modern Times: Biographies and Portraits.* Westwood, Mass.: Faxon, 1970. Tells where to find good biographies and portraits of 13,000 prominent women of all periods from all over the world.

James, Edward T., and Janet W. James, eds. *Notable American Women,*

1607–1950: A Biographical Dictionary. 3 vols. Cambridge, Mass.: Belknap Press of Harvard University, 1971. Begins with an introductory survey of the history of women in America, then presents signed articles analyzing the lives of American women who have made notable contributions to various fields of knowledge.

Krichmar, Albert. *The Women's Rights Movement in the United States, 1848–1970: A Bibliography and Sourcebook.* Metuchen, N.J.: Scarecrow Press, 1972. A bibliographic guide, divided into such sections as economic status, education, religion, and biography. Includes author and subject indexes.

Lerner, Gerda, ed. *Black Women in White America.* New York: Pantheon Books, 1972. A documentary history of black women in U.S. history. Covers such topics as slavery, education, and work in prejudiced environments.

Lifton, Robert Jay, ed. *The Woman in America.* Boston: Houghton Mifflin, 1965. A collection of essays resulting from the Daedalus Conference on Women, held in Boston in 1964. Considered historically important. Includes numerous bibliographical references.

Matthiasson, Carolyn J., ed. *Many Sisters: Women in Cross-Cultural Perspective.* New York: The Free Press, 1974. Written entirely by women anthropologists and sociologists, this anthology examines the roles of women in various cultures of the world.

Millett, Kate. *Sexual Politics.* Garden City, N.Y.: Doubleday, 1970. A volume that caused a great stir when first published. Presents evidence for the fact that throughout history sexual politics have kept women out of areas where they could acquire power. The book traces the vocabulary of sexual power in varying texts. Includes a bibliography and index.

O'Neill, William L. *The Woman Movement: Feminism in the United States and England.* New York: Barnes & Noble, 1969. Deals with all aspects of women's rights. Includes bibliographical references.

Reiter, Rayna R., ed. *Toward an Anthropology of Women.* New York: Monthly Review Press, 1975. A collection of addresses, essays, and lectures on the role of women from an anthropological perspective.

Rossi, Alice S. *The Feminist Papers: From Adams to Beauvoir.* New York: Columbia University Press, 1973. A collection of the essential works of feminism in abridged form.

Steiner-Scott, Elizabeth, and Elizabeth P. Wagle. *New Jersey Women, 1770–1970: A Bibliography.* New York: G. K. Hall, 1977. A guide to works covering general aspects of women over the last 200 years.

Stimpson, Catharine R., ed. (In conjunction with the Congressional Information Service.) *Discrimination against Women: Congressional Hearings on Equal Rights in Education and Employment.* New York: Bowker, 1973. A well-edited version of the 1970 hearings of the government Special Subcommittee on Education.

Wheeler, Helen. *Womanhood Media: Current Resources about Women.* An annotated list of over 300 books, with a section on nonbook materials, all relating to the role of women in society. Evaluates the treatment of women in general reference works.

Women's Work and Women's Studies, 1973–74. Old Westbury, N.Y.: Feminist Press, 1977. Provides abstractions of books, articles, and research on women's activities. Includes information on current feminist activism and an author index.

JOURNALS ABOUT WOMEN

Aphra
Everywoman
Feminist Studies
Journal of Female Liberation
NOW Acts
The Pedestal
Up from Under
The Woman Activist
Women: A Journal of Liberation
Women's Rights Law Reporter

five

Doing the research

5a
Assembling a working bibliography

The bibliography is a list of sources on the research topic. These sources will range from encyclopedia entries to magazine articles, from scholarly essays to chapters of books and information stored on microform. The *working bibliography* is made up of those sources consulted for information; the *final bibliography* is an alphabetical list of those sources actually used in the paper.

The working bibliography is assembled as the researcher scans the references and card catalog for information on the subject. Promising sources are noted down on 3×5 bibliography cards (to be distinguished from the 4×6 note cards). The bibliography card should contain information about the sources to be consulted, along with a brief note on why it is likely to be useful. See example on page 77.

This researcher, who was writing a paper on Rasputin, had no way of knowing whether or not the book would be useful without first skimming it. But as she thumbed through the card catalog, she compiled several bibliography cards on books, giving her numerous titles to consult and skim through.

Generally a student will end up with many more sources in the working bibliography than are listed in the final bibliography. This is as it should be. Many sources will be consulted, but few chosen. Students must literally grope their way through the maze of sources available on the subject. False starts and dead-end trails are to be expected. Books will lure one on with a promising table of contents and title, but once skimmed, will prove to be excessively technical, dated, or simply beside the point. The researcher must good-naturedly ignore the irrevelant and worthless sources, while studiously tracking down those articles, essays, and books that promise to be worthwhile and useful.

A single bibliography card should be used for each source. Bibliography cards are better than a scrap of paper or a page in one's notebook because (1) they can easily be carried in the pocket; (2) they can readily be set aside, if a source proves useless; (3) they can be added to if a new source is found; and (4) they can be shuffled into alphabetical order, which is how the entries have to be listed in the final bibliography.

Scanning the card catalog, the student doing the paper on Rasputin found numerous promising titles and prepared a bibliography card for each. Moreover, entries found under "Rasputin" in the subject index of the card catalog also referred her to cross-listings such as "Russian History," "Nicholas II," "Russia, 1894–1917," and "Russian Court and Courtiers." Some of these listings led to other promising sources, all of which were recorded on separate bibliography cards.

Having pored over the card catalog, the student consulted the

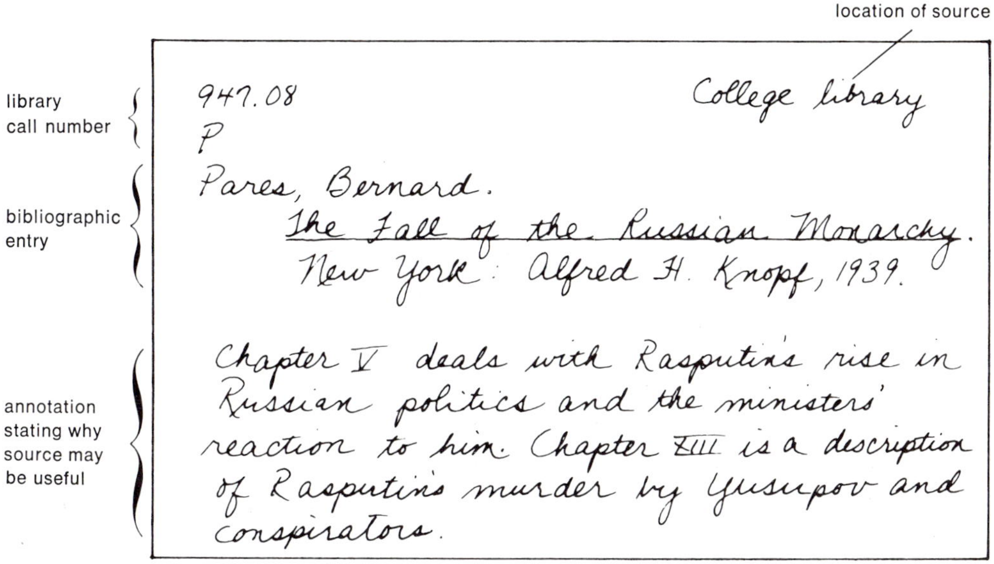

location of source

library
call number

> 947.08
> P
> College library

bibliographic
entry

> Pares, Bernard.
>   *The Fall of the Russian Monarchy.*
> New York: Alfred H. Knopf, 1939.

annotation
stating why
source may
be useful

> Chapter V deals with Rasputin's rise in
> Russian politics and the ministers'
> reaction to him. Chapter XIII is a description
> of Rasputin's murder by Yusupov and
> conspirators.

Figure 5-1   Bibliography card for a book

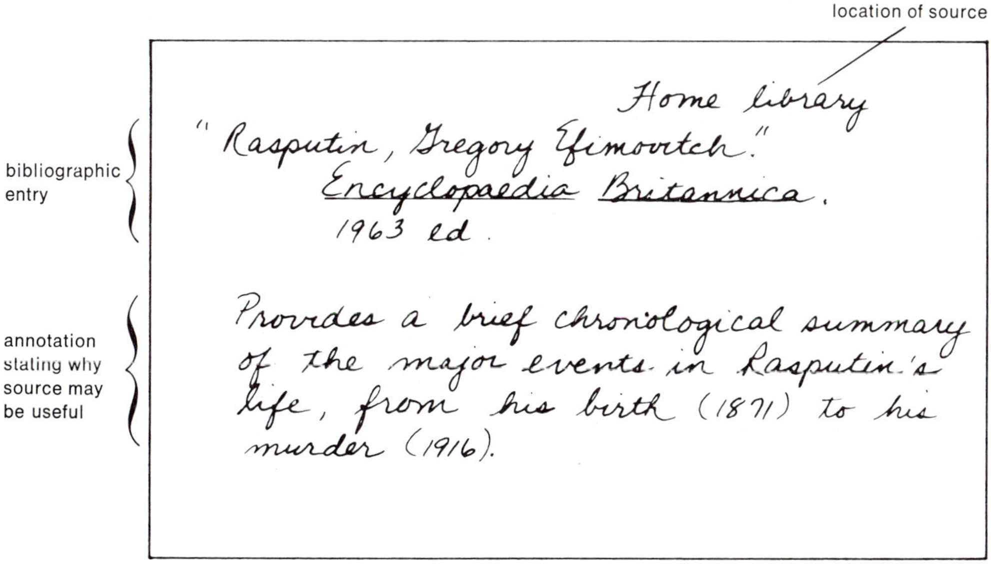

location of source

bibliographic
entry

> Home library
> "Rasputin, Gregory Efimovitch."
>   *Encyclopaedia Britannica.*
>   1963 ed.

annotation
stating why
source may
be useful

> Provides a brief chronological summary
> of the major events in Rasputin's
> life, from his birth (1871) to his
> murder (1916).

Figure 5-2   Bibliography card for an encyclopedia article

Encyclopaedia Britannica on "Rasputin," finding information there whose usefulness she summarized on the bibliography card found on page 77. Moreover, the bibliography at the end of the encyclopedia entry also referred her to several other sources.

The student then checked several references including the *Readers' Guide to Periodical Literature,* the *Social Science Index,* and the *Humanities Index* for articles about Rasputin. The back issues of these references were also checked for articles about Rasputin written within the past fifteen years. Periodical sources indexed in these references were entered on bibliography cards, as in Figure 5-3.

While researching periodical sources, the student came across an entry about a *Los Angeles Times* interview with Rasputin's daughter, who described her father somewhat differently than did most of his biographers. This newspaper source was entered on a bibliography card (Figure 5-4). The interview also mentioned that Maria Rasputin had just published a book about her father: *Rasputin: The Man behind the Myth.* Checking the *Book Review Digest,* the student found that the book was adjudged by reviewers to contain important new information about Rasputin; she therefore entered the title on a bibliography card.

Bibliography cards were also prepared for the entries from various other references, such as the *Who Was Who in the USSR* article about Rasputin. Further, the student discovered two book titles about Rasputin from reviews listed in the *Book Review Digest,* and although both titles were unavailable from either the city or the college library, she entered them on bibliography cards and put in a request for the books through the interlibrary loan service.

5a-1   The proper form for bibliography cards

- Record each source in ink on a separate 3×5 card.
- Use the same form on the bibliography cards as will be used later in the final bibliography. This makes it possible to prepare the final bibliography by simply transcribing from the cards those titles actually used in writing the paper. The following basic information must be listed on the cards:

    Name of author(s)
    Title of work
    Facts of publication
    Page(s) of information

- In the upper right-hand corner of the card, name the library or place where the source was found, as for example, "Main City Library."
- In the upper left-hand corner of the card, cite the library call number of the source, so that it can be easily found even if reshelved.

location of source

bibliographic entry

City library

Halliday, E. M.
"Rasputin Reconsidered."
Horizon, 9 (Autumn 1967), 152-54.

annotation stating why source may be useful

This article came out after Prince Yusupov's book *Lost Splendor*, in which Yusupov admits killing Rasputin. The article promises to re-evaluate Rasputin's character and role in Russian history.

Figure 5-3 Bibliography card for a periodical

location of source

Microfilm from
L.A. Times

bibliographic entry

" Interview with Rasputin's Daughter."
Los Angeles *Times*, 9 June 1976,
Sec. I, pp. 1, 10, 11.

annotation stating why source may be useful

Interviewed as a dying old woman, Maria Rasputin insists that her father was a gentle, good man, subject to many temptations.

Figure 5-4 Bibliography card for a newspaper article

5a-2   Where to look for information

- Check the encyclopedia for general information on the subject. For further sources, check the bibliography at the end of the encyclopedia article.
- For definitions of technical or controversial terms, check the various standard dictionaries.
- Check the card catalog under the subject heading. Also, check any cross-listings noted on the subject cards.
- Check the various periodical indexes for magazine articles on the subject. If the subject is in the Social Sciences, be sure to check the *Social Science Index.* Likewise, if the subject falls under the Humanities or under Education, check the *Humanities Index* or the *Education Index* for journal articles on the subject.
- Check the specialized references available on the subject.
- Check the *Book Review Digest* for summaries of the contents of reviewed books.
- Check the various *Who's Who* volumes for information about note-worthy people.
- For information about places and countries, consult gazetteers and atlases.

5a-3   Skimming for major ideas

Researchers seldom have time to faithfully read every book or article written about their subject. Instead, the experienced researcher will initially skim a source to determine its usefulness. In skimming, one searches for major ideas in a piece of writing merely to confirm its appropriateness as a research source. If an initial skimming indicates that source is helpful and to the point, it can be read carefully later. However, if the source appears to be farfetched, ponderous, dated, irrelevant, or otherwise useless, then it should be set aside and more promising leads pursued. Do not, however, destroy the bibliography card of the discarded source, since you may wish to return to it later.

Skimming, like most skills, improves with practice. Here are some hints on how to skim a piece of writing for major ideas:

- Glance at the preface of a book. Often an author will state there what the book is about. Likewise, an afterword will often recount the major ideas of a book.
- Look up the subject in the index of the book. Frequently one can tell from the number of pages devoted to the subject whether or not the book is likely to be useful. For instance, if you were looking in a Russian history book for information on Rasputin, and saw from its index that it contained only two pages about him, you should probably move on to some other source.

- Read the chapter headings. Often these will reveal what the chapter is about. Likewise, the major ideas in a chapter are usually summarized in the headnotes to its various sections.
- Read the first and last two sentences in a paragraph to find out what information it contains. Generally, the main idea of a paragraph is stated in its initial sentences, and summed up in its final sentences.
- Glance at the opening paragraph of an article, essay, or book chapter. Often the author's thesis will be stated in the first paragraph or two of an article or essay. Similarly, the thesis of a chapter may be given in its initial paragraph.
- Glance at concluding paragraphs in an article, essay, or book chapter. Often these final paragraphs will sum up the discussion and restate major ideas.
- Run your eye down the page, reading randomly every fourth or fifth sentence. Most readers who do this can get a fair inkling of what the material is about.

5a-4 Evaluating sources

All sources are not created equal. They vary in quality of scholarship, force of argument, and accuracy of detail. Some sources are useful, scholarly, and accurate; others are worthless, silly, and misleading. For example, a student writing a paper on human evolution would be grievously mistaken in taking the fossil remains of the Piltdown Man to be the "missing link"—no matter how many library sources said so. In a brief burst of glory the Piltdown Man was hailed as the "missing link" in human evolution. Many articles and books in the library still make this claim, though their authors would now dearly love to retract, since the Piltdown Man has been exposed as an elaborate hoax. Anthropologists know all about the Piltdown Man's checkered career, though a student researcher might not. All fields are similarly littered with past errors duly preserved in the collections of libraries. Yet the student researcher, who is often a novice in the subject, must nevertheless dicriminate between error and truth in the writings of experts—a tricky thing to do.

Fortunately, there are some common-sense guidelines for evaluating the quality of sources. First, the research should always use the most recent source that can be found, so as to have a better chance of quoting only state-of-the-art opinion. If two sources exist that differ only in date, the later one should always be used.

Second, the controversial or even commonplace assertions of one source should always be verified against the opinions of another. No student who conscientiously researched the literature on human fossils would be duped by early claims about the Piltdown Man, for these have been thoroughly discredited in later writings. The authors in any field often write about and comment on the work of their peers. The diligent researcher soon perceives a consensus of opinion among the experts that allows the researcher to judge the reputation of an author or source.

Third—and this is admittedly difficult to do—student researchers should themselves try to evaluate the evidence and logic of any source they intend to use. Such an evaluation is often within the abilities of students, especially if they have followed the advice given earlier and not chosen an excessively technical topic. For instance, a student doing a paper on the possible existence of UFO's is surely capable of analyzing the testimony of someone who claims to have seen a UFO. Common sense and attention to detail are the only requirements for evaluating this kind of source and many others.

Finally, the opinions of critics can give the student an inkling of how professional readers have evaluated and received a work. The *Book Review Digest* is a good source for critical opinions on a wide variety of books. The student can also check the credentials of an author in any of the various biographical dictionaries or *Who's Who* volumes. This sort of information tells a researcher whether or not an author is indeed qualified to write as an expert in a certain field, or whether the author is merely an interloper bent on making sensational pronouncements and charges.

5a-5 Primary and secondary sources

A primary source is original writing *by* an author; a secondary source is writing *about* an author. Letters, memoirs, autobiographies, novels, short stories, poems, plays, personal notes, diaries, and the like are therefore all primary sources. Critical reviews, biographies, articles in scholarly journals, and book-length critical works are secondary sources.

Primary sources involve no middleman and are preferable to secondary sources for certain kinds of papers. A paper about the life of Shelley, for instance, will probably draw heavily on such primary sources as Shelley's letters and poems. But such secondary sources as the opinions of Shelley's critics and biographers can help the student interpret these primary sources, many of which will seem nearly meaningless to the student unfamiliar with the society in which Shelley lived and wrote.

5b

Note-taking

The information uncovered on your topic through research should be transcribed onto 4×6 note cards and eventually incorporated into the body of the paper. Bear in mind, as you read and take notes, that a research paper should contain a variety of material taken from different sources. It is not enough to simply write down your own ideas and speculations, while ignoring everyone else's opinion on the subject. Your own ideas should be derived from evidence and information uncovered on the subject through research, and the reader should be made aware not only of your conclusions, but also of the substance and reasoning that led you to them.

Students are often puzzled about how much of the paper should consist of their original writing, and how much of material drawn from researched sources. No exact rule exists. You should not write a paper consisting of a string of quotations and paraphrases but containing nothing of your own. Nor should you glut the paper entirely with your own notions, with only a token quotation or paraphrase added here and there to give the illusion of research. Ideally, the paper should consist of information from sources blended judiciously with your own commentary and interpretation. Certainly you should say what you think, but you should also say why you think it—what evidence exists to support your opinions; which authorities on the subject agree with you; and why those of a different opinion are probably in error. In sum, the paper demands not merely opinionated conclusions, but conclusions supported by other opinions.

5b-1   Format of the note cards

- Use 4×6 cards for note-taking. Large enough to accommodate fairly long notes, 4×6 cards are also unlikely to be confused with the smaller 3×5 bibliography cards.
- Write in ink so that the cards can be shuffled without blurring the notes.
- Write down only one idea or quotation on each card. Cards with only a single note can be put in any sequence simply by shuffling. If the note is so long that two cards have to be used, staple them together.
- Identify the source of the note in the upper right-hand corner of the card. Since the bibliography card already lists complete information on the source, use only the author's last name or key words from the title followed by a page number. For example, use "Fülöp-Miller, p. 10," or "Holy Devil, p. 10," to identify *Rasputin, the Holy Devil,* by René Fülöp-Miller, on a note card.
- Jot down in the upper left-hand corner of the card a general heading for the information the card contains. These headings make it easy to organize the notes by shuffling the cards.

5b-2   Kinds of note cards

The notes gathered from your research must be blended into the body of the paper to provide documentation, proof, and evidence in support of the thesis. These notes are of four kinds: the *summary*, the *paraphrase*, the *quotation*, and the *personal comment*.

a. The summary

A summary is a condensation of significant facts from an original piece of writing. A chapter is condensed into a page, a page into a paragraph, or a paragraph into a sentence, with the condensation in each case retaining the essential facts of the original. Consider the following summary of a five-page description of Rasputin:

Fülöp-Miller, pp. 3-10.   Rasputin's appearance

Rasputin's appearance was a combination of coarse, unkempt peasant burliness and mystical, poetic religiosity. He was at once repulsive and attractive. Strangers who met him were first disgusted by such details as his pock-marked skin and his dirty fingernails, but inevitably they came under the spell of his urgent, probing blue eyes.

Figure 5-5   Sample note card containing a summary

Common sense should govern your use of the summary. Some facts need to be quoted in detail, but others do not, and can be just as effectively summarized. For instance, the note card was taken from a paper on Rasputin that dealt mainly with the historical truth about the man, not with his physical appearance. Without numbering every pock or pimple, it was therefore enough for the student to summarize that Rasputin had a pockmarked face that made him look repulsive. In another context, say in a paper on the physical disfigurement of famous people, it might have been necessary for the student to quote generously from the five-page description which, in this instance, she needed only to summarize.

b. The paraphrase

To paraphrase means to say in one's own words what someone else has said. The paraphrase—unlike the summary—does not condense, but restates a passage in approximately the same number of words as the original, using the syntax and vocabulary of the paraphraser. Ordinarily, the paraphrase is the most frequently used note in a research paper.

Paraphrasing achieves two purposes: first, it shows that the student has mastered and assimilated the material to the extent of being able to state it in his or her own words. Second, it gives the paper an even, consistent style, since both original and source material are cast in the words of the student writer. Below is a short passage from *The Fall of the Russian Monarchy* by Bernard Pares, followed by an appropriate student paraphrase:

> Meanwhile Rasputin, as he appears to have done earlier, disappeared into the wilds of Russia. Here too he was true to an historical type. Always, throughout Russian history, there had been *stranniki* or wanderers who, without any ecclesiastical commission, lived in asceticism, depriving themselves of the most elementary of human needs, but gladly entertained by the poor wherever they passed. Some of them went barefoot even throughout the winter and wore chains on their legs. This self-denial gave them a freedom to address as peasant equals even the Tsars themselves, and there are many instances of their bold rebuke scattered over Russian history.

Pares, pp. 134-35.   Rasputin as nomad, ca. 1902

For some time Rasputin became like the well-known stranniki, those wandering ascetics who, without official priestly license, wandered all over Russia depending, wherever they passed, on the poor for food and shelter. Some of the nomads even walked barefoot in the freezing Russian winter with chains clinking around their legs. This kind of self-denial bestowed on them the peculiar right to address even a Tsar as their peasant equal. In this role of half priest half beggar, Rasputin roamed the wilds of Russia.

Figure 5-6 Sample note card containing a paraphrase

Fülöp-Miller, p. 366.   The murder of Rasputin

Farewell letter from Empress Alexandra to the
murdered Rasputin:

" My dear martyr, grant me your blessing to
accompany me on the sorrowful road I
have still to tread here below. Remem-
ber us in Heaven in your holy prayers.
Alexandra."

Figure 5-7 Sample note card containing a quotation

c. The quotation

The quotation reproduces an author's words exactly as they were spoken
or written, preserving even peculiarities of spelling, grammar, or punctuation. Use of an occasional quotation is justified only where the
authority of the writer is being evoked, or where the original material
is so splendidly expressed as to be altogether ruined by any attempt at
either summary or paraphrase.

Student papers are commonly flawed by the overuse of quoted
material. Moreover, many teachers regard the excessive inclusion of
quotations as a sign of padding, and respond with appropriate hostility
and suspicion. A good rule of thumb is therefore to limit quoted material
to no more than ten percent of the total paper. Another good rule is to
quote only when the authority of the writer is needed, or when the
material simply cannot be either paraphrased or summarized.

The rules for placing quotations on note cards are:

- Place quotation marks around the quotation.
- Introduce the quotation or place it in proper context.
- Copy quotations exactly as they are written. (See pp. 114–18 for how
  to introduce quotations, and pp. 119–23 for how to use ellipses.)

Occasionally, a summary or paraphrase is combined with a quotation
on a note card, the key phrases or words from the original source being

used to add literary flavor or authenticity to the note. Below is an original passage from *The Fall of the Russian Monarchy* by Bernard Pares, followed by a note card that combines a paraphrase with a quotation from this source.

> Nothing is more untrue than the easy explanation that was so often given, that he became the tool of others. He was far too clever to sell himself to anyone. He did not ask for presents and had no need; he had only to accept all that was showered upon him, and that he did briefly and almost casually, in many cases at once passing on the largess to the poor; his position was that of one who plundered the rich for the poor and was glad to do it.

Pares, pp. 140, 141.   Rasputin's generosity to the poor

Some critics have accused Rasputin of becoming "the tool of others" in order to acquire expensive personal gifts or other material advantage. Nothing could be further from the truth. Rasputin was too clever "to sell himself to anyone." He did not need to. All he had to do was sit back and accept all the luxuries offered to him by high society. And, in fact, one of his favorite roles was that of a Russian Robin Hood who "plundered the rich for the poor" by taking gifts offered and immediately passing them on to people in need.

Figure 5-8 Sample note card combining paraphrase and quotation

d. The personal comment

Personal-comment notes can be used to record any ideas, conjectures, or conclusions that occur to you during the research. These notes are generally used to explicate a fuzzy statement, stress a particular point, draw a conclusion, clarify an issue, identify an inconsistency, or introduce a new idea. Jot down these ideas as they dawn on you. If the personal-comment note deals with material contained on another card, staple the two cards together. An example of a personal-comment note card is given on page 88.

Personal Comment   The Czarina's initial attraction to Rasputin

It becomes clear, from all accounts describing the first meeting between Alexandra and Rasputin, that initially this peasant monk gained entrance to the Czarina's confidence by offering hope for the health of her hemophiliac son, at a time when she was utterly sunk in grief and despair. In the grip of maternal terror, she wanted to believe that God had sent a simple peasant to perform miracles.

Figure 5-9   Sample note card containing a personal comment

5c

Plagiarism: what it is and how to avoid it

Plagiarism is the act of passing off another's words and ideas as one's own. The question of when one has plagiarized and when one has simply asserted a general truth from an unknown source, can be sometimes puzzling. In a cosmic sense, the process of learning is made up of countless tiny crimes of plagiarism, since we all borrow freely from one another. No generation speaks a language of its own invention; few people are creators of the proverbs and sayings that they utter daily. The mother who tells her child, "A thing of beauty is a joy forever," is plagiarizing from the poet John Keats; the father who warns his son, "Hell hath no fury like a woman scorned," has plagiarized from the playwright William Congreve. Innumerable other examples can be given to show how we freely and wantonly borrow ideas and expressions from one another.

Blatant plagiarism, however, involves the conscious and deliberate stealing of another's words and ideas, generally with the motive of earning undeserved rewards. The student who copies the paper of a friend is guilty of blatant plagiarism. Likewise, the student who steals an idea from a book, expresses it in his or her own words, and then passes it off as original, has committed an act of plagiarism.

The conventions of writing research papers dictate that students must acknowledge the source of any idea or statement not truly their own. This acknowledgment is made in a note specifying the source and author of borrowed material. All summaries, paraphrases, or quotations must be acknowledged in a note; only personal comments may remain undocumented. In sum, to avoid plagiarism students must:

- Provide a note for any idea borrowed from another.
- Place quoted material within quotation marks.
- Provide a bibliography entry at the end of the book for every source that appears in a footnote.

Not every assertion is documentable, nor is it necessary for students to document matters of general and common knowledge. For instance, it is commonly known that the early settlers of America fought wars with the Indians—an assertion a student could safely make without a note. Similarly, a student could write. "Russia was in turmoil during the years preceding the Bolshevik Revolution," without adding a note, since the turmoil of prerevolutionary Russia is common knowledge. As a rule of thumb, a piece of information that occurs in five or more sources may be considered general knowledge. Proverbs, and sayings of unknown origins, are also considered general knowledge and do not have to be documented.

The following, however, must be accompanied by a note specifying author and source:

- Any idea derived from any known source.
- Any fact or data borrowed from the work of another.
- Any especially clever or apt expression, whether or not it says something new, that is taken from someone else.
- Any material lifted verbatim from the work of another.
- Any information that is paraphrased or summarized and used in the paper.

In writing research papers, students are expected to borrow heavily from the works of experts and authorities—indeed, this is partly the purpose of the research; but they are also expected to acknowledge the source of this borrowed material.

To illustrate plagiarism in different degrees, we have reproduced a passage from a book, followed by three student samples, two of which are plagiarisms.

Original passage   Alexander III died on 20 October, 1894, and was succeeded by his son Nicholas. The new emperor was more intelligent and more sensitive than his father. Both those who knew him well, and those who had brief and superficial contact with him, testify to his exceptional personal charm. The charm was, however, apparently associated with weakness and irresolution. Nicholas appeared to agree with the last person he had talked to, and no one could tell what he would do next.

Student Version A
(*plagiarized*)

When Alexander III died on October 20, 1894,

he was followed by his son Nicholas, who was

more intelligent and more sensitive than his

father.   People who knew him well and also

some who knew him only superficially testify

that he was exceptionally charming as a

person.   This charm, however, was associated

with weakness and an inability to make

decisions.   Nicholas always seemed to agree

with the last person he had talked to, and no

one could predict what he would do next.

This is an example of outright plagiarism. No documentation of any sort is given. The student simply repeats the passage almost verbatim, as though he or she had written it.

Student Version B
(*plagiarized*)

When Alexander III died on October 20, 1894,

he was followed by his son Nicholas, who was

more intelligent and more sensitive than his

father. People who knew him well, and also

some who knew him only superficially, testify

that he was exceptionally charming as a

person. This charm, however, was associated

with weakness and an inability to make

decisions. Nicholas always seemed to agree

with the last person he had talked to, and no

one could predict what he would do next.[3]

      [3] Hugh Seton—Watson, The Russian Empire,
1801—1917, Vol. III of The Oxford History of
Modern Europe (Oxford: Oxford University
Press, 1967), p. 547.

Though documented with a footnote, the passage is still a plagiarism because the student has merely changed a word or two of the original, without doing a proper paraphrase.

Student Version C
(*acceptable*)

      Emperor Nicholas II, who came to the throne

of Russia following the death of his father,

Alexander III, was apparently a man of

exceptional personal charm and deep

sensitivity. Ample testimony has come to us

from both intimate as well as casual

acquaintances, indicating that indeed he

possessed a magnetic personality. However,

the general consensus is also that he was a

man who lacked the ability to make hard

decisions, preferring to agree with the last

person he had seen, and thus making it

impossible to predict what he would do next.[3]

      [3] Hugh Seton—Watson, The Russian Empire,
1801—1917, Vol. III of The Oxford History of
Modern Europe (Oxford: Oxford University
Press, 1967), p. 547.

The above illustrates an acceptable use of the material. The original is properly paraphrased and its source documented with a footnote.

six

The thesis and the outline

6a

The thesis: definition and function

The thesis is a statement that summarizes the central idea of the paper. By convenience and custom, this statement is usually the final sentence of the opening paragraph, as in the following example:

```
             The Bilingually Handicapped Child


    There are approximately five million children in the United

States who attend public schools and speak a language other than

English in their homes and neighborhoods.  Many of these chil-

dren are handicapped in communication and thought processes, and

have to repeat the first grades in school several times.  The

bilingual child is usually unable to conceptualize in the Eng-

lish language taught at school, since he is from a different

cultural and language background.  Early compensatory educa-

tional programs would give the bilingual child a head start and

he would be better prepared for handling school work.
```

The underlined sentence is the thesis—the central idea for which the writer intends to argue. Once readers have gotten through this first paragraph, the aim of the paper is abundantly clear to them; they know what to anticipate.

The thesis serves at least three functions. First, it establishes a boundary around the subject that discourages the writer from wandering aimlessly. Most of us are often tempted to stray from the point when we write. We begin by intending to write a paper about Rasputin's place in history, then stumble onto some fascinating fact about Russian monasteries and become eager to somehow work it in. With a clear thesis before us, however, we are less likely to be seduced by a digression. Formulated before the actual writing of the paper begins, the thesis commits us to argue one point, discuss one subject, clarify one issue. Writers so committed will not leapfrog from topic to topic, nor free-associate erratically from one minor point to another.

Second, the thesis—if worded properly—can chart an orderly course for the essay, making it easier to write. Consider for instance this thesis:

>   Two defects in the design of the <u>Titanic</u> contributed to her
>
>   sinking: her steering was sluggish and unresponsive, even for a
>
>   ship of her immense size; her traverse bulkheads, which should
>
>   have made her virtually unsinkable, did not extend all the way
>
>   up to her deck.

The course before the writer is as plain as day: first, the sluggish steering of the *Titanic* must be discussed and clarified with appropriate facts and details; second, the design of her traverse bulkheads must be dealt with, and the defect thoroughly explained. The writer's job is easier because the thesis has conveniently divided the paper into two parts, establishing not only the topics to be discussed, but also their sequence. It is better and easier by far to write about such a thesis than to write randomly about the sinking of the *Titanic*.

Third, the thesis gives the reader an idea of what to expect, making the paper consequently easier to read. Textbooks have elaborate chapter headings and section headnotes just for this purpose. Newspaper stories are captioned and headlined for a similar reason. It is easier to read virtually anything if we have an idea of what to anticipate since the anticipation narrows and focuses our attention. A paper without a thesis creates no such anticipation in a reader and is therefore more difficult to follow.

6a-1 Finding the thesis

There is no chicken-and-egg mystery about which comes first—the notes or the thesis. One cannot formulate a thesis about a subject unless one first knows a great deal about it. Ordinarily, students will therefore be well into the research and notes before they can formulate the thesis.

Some groping over the notes may be necessary before a suitable thesis occurs to you. Basically, you are looking for a central idea that summarizes the information you have gathered on the subject. Consider for instance the paper on Rasputin, which we have been using as our prime example. The student, after much reading and note-taking, discovered that despite his diabolic reputation, Rasputin did do some good. Specifically, she discovered that: (1) Rasputin had intense religious feelings; (2) he had a passionate desire for peace in Russia; (3) he was deeply devoted to his family and friends. She therefore summarized her findings about Rasputin in the following thesis:

> Thesis: After six decades of being judged a demoniacal liber-
>
> tine, Rasputin now deserves to be viewed from another

```
point of view--as a man who was intensely religious, who

passionately desired peace, and who was deeply devoted

to his family and friends.
```

Notice that the thesis, as worded, specifies exactly what the writer has to do, and what information she will need to do it. To begin with, she will have to document Rasputin's reputation as a demoniacal libertine. Having done that, she will have to support her three contrary assertions: that Rasputin was intensely religious, that he passionately desired peace, and that he was deeply devoted to his family and friends. The thesis, moreover, suggests exactly the kind of information that the student will need to write the paper. First, she must cite historical opinion that portrays Rasputin as a demoniacal libertine. Second, she will need to produce anecdotal material, eyewitness accounts, biographical opinions, and similar evidence that support her contrary assertions about Rasputin.

6a-2 Rules for wording the thesis

To be useful, the thesis must be properly worded. A vague, confused, or lopsided thesis will either inflict similar miseries on the paper, or cause the writer to flounder helplessly among a disarray of note cards. Properly worded, the thesis should: (1) be clear, comprehensible, and direct; (2) predict major divisions in the structure of the paper; (3) commit the writer to an unmistakable course, argument, or point of view. The thesis on Rasputin is clear, implies a four-part division in the structure of the paper, and obligates the writer to argue a single proposition: that Rasputin was harshly judged by history. Likewise, the thesis on the *Titanic* disaster is clear and direct, divides the paper into two principal parts, and commits the writer to a single argument: that the ocean liner sank because of defects in her steering and bulkheads. Listed below are a series of rules to guide you in properly wording your thesis.

■ *The thesis should commit the writer to a single line of argument.* Consider for instance this example:

Poor
```
The Roman theater was inspired by the Greek theater,

which it imitated, and eventually the Romans produced

great plays in their theatrons, such as those by Plautus,

who was the best Roman comic writer because of his

robustness and inventiveness.
```

A single topic is difficult enough to research and write about; with two topics in a single paper, the writer's task becomes almost impossible. The above thesis threatens to wrench the paper into two contrary directions: it commits the student to cover both the origins of Roman theater and the theatrical career of Plautus, one of Rome's greatest comic playwrights. This dual thesis came about because the student had laboriously accumulated two sets of notes—one on the origins of Roman theater and another on the career of Plautus—and was determined to devise a thesis that would allow him to use both. The result is this curiously dual thesis that skews the paper into two contrary directions. Persuaded to relinquish the notes on the origins of the Roman theater and to focus the paper entirely on the career of Plautus, the student drafted the following improved thesis:

Better   Because of his robust language and novel comic plots,

Titus Maccicus Plautus can be considered the best Roman

comic playwright, whose plays are still successfully

staged today.

The paper is now committed to a single line of argument, and its focus is therefore vastly improved.

■ *The thesis should not be worded in figurative language.* The reasoning behind this rule is obvious: figurative language is too muddled and oblique to constitute the central idea of a paper. Consider this thesis:

Poor   Henry James is the Frank Lloyd Wright of the American

novel.

No doubt the writer knew exactly what she meant by this allusion, but its significance is murky to a reader. If one cannot understand the central idea of a paper, what hope does one have of understanding the paper? The following plainly expressed thesis is vastly better:

Better   The novels of Henry James have internal consistency

because of the way he unifies his themes, patterns his

episodes, and orders his images.

■ *The thesis should not be vaguely worded.* Vagueness may tantalize, but it does not inform. Moreover, a paper with a vague thesis is a paper without direction, and all the more difficult to write. Consider this example of a vague thesis:

Poor   Cigarette smoking wreaks havoc on the body.

Doing a paper on such a thesis will truly put a writer to the test. The thesis suggests no direction, provides no structure, proposes no arguments. Contrast it with this improved version:

Better   Cigarette smoking harms the body by constricting the

blood vessels, accelerating the heartbeat, paralyzing the

cilia in the bronchial tubes, and activating excessive

gastric secretions in the stomach.

The writer knows exactly what points he must argue, and in what order.

- *The thesis should not be worded as a question.* The thesis worded as a question seldom provides the kind of obligatory direction to a paper that the thesis phrased as an assertion provides. Here is an example:

Poor   Who makes the key decisions in U.S. cities?

This thesis offers neither structure nor direction to the writer. Below is the improved version, worded as an assertion:

Better   Key decisions in large U.S. cities are made by a handful

of individuals, drawn largely from business, industrial,

and municipal circles, who occupy the top of the power

hierarchy.

Another good reason for not wording the thesis as a question is the strong presumption behind the research paper assignment—that students will learn how to use research to find answers.

- *The thesis should be as concise as possible.* If ever a writer should try for conciseness, it is in the drafting of the thesis. A long, cumbersome thesis is likely to muddle the writer and send the paper flying off in different directions. The reader who cannot fathom the thesis of a paper is even less likely to make sense of its contents. Here is a muddled thesis:

Poor   Despite the fact that extensive time consumed by
television detracts from homework, competes with
schooling more generally, and has contributed to the
decline in the Scholastic Aptitude Test score averages,
television and related forms of communication give the
future of learning its largest promise, the most
constructive approach being less dependent on limiting
the uses of these processes than on the willingness cf
the community and the family to exercise the same
responsibility for what is taught and learned this way as
they have exercised with respect to older forms of
education.

This is of course garbled nonsense. Pity the student who has written a
paper based on this tortured thesis. Here is an improved version:

Better   While numerous studies acknowledge that the extensive
time spent by students watching television has
contributed to the decline in the Scholastic Aptitude
Test scores, leading educators are convinced that
television holds immense promise for the future of
learning, provided that the family and the community will
prudently monitor its use.

To paraphrase an old saying, "Like thesis, like paper." A muddled,
incoherent thesis will generate an equally muddled and incoherent
paper.

6a-3 Placing the thesis

By common consent, the thesis is usually placed as the final sentence of
the first paragraph—a position that gives the writer a chance to make
some catchy opening remarks, yet is still emphatic enough to draw

attention to the thesis. Some variation in placement of the thesis does exist, but most teachers distinctly prefer it to be stated as the final sentence of the initial paragraph. Here are three examples of theses introduced in this customary place:

He is a vagabond in aristocratic clothing—shabby but grand. As he scurries along in his cutaway and derby hat, aided by a cane, he is obviously a tramp, but a tramp with the impeccable manners of a dandy. He is willing to tackle any job, but seldom does it properly. He often falls in love, but usually the affair sours in the end. His only enemies are pompous people in places of authority. The general public adores him because he

Thesis is everyman of all times. Charlie Chaplin's "Tramp" has remained a favorite international character because he is a character with whom the average person can empathize.

A quarter of a million babies are born each year with birth defects. Of these defects, only 20 percent are hereditary. Most of them could have been prevented because they are the tragic results of poor prenatal

Thesis care. An unfavorable fetal environment, such as can be caused by malnutrition in the mother or her use of drugs, is a primary cause of many kinds of birth defects.

Theodor Seuss Geisel writes and illustrates zany children's books, usually in verse, under the pseudonym of "Dr. Seuss." He has written twenty-six best sellers over a period of thirty years, and they are all still in print. In story after story, this author creates a

100

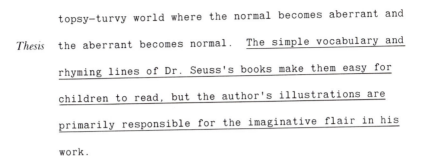

Thesis

topsy–turvy world where the normal becomes aberrant and the aberrant becomes normal. <u>The simple vocabulary and rhyming lines of Dr. Seuss's books make them easy for children to read, but the author's illustrations are primarily responsible for the imaginative flair in his work.</u>

6b

The statement of purpose

Some research papers have no thesis, but instead have a statement of purpose. Unlike the thesis—which summarizes the central idea of the paper—the statement of purpose is merely an announcement of what the writer proposes to do. Here are some examples:

The purpose of this paper is to describe the builders of the great Pyramid of Egypt and to explain the techniques used in its construction.

The aim of this paper is twofold: first, to define earthquakes; second, to investigate their major causes.

In this paper I intend to examine the destructive power of a thermonuclear blast, and to suggest some safety measures that can be taken in the event of a nuclear attack.

This paper will analyze the present California juvenile reform system and its procedures for rehabilitating convicted delinquents.

The purpose statement has the advantage of allowing the writer to consolidate several separate ideas into a single purpose. The other side of this coin, however, is that a broad statement of purpose will often

101

lure the inexperienced writer in miscellaneous and unrelated directions. Purpose statements merely propose a blanket justification for a paper, providing neither structure, order, nor direction for the writer. The novice writer attempting to write a paper according to a statement of purpose therefore runs a greater risk of rambling.

Frequently, it is useful to formulate a purpose statement in the early stages of the research, simply to give the project some firm justification. For instance, one might devise the following statement of purpose for a proposed paper on the architecture of Frank Lloyd Wright: "The purpose of this paper is to prove the influence of Oriental philosophy on Frank Lloyd Wright and on his concept of organic architecture." But when you are actually ready to begin writing, it is advisable to change this statement of purpose into a thesis, such as: "Oriental philosophy influenced Frank Lloyd Wright's concept of organic architecture, affecting primarily the architect's use of form, colors, and space in his designs." By then, if you have done your research diligently, you will know what you are writing about, and can substitute the more specific thesis for the less specific statement of purpose. It is also a good general rule to use a statement of purpose in a report paper, and a thesis in a thesis paper.

The outline

The outline is an ordered listing of the topics covered in the paper. Varying in complexity and style, outlines are nevertheless useful to both the writer and the reader. The writer who writes from an outline is less likely to stray from the point, or to commit a structural error such as overdeveloping one topic while skimping on another. The reader, on the other hand, benefits from the outline as a complete and detailed table of contents.

6c-1 Visual conventions of the outline

The conventions of formal outlining require that main ideas be designated by Roman numerals such as I, II, III, IV, V, and so on. Subideas branching off from the main ideas are designated by capital letters A, B, C, D, etc. Examples of these subideas are designated by Arabic numerals 1, 2, 3, 4, and so forth. Details supporting the examples are designated by lower-case letters a, b, c, d, etc. Here is an example of the proper form of an outline:

```
I.  Main idea

    A.  Subidea
    B.  Subidea
        1.  Example of a subidea
        2.  Example of a subidea
            a.  Detail
            b.  Detail

II.  Main idea
```

The presumption behind this sort of arrangement is obvious: namely, that students will not merely generalize, but will support their contentions and propositions with examples and details. Indeed, that is exactly what the writer of a research paper is expected to do—to make assertions that are supported by concrete examples and specific details. If you have done your research badly and have not been diligent in gathering specific facts about the topic, this deficiency will now become painfully obvious.

Notice that every category must be subdivided at least once, since it is impossible to divided anything into fewer than two parts. An outline dividing the subject into three or four levels—that is, down to examples or details—is generally adequate for most college-level research papers. If further subdivisions are necessary, the format is as follows:

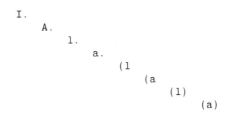

The basic principle remains the same: larger ideas or elements are stacked to the left, with smaller ideas and elements to the right.

6c-2 Equal ranking in outline entries

The logic of an outline requires that each entry be based on the same organizing principle as another entry of equal rank. All capital-letter entries must consequently be equivalent in importance and derived from the same organizing principle. Notice the lack of equal ranking in the following example:

```
I.   Rousseau gave the people a new government to work toward.

     A.  It would be a government based on the general will.
     B.  The new government would serve the people instead of
         the people serving the government.
     C.  The people tore down the Bastille.
```

The C entry is out of place because it is not of equal rank with entries A and B. A and B are subideas that characterize the new government proposed by Rousseau; C is a statement that describes the revolt of the French people against the old government.

6c-3 Parallelism in outline entries

The clarity and readability of an outline are immeasurably improved if its entries are worded in similar grammatical form. Notice the lack of parallelism in the following outline:

```
I.   The uses of the laser in the military

     A.  For range-finding
     B.  For surveillance
     C.  To illuminate the enemy's position
```

Entries A and B consist of a preposition followed by a noun, while entry C is worded as an infinitive phrase. C should therefore be reworded to make it grammatically similar to entries A and B:

```
I.   The uses of the laser in the military

     A.  For range-finding
     B.  For surveillance
     C.  For illuminating an enemy's position
```

The outline is now easier to read because its entries are grammatically parallel.

6c-4 Types of outlines

The three main types of outlines are: the topic outline, the sentence outline, and the paragraph outline. The formats of these different outlines cannot be mixed or combined; one type of outline must be used exclusively.

a. The topic outline

The topic outline words each entry as a phrase, breaking down the subject into major subheadings. Topic outlines are particularly useful for outlining relatively simple subjects. Here is a topic outline of the paper on Rasputin:

```
                    Rasputin's Other Side


Thesis: After six decades of being judged a demoniacal liber-
        tine, Rasputin now deserves to be viewed from another
        point of view--as a man who was intensely religious, who
        passionately desired peace, and who was deeply devoted
        to his family and friends.


    I.  The ambiguity of the real Rasputin

        A.  His birth
        B.  Popular historical view
            1.  His supporters
            2.  His detractors

   II.  Rasputin's religious feelings

        A.  His rich nature and exuberant vitality
        B.  His simple peasant faith

  III.  Rasputin's desire for peace in Russia

        A.  His concern for the Russian underdog
            1.  His loyalty to the peasantry
            2.  His opposition to anti-Semitism
        B.  His opposition to all wars

   IV.  Rasputin's gentle, compassionate side

        A.  His kindness to the Romanovs
        B.  His love for family
```

Notice that the thesis of the paper is placed as a separate entry in the outline immediately after the title. It is also customary to omit "introduction" and "conclusion" entries.

b. The sentence outline

The sentence outline uses a complete grammatical sentence for each entry. (Some instructors allow the entries to be worded as questions, but most prefer declarative sentences.) Sentence outlines are especially well suited for complex subjects, the detailed entries giving the writer an excellent overview of the paper. Here is a sentence outline of the paper on Rasputin:

Rasputin's Other Side

Thesis: After six decades of being judged a demoniacal libertine, Rasputin now deserves to be viewed from another point of view—as a man who was intensely religious, who passionately desired peace, and who was deeply devoted to his family and friends.

I. The real Rasputin is difficult to discover.

    A. The birth of Rasputin coincided with a "shooting star."
    B. The popular historical view of Rasputin portrays him as primarily evil.
       1. Supporters called him a spiritual leader.
       2. Detractors called him a satyr and charged that his depraved faithful were merely in awe of his sexual endowments.

II. Rasputin had intense religious feelings.

    A. He had a rich nature and exuberant vitality.
    B. He had a simple peasant faith in God.

III. Rasputin's passionate desire for peace in Russia revealed itself in several ways.

    A. He was concerned for the Russian underdog.
       1. He wanted a Tsar who would stand mainly for the peasantry.
       2. He spoke out boldly against anti-Semitism.
    B. Because of his humanitarian spirit, he was opposed to all wars.

IV. Rasputin had a gentle, compassionate side.

    A. He showed great kindness to the Romanovs.
    B. Maria Rasputin tells of her father's love for his family.

c. *The paragraph outline*

The paragraph outline records each entry as a complete paragraph, thus providing a condensed version of the paper. This form is useful mainly for long papers whose individual sections can be summarized in whole paragraphs, but is seldom recommended by instructors for ordinary college papers. Here is the Rasputin paper in the form of a paragraph outline:

Rasputin's Other Side

Thesis: After six decades of being judged a demoniacal
libertine, Rasputin now deserves to be viewed from
another point of view—as a man who was intensely
religious, who passionately desired peace, and who was
deeply devoted to his family and friends.

I. Rasputin himself always attached great significance to
the fact that at the time of his birth, a shooting star
was seen streaking across the horizon. He saw this phe-
nomenon as an omen that he was fated to have influence
and special powers. The popular historical view of Rasputin paints him primarily as evil. In his day, however,
he attracted numerous supporters who viewed him as their
spiritual leader. But he also had many detractors who
called him a satyr and accused his followers of sexual
depravity.

II. Rasputin had intense religious feelings. So filled with
exuberance and vitality was he that he could stay awake
until the early hours of the morning, dancing and drink-
ing in frenzied religious fervor. He did not have the
theology of a sophisticated church cleric, but rather he
expressed his religion in the simple terms of a Russian
peasant.

III. Rasputin's passionate desire for peace in Russia revealed
itself in several ways. For instance, he was concerned
for such Russian underdogs as the peasants and the Jews,
always encouraging the Tsar to protect these unfortunate
groups. Also, his humanitarian and pacifist nature made
him a determined opponent of all wars.

IV. Rasputin had a gentle, compassionate side. He was completely devoted to the Tsar's family and was known to
have had a calming influence on the hemophiliac son of
the Tsar. Maria Rasputin gives a glowing report of her
father's kindness and love.

6c-5 The decimal notation of an outline

Other outline forms exist that use various methods of indenting, labeling,
and spacing. One form that has been gaining favor in business and
science is the decimal outline. Based on the decimal accounting system,
this outline form permits an infinite number of possible subdivisions
through the simple addition of another decimal place. Here is the body
of the Rasputin paper notated in the decimal outline form:

Rasputin's Other Side

1. The ambiguity of the real Rasputin
    1.1. His birth
    1.2. Popular historical view
        1.2.1. His supporters
        1.2.2. His detractors

2. Rasputin's religious feelings
    2.1. His rich nature and exuberant vitality
    2.2. His simple peasant faith

3. Rasputin's desire for peace in Russia
    3.1. His concern for the Russian underdog
        3.1.1. His loyalty to the peasantry
        3.1.2. His opposition to anti-Semitism
    3.2. His opposition to all wars

4. Rasputin's gentle, compassionate side
    4.1. His kindness to the Romanovs
    4.2. His love for family

Notice that though a decimal notation is used, this outline arranges its entries on the same indentation principle used in other outlines, with larger ideas stacked to the left, and smaller ideas to the right.

seven

Transforming the notes into a rough draft

7a

Preparing to write the rough draft: a checklist

The following is a practical checklist of things you should do before beginning to write the rough draft:

- You should formulate a thesis. The research paper is the sort of writing that requires considerable premeditation from a writer. Information sifted from the sources and assembled on the note cards has to be carefully grafted into the main body of the paper. Arguments have to be thought out in advance and checked against the opinions of experts. In sum, no matter how spontaneous a writer you may be, you should nevertheless have a definite thesis in mind before you begin to write the rough draft.
- You should go over the note cards, picking out those cards relevant to the thesis, and setting aside all others. Bear in mind, moreover, that you are very likely to have more notes than you can use. To attempt to cram every single note into the paper is to be misled by an impulse that has ruined thousands of papers. You must exercise selectivity over the note cards, based upon the wording of the thesis, or the paper will end up an incoherent muddle of unrelated notes.
- You should shuffle the cards until they are organized in the order in which they will be used. This order in turn will be dictated by the wording of the thesis, and the nature of the information entered on the individual cards.
- You should sketch an outline of the paper, breaking down the thesis into an ordered listing of topics. This is the stage at which you should experiment with different approaches to your research subject. Juggle the topics until they are aligned in the most logical and emphatic order. If necessary, rephrase the thesis until it generates a more definite structure to the paper.

Once you have formulated the thesis, sorted the cards in their proper sequence, and drafted the outline, you are ready to begin writing the rough draft. Work from the outline and note cards. Triple space the rough draft to allow room for penciling in afterthoughts or scribbling down corrections to the sentences. Use a separate sheet for each paragraph so that additional ideas, words, or phrases that occur to you can be tacked on to the paragraphs without creating an unreadable jumble. Keep a dictionary and thesaurus handy, using the first to avoid misspelled or incorrect words, and the second to insure word precision and variety.

7b

Incorporating the notes into the flow of the paper

All notes should be blended smoothly into the natural flow of the paper—this is the prime rule for writing the rough draft. Documentation should add clarity, not clutter. Paraphrases, summaries, and personal-comment notes should be edited for smoothness. Quotations of course have to be used verbatim, and must not be tampered with. Transitions between ideas should be made logically and smoothly. The paper should not seem a cut-and-paste hodgepodge bristling with numerous unrelated quotations. In sum, the student must observe the rhetorical principles of unity, coherence, and emphasis (see 7d).

7b-1 Using summaries and paraphrases

The sources of summaries and paraphrases must be given in footnotes or endnotes, but do not need to be mentioned in the text. Below is an example of a paraphrase used without mention of its source in the text:

> When the court life of Russia died out at the imperial palace of Tsarskoe Selo, all kinds of political salons suddenly made their appearance in various sections of St. Petersburg. While these new salons became the breeding ground for the same kinds of intrigues, plots, counterplots, and rivalries that had taken place at the imperial palace, somehow their activities seemed dwarfed and their politics lacked the grandeur and dazzle that had accompanied the political style at the palace.[1]

---

[1] René Fülöp-Miller, Rasputin, the Holy Devil (New York: Garden City Publishing Co., Inc., 1927), p. 101.

In this case, documentation of the paraphrase with a footnote is sufficient. However, the writer who wishes to state a paraphrase more emphatically, or to throw the weight of an expert or authority behind the summary, should mention the source in the text, as in the following example:

As Hugh Seton-Watson points out in the Preface to his book on

the Russian empire, most people tend to forget that the Russian

empire was multi-national and therefore peopled with many non-

Russian citizens, most important of which were the Polish.[2]

　　[2] The Russian Empire, 1801-1917, Vol. III of The Oxford
History of Modern Europe (Oxford: Oxford University Press,
1967), p. ix.

The summary here is more emphatic because it is coupled with the name of the authority whose work is being summarized.

Sometimes students become so bedazzled by the writing style of a source, that they unwittingly cast their summaries in its flavor and language; the result is a discordant mixture of styles within a single paragraph. Here is an example:

The hull of the Titanic was traversed by watertight bulkheads,

capable of withstanding enormous pressure.　The engineering no-

tion was that if the ship sprang a leak, water would seep into

individual compartments and be harmlessly trapped.　At worse,

the liner would list, and her passengers be slightly uncomforta-

ble as she limped her way back to port.　Metallurgical fabrica-

tion techniques employed in the construction and deployment of

each bulkhead were consonant with the best engineering and me-

tallurgical knowledge extant at the time of the Titanic's con-

struction.　In short, the Titanic, though considered "unsinka-

ble," was neither better nor worse built than any of her other

sisters then at sea.

The underscored sentence is a summary of information found in a book on marine engineering. Notice how stylistically different the summary seems from the writing in the rest of the paragraph. Having pored over the book, the student then unconsciously mimicked its wooden flavor when writing the summary. Before using it, she should have edited the summary to blend it in with the style of the paragraph. Here is an improved version:

```
The hull of the Titanic was traversed by watertight bulkheads,

capable of withstanding enormous pressure.  The engineering no-

tion was that if the ship sprang a leak, water would seep into

individual compartments and be harmlessly trapped. At worse,

the liner would list, and her passengers be slightly uncomforta-

ble as she limped her way back to port.  These bulkheads were

built according to the best metallurgical techniques known at

the time of the Titanic's construction.  In short, the Titanic,

though considered "unsinkable," was neither better nor worse

built than any of her other sisters then at sea.
```

7b-2 Using quotations

Quotations must be reproduced in the exact phrasing, spelling, capitalization, and punctuation of the original. Staple or paste the quotation note card to the rough draft rather than copying the quotation. Later, when you write the final draft, you will have to transcribe the quotation from the note card onto the paper. By stapling the note card to the rough draft, you avoid having to transcribe quotations twice, thus reducing the chance of error.

Any modification made in a quotation—no matter how minor—must be indicated either in a note placed in square brackets within the quotation, or in parentheses at the end of the quotation.

```
Milton was advocating freedom of speech when he said, "Give me

the liberty to know, to think, to believe, and to utter freely

[emphasis added] according to conscience, above all other liber-

ties."³
```

For more on the use of square brackets to indicate interpolations, see p. 119.

Quotations must fit logically into the syntax of surrounding sentences, so as not to produce an illogical or mixed construction. The following quotation is poorly integrated:

```
Chung-Tzu describes a sage as "suppose there is one who insists

on morality in all things, and who places love of truth above

all other values."
```

Here is the same quotation properly integrated into the sentence:

```
Chung-Tzu describes a sage as "one who insists on morality in

all things, and who places love of truth above all other

values."
```

Here is another example of a badly integrated quotation:

```
The poet showed his belief in self-criticism by writing that "I

am a man driven to scold myself over every trivial error."
```

Here is the quotation properly handled:

```
The poet showed his belief in self-criticism when he wrote this

about himself: "I am a man driven to scold myself over every

trivial error."
```

a. Overuse of quotations

No passage in the paper should consist of an interminable string of quotations. A mixture of summaries, paraphrases, and quotations is smoother and easier to read; moreover, such a mixture gives the impression that students have done more than "cut and paste" from books and articles they have read. Here is an example of a paragraph littered with too many quotations:

```
According to McCullough, "the groundswell of public opinion

against the Japanese started in the early 1900s."¹²  This is when

the United States Industrial Commission issued a report stating

that the Japanese "are more servile than the Chinese, but less
```

obedient and far less desirable."[13]   At about the same time, the
slogan of politician and labor leader Dennis Kearney was "the
Japs must go."[14]   The mayor of San Francisco wrote that "the Japanese cannot be taken into the American culture because they are
not the stuff of which American citizens are made."[15]   In 1905,
writes McCullough, "the Japanese and Korean Expulsion League
held its first meeting and spawned many other such similar organizations."[16]

Here is an improved version, which deftly turns many of the quotations
into summaries and paraphrases, resulting in a cleaner, less cluttered
paragraph:

The anti-Japanese movement in America goes back to the turn of
the century, when the United States Industrial Commission
claimed that the Japanese "are more servile than the Chinese,
but less obedient and far less desirable."[12] At about the same
time, the slogan of politician and labor leader Dennis Kearney
was "The Japs must go!" while the mayor of San Francisco insisted that it was impossible for the Japanese to assimilate
into our culture and that they were "not the stuff of which
American citizens are made."[13] Appropriately, the Japanese and
Korean Expulsion League was formed in 1905 and a number of other
anti-Japanese societies followed.[14]

Notice, by the way, that the improved version contains fewer notes
than the original. In the first version, the student was forced to document
every quotation, even though successive quotations sometimes came
from the same source. The blend of summaries, paraphrases, and
quotations not only reduced clutter, but also cut down on the number
of notes by combining references from the same source into a single
sentence and under a single note. In the original paragraph, for instance, notes 12 and 13 refer to two quotations from the same source—

a book by a woman named McCullough. The improved version para-phrases the first quotation while using the second, and combines both in a single sentence that is documented by a single note.

b. Using brief quotations

Brief quotations (four lines or less) may be introduced with a simple phrase:

```
Betty Friedan admits that it will be quite a while before women

know "how much of the difference between women and men is cul-

turally determined and how much of it is real."5
```

```
"God is the perfect poet," said Browning in "Paracelsus."6
```

```
Hardin Craig suggests that "in order fully to understand and ap-

preciate Shakespeare, it is necessary to see him as a whole."7
```

```
In Shakespeare's Antony and Cleopatra, Cleopatra prefers "a

ditch in Egypt" as her grave to being hoisted up and shown to

the "shouting varletry of censuring Rome." (Ant. IV.i.55-60)
```

```
According to David Halberstam, when McNamara began to take over

the Vietnam problem, "there was a growing split between the ci-

vilians and the military over the assessment of Vietnam."8
```

```
In contrast to Eichmann's concept of justice, Thoreau believed

that "a true patriot would resist a tyrannical majority."9
```

Note that if the quotation is grammatically part of the sentence in which it occurs, the first word of the quotation does not need to be capitalized, even if it is capitalized in the original.

Original quotation "Some infinitives deserve to be split."
Bruce Thompson

Quotation used as Bruce Thompson affirms what writers have always
part of a sentence
            suspected, namely that "some infinitives deserve

            to be split."

Moreover, if the quotation is used at the end of a declarative sentence, it will be followed by a period whether or not a period is used in the original.

Original quotation   "Love is a smoke rais'd with the fume of sighs; . . ."
                                                        Shakespeare

Quotation used in a In Act I Romeo describes love as "a smoke
declarative sentence
            rais'd with the fume of sighs."

Finally, you should strive for variety in the introduction of quotations, rather than ploddingly serving them up with the same words and phrases. If you introduce one quotation with, "So-and-so says," try something different for the next, such as, "In the opinion of at least one critic," or "A view widely shared by many in the field affirms that," and so on.

Here is a list of words and expressions that can be used to give variety to your introductions of quotations:

contend	reveal
affirm	state
believe	think
insist	verify
mention	bring to light
report	

Another view <u>contends</u> that...

It has been <u>affirmed</u> by at least one writer that . . .

Some <u>believe</u>, along with Professor . . . , that . . .

This point was <u>brought to light</u> by Jane Brown, who summed up

the argument by saying that . . .

c. Using long quotations

Unlike quotations of four lines or less, longer quotations need to be introduced by a formal sentence, placed in context, and properly explained. Moreover, long quotations must be set off from the text by triple spacing, indented ten spaces from the left margin, and typed with double spacing but without quotation marks (unless the quotation itself contains quotation marks, such as for a title or for dialogue). If the quotation consists only of a single paragraph, or if the opening sentence of the quotation is not the start of a paragraph, then the first line of the quotation need not be indented more than the rest of the quotation; however, if two or more paragraphs are quoted, then the sentence beginning each paragraph should be indented three spaces more than the body of the quotation. Each long quotation should be preceded by a colon:

> The final paragraphs of "A Rose for Emily" bring to a horrifying climax all elements of Gothic horror that have pervaded the story:

quotation set apart from the text by triple spacing

opening sentence of paragraph indented 3 spaces

body of quotation indented 10 spaces from left margin

> For a long while we just stood there, looking down at the profound and fleshless grin. The body had apparently once lain in the attitude of an embrace, but now the long sleep that outlasts love, had cuckolded him. What was left of him, rotted beneath what was left of the nightshirt, had become inextricable from the bed in which he lay; and upon him and upon the pillow beside him lay that even coating of the patient and biding dust.

opening sentence of second paragraph indented 3 spaces

> Then we noticed that in the second pillow was the indentation of a head. One of us lifted something from it, and leaning forward, that faint and invisible dust dry and acrid in the nostrils, we saw a long strand of iron-gray hair.[10]

Figure 7-1   A long quotation

d. Using quotations from poetry

Unless the stanzaic line needs to be preserved for stylistic emphasis, short passages of verse should be enclosed by quotation marks and incorporated into the text. Quotations of two or three lines may also be part of the text, but with the lines separated by a slash (/) with a space on each side of the slash:

> The line "I have been half in love with easeful Death" expresses
>
> a recurrent theme in Keats's poetry——the desire for permanent
>
> residence in a world free from pain and anguish.[11]

> "The raven's croak, the low wind choked and drear, / The baffled
>
> stream, the gray wolf's doleful cry" are typical Romantic images
>
> used by William Morris to create a mood of idle despair.[12]

Verse quotations that exceed three lines should be separated from the text by triple spacing, indented ten spaces from the left margin (or less, if the line is so long that it would cause the page to look unbalanced), double-spaced without quotation marks (unless the poem itself contains quotation marks), and introduced with a colon. The spatial arrangement of the original poem (indentation and spacing within and between lines) should be reproduced with accuracy:

> In the following lines from "You Ask Me Why, Tho' Ill at Ease,"
>
> Tennyson expresses the poet's desire for freedom to speak out:
>
> > It is the land that freemen till,
> >
> > That sober-suited Freedom chose,
> >
> > The land, where girt with friends or foes
> >
> > A man may speak the thing he will.[13]

The quotation beginning in the middle of a line of verse should be reproduced exactly that way and not shifted to the left margin:

> As Cordelia leaves her home, exiled by Lear's folly, she reveals
>
> full insight into her sisters' evil characters:

```
         I know you what you are;

     And like a sister am most loath to call

     Your faults as they are nam'd.  Love well our father:

     To your professed bosoms I commit him:

     But yet, alas, stood I within his grace,

33   I would prefer him to a better place. (Lr. I.i.272-77)
```

e. Using a quotation within another quotation

Use single quotation marks to enclose a quotation within another brief quotation:

```
Rollo May is further exploring the daimonic personality when he

states that "in his essays, Yeats goes so far as to specifically

define the daimonic as the 'Other Will.' "
```

For quotations within long, indented quotations, use double quotation marks.

f. Punctuating quotations

The rules for punctuating quotations are few and simple:

■ Place commas and periods inside the quotation marks:

```
"Three times today," Lord Hastings declares in Act III, "my

foot-cloth horse did stumble, and started, when he look'd upon

the Tower, as loath to bear me to the slaughter-house."
```

■ Place colons and semicolons outside the quotations marks:

```
Brutus reassures Portia, "You are my true and honourable wife,

as dear to me as are the ruddy drops that visit my sad heart";

consequently, she insists that he reveal his secrets to her.
```

■ Place question marks and exclamation marks inside the quotation marks if they are part of the quotation, but outside if they are not:

```
King Henry asks, "What rein can hold licentious wickedness when

down the hill he holds his fierce career?"
```

But:

```
Which Shakespearean character said, "Fortune is painted blind,

with a muffler afore her eyes"?
```

g. Interpolations in quoted material

Personal comments or explanations within a quotation must be placed in square brackets (not parentheses), which may be handwritten if no such key exists on your typewriter. The word "sic" within square brackets means that the quotation—including any errors—has been exactly copied.

```
The critical review was entitled "A Cassual [sic] Analysis of

Incest and Other Passions."
```

The "sic" indicates that "cassual" is reproduced exactly as it is spelled in the quotation.

Here is an explanatory interpolation, also set off in square brackets:

```
Desdemona answers Emilia with childlike innocence: "Beshrew me

if I would do such a wrong [cuckold her husband] for all the

whole world."
```

h. The ellipsis

The ellipsis—three dots (. . .) with a space before and after each dot—is used to indicate the omission of material from a quotation. Such omissions are necessary when only a part of the quotation is relevant to the point you are making. Use of the ellipsis, however, does not free a researcher from an obligation of remaining faithful to the intent of the author's original text. The following example illustrates the misuse of the ellipsis to distort an author's meaning:

Original   Faulkner's novels have the quality of being lived, absorbed, remembered rather than merely observed.

Malcolm Cowley

Quotation   Malcolm Cowley further suggests that "Faulkner's

novels have the quality of being . . . merely

observed."

If you are quoting no more than a fragment and it is clear that something has been left out, no ellipsis is necessary:

Malcolm Cowley refers to Faulkner's "mythical kingdom."

But when it is not clear that an omission has been made, the ellipsis must be used.

- *Omissions within a sentence* are indicated by three spaced dots:

Original   Mammals were in existence as early as the latest Triassic, 190 million years ago, yet for the first one hundred and twenty million years of their history, from the end of the Triassic to the late Cretaceous, they were a suppressed race, unable throughout that span of time to produce any carnivore larger than cat-size or herbivore larger than rat-size.

Quotation   Adrian Desmond, arguing that the dinosaurs were once

dominant over mammals, points out that "mammals were

in existence as early as the latest Triassic . . . yet

for the first one hundred and twenty million years of

their history . . . they were a suppressed race,

unable to produce any carnivore larger than cat-size

or herbivore larger than rat-size."

Two omissions are made in the quotation, and both indicated by an ellipsis of three spaced dots.

- *Omissions at the end of a sentence* use a period followed by three spaced dots:

Adrian Desmond, arguing that the dinosaurs were once dominant

over mammals, points out that the mammals were, for millions of

years, "a suppressed race, unable throughout that span of time

to produce any carnivore larger than cat-size. . . ."

Notice that the first dot is a period, and is placed immediately after the last word without an intervening space.

If the ellipsis is followed by parenthetical material at the end of a sentence, use three spaced dots and place the sentence period after the final parenthesis:

```
Another justice made the following, more restrictive, statement:

"You have the right to disagree with those in authority . . .

but you have no right to break the law . . ." (Martin, p. 42).
```

■ *Omissions of a sentence or more* are also indicated by four dots, but with this proviso: that a complete sentence must both precede and follow the four dots. Here is an example:

Original

Manuscript Troana and other documents of the Mayas describe a cosmic catastrophe during which the ocean fell on the continent, and a terrible hurricane swept the earth. The hurricane broke up and carried away all towns and forests. Exploding volcanoes, tides sweeping over mountains, and impetuous winds threatened to annihilate humankind, and actually did annihilate many species of animals. The face of the earth changed, mountains collapsed, other mountains grew and rose over the onrushing cataract of water driven from oceanic spaces, numberless rivers lost their beds, and a wild tornado moved through the debris descending from the sky.

Unacceptable use of four dots to mark an omission

```
That species of animals may have been made extinct

by some worldwide catastrophe is not unthinkable.

Immanuel Velikovsky states that according to

"Manuscript Troana and other documents. . . . The

face of the earth changed, mountains collapsed,

other mountains grew and rose over the onrushing

cataract of water driven from oceanic spaces,

numberless rivers lost their beds, and a wild

tornado moved through the debris. . . ."
```

The quotation is unacceptably reproduced because the fragment

"*Manuscript Troana* and other documents," rather than an entire sentence, is placed before the four dots. Here is an acceptable use of this material:

```
That species of animals may have been made extinct by some

worldwide catastrophe is not unthinkable.   Immanuel Velikovsky

states that "Manuscript Troana and other documents of the Mayas

describe a cosmic catastrophe. . . . The face of the earth

changed, mountains collapsed, other mountains grew and rose over

the onrushing cataract of water driven from oceanic spaces, num-

berless rivers lost their beds, and a wild tornado moved through

the debris. . . ."
```

Complete sentences are reproduced before and after the four periods, which satisfies the convention.

- *Omissions of long passages,* such as several stanzas, paragraphs, or pages, are marked by a single typed line of spaced dots.

```
Speaking through the prophet Amos, the God of the Israelites

warns sternly:

                 For you alone have I cared

                 among all the nations of the world;

                 therefore will I punish you

                 for all your iniquities.

                 .  .  .  .  .  .  .  .  .

                 An enemy shall surround the land;

                 your stronghold shall be thrown down

                 and your palaces sacked.

                           (Amos iii.2-12, The New English Bible)
```

- *Omissions that immediately follow an introductory statement* require no ellipsis.

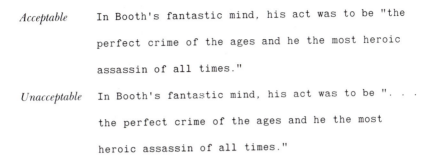

Although an omission has been made in the beginning of the quotation, the use of an ellipsis following the introductory remark is unnecessary.

7b-3 Using personal comments

Students are expected to do more in the paper than simply preside over the opinions of their sources. Naturally, the bulk of the paper will consist of material accumulated in research. But without the interpretation of the student, none of this material is likely to make any sense to a reader. A prime function of the personal comment, therefore, is to supply the reader with information otherwise unobtainable from the stark research data. Personal comments serve to interpret material, mark transitions from one idea to another, and draw conclusions. In a manner of speaking, the thesis statement can also be regarded as an elaborate personal comment in which the student enunciates a general design and focus for the entire paper.

The example below illustrates the use of the personal comment to interpret material. The student's paper is on the career of Pope Innocent III; the discussion in the preceding paragraph centered on a crusade that Innocent III had just called for. Interjecting a personal comment, the student interprets the motive of Innocent III in launching this crusade:

```
Innocent III's call for this crusade shows that he was trying to

establish that the Papacy was the temporal authority on earth.

As the head of Christendom, he couldn't tolerate any philosphy

that would divert attention away from the teaching of the Catho-

lic church.
```

Personal comments are also used to establish smooth transitions as the discussion moves from one idea to another. Here is an example, taken from this same student paper. The preceding paragraph has just summarized the reaction of Innocent III to the heresy of the Cathars.

> The heresy of the Cathars was not the only anti—Catholic philos-
> ophy that Innocent III endeavored to crush. He desired to crush
> the heresy of the Moslems as well.

The paper then moves on to a discussion of the efforts of Pope Innocent III to crush the Moslems.

Finally, the personal comment is widely used to make summations and draw conclusions. The paper on Innocent III ended with this summation of the Pontiff's career:

> Innocent III's pontificate was the zenith of the medieval pa-
> pacy. He involved himself in world affairs by endeavoring to
> stop heresy and by exerting his authority over kings. He
> crushed the Cathar heresy and brought the Greek church under his
> control. He used the kings of Europe like pawns on a chess-
> board. Therefore one can conclude that Innocent III made the
> theory of papal theocracy into a reality.

7c
Endnotes or footnotes

Widespread disagreement exists on whether research papers should use endnotes or footnotes. Endnotes are lumped together at the end of the paper, while footnotes are placed at the bottom of the page on which the documented source occurs. Endnotes have become the preferred form of the *MLA Handbook* and in time will probably replace footnotes at most colleges and universities. Nevertheless, footnotes are still widely used because of the convenience in having a source and its citation appear immediately on the same page. Be sure you know which form of documentation your instructor requires you to use.

7c-1   Format for endnotes

Endnotes occur in the following format, and are typed together on a separate sheet at the end of the paper:

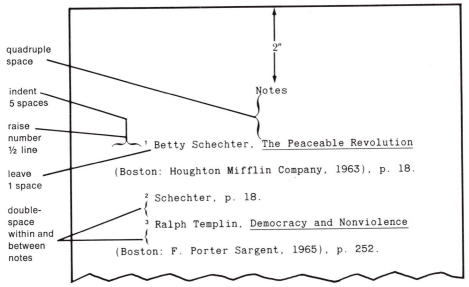

Figure 7-2 Format for endnotes

7c-2 Format for footnotes

Footnotes are placed at the bottom of the page on which the cited source occurs, and in the following format:

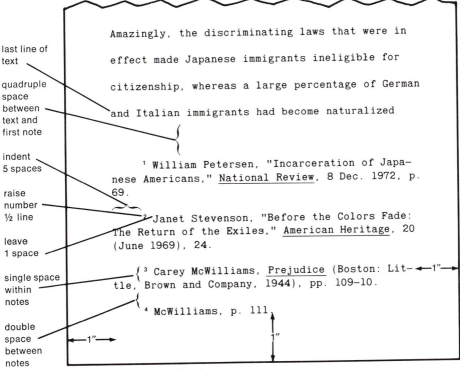

Figure 7-3 Format for footnotes

7c-3 Numbering of notes

Notes are numbered by Arabic numerals elevated one half space above the line and placed as close as possible to the end of the material cited. All notes should be numbered consecutively throughout the paper (1, 2, 3, etc.). Note numbers are not followed by periods or enclosed in parentheses. Moreover, they follow without space all punctuation marks except the dash.

7c-4 Proper placement of note numbers

The prime rule is that a note number should be placed as near as possible to the *end* of cited material.

Wrong In <u>A Matter of Life</u> Bertrand Russell emphasizes that

law "substitutes a neutral authority for private

bias,"[13] and he believes this to be the main advantage

of the law.

Better In <u>A Matter of Life</u> Bertrand Russell emphasizes that

law "substitutes a neutral authority for private

bias," and he believes this to be the main advantage

of the law.[13]

However, if cited material is followed by material quoted or paraphrased from another source, then each note should be placed immediately after the material to which it refers.

Whereas Herbert Read suggests passive resistance as "the weapon

of those who despair of justice,"[14] Ralph Templin warns that

nonviolence must never overlook evil for the sake of peace.[15]

(In the preceding example, note 14 cites quoted material from one source, while note 15 cites paraphrased material from another source.)

Finally notes should not be placed immediately after an author's name, or immediately after the verb or colon that introduces a documented passage:

Wrong	Justice Abe Fortas¹ states, for example, that civil disobedience should be directed only against "laws or practices that are the subject of dissent."
Wrong	Justice Abe Fortas states,¹ for example, that civil disobedience should be directed only against "laws or practices that are the subject of dissent."
Right	Justice Abe Fortas states, for example, that civil disobedience should be directed only against "laws or practices that are the subject of dissent."¹

7d
Writing the paper with unity, coherence, and emphasis

7d-1 Unity

The rhetorical principle of unity dictates that a paper should stick to its chosen thesis without rambling or digressing. If the thesis states that Japanese art influenced French Impressionism, the paper should cover exactly that subject and nothing more. If the thesis proposes to contrast the life styles of inner city residents and suburban dwellers, the paper should concisely pursue such a contrast, ignoring all side issues no matter how personally fascinating to the writer.

To observe the principle of unity, a writer has merely to follow the lead of the thesis. Properly drafted, the thesis will predict the content of a paper, control its direction, and obligate the writer to a single purpose. The writer introduces only material relevant to the thesis, suppressing the urge to dabble in side issues or to stray from the point. Such admirable single-mindedness will produce a paper written according to the principle of unity, and consequently easier for a reader to follow.

The principle of unity should govern the progression of ideas within an individual paragraph as well as throughout the entire structure of an essay. Paragraphs should be written to scrupulously deliver exactly what the topic sentence promises, for the content of a paragraph is controlled by its topic sentence much as the structure and direction of an essay are

129

determined by its thesis. Here is an example of a paragraph that fails to observe the principle of unity; notice the underscored irrelevant sentences that destroy its unity.

Topic sentence The Beatles' target was the values of society and the problems those values created. The music of the Bea-tles, along with their unorthodox clothing and long hair, banded together the NOW generation. They made so-cial comments and aired subjects that had never before been publicly discussed. "Help," for example, is an attempt to see the seriousness of life instead of its lighthearted fun and romance. "She's Leaving Home" tells of parents who think they have given their daugh-ter everything, when in reality their materialism left no room for communication. This is the first time that teenagers were performing for teenagers. It was a revolt against listening to what grownups decided teenagers should listen to. Songs such as "Eleanor Rigby" exposed the haunting loneliness of alienated people living in the twentieth century. The Hippies' insistence on free emotions was stressed in the album "Revolver." The Beatles were word conscious and extremely adept with puns and wit. The Beatles even promoted a new style of love—a love that was free and unrestrained instead of the strict, moral "until death do us part" type of love exalted by previous generations. My favorite Beatle was John Lennon. In short, the Beatles united the youth but left each individual to choose his own approach to social values.

The unity of the paragraph is vastly improved if the irrelevant sentences are omitted. Be sure to prune similar irrelevancies out of your own paragraphs.

7d-2 Coherence

Coherence is said to exist in a paragraph whose sentences are arranged in a clear, logical, and intelligible order. If the sentences of a paragraph are illogically or unintelligibly arranged, the paragraph is said to be incoherent, as for instance this one:

> In the past year it's been through times of extreme highs and lows in my emotional outlook on life. The trend of any life seems to follow this general pattern. Some of the high moments were meeting new people that turned out to be much more than mere acquaintances, having the newly met person turn into a friend a person could know for the rest of their life. Also competing in sports and in the area of track and field and baseball. Meeting and going out with a few girls, which in our relationship between each other bloomed into a special kind of affection for ourselves.

The paragraph is so muddled and incoherent that it is nearly impossible to read.

Incoherent writing is primarily caused by a writer's inability to perceive the paragraph as a whole. Instead, the writer becomes preoccupied with individual sentences, and fashions them as though they existed in isolation on the page. The result is the splintered writing seen in the paragraph above. To avoid incoherence, a writer must conceptualize the paragraph as a unit of expression to which individual sentences contribute an increment of meaning. Sentences must be written down in such a way as to coexist harmoniously with their neighbors. Here are some ways to achieve coherent paragraphs.

a. Avoiding mixed constructions

Mixed constructions are sentences that begin in one grammatical pattern and then abruptly switch to another. Here are some examples, along with suggested improvements:

Mixed	Whereas parents insist on stifling their children's independence, they encourage rebellion.
Improved	When parents insist on stifling their children's independence, they encourage rebellion.
Mixed	With every new service on the part of the government suggests that our taxes are going to be raised.
Improved	Every new service on the part of the government suggests that our taxes are going to be raised.
Mixed	Of the two plays King Lear and Antony and Cleopatra are rather opposite of each other regarding the overall themes in them.
Improved	The overall themes of Shakespeare's King Lear and Antony and Cleopatra differ considerably.
Mixed	Such a metaphor is typical of the Cavalier poets, which they attempted to be cynical and casual about love.
Improved	Such a metaphor is typical of the Cavalier poets, who attempted to be cynical and casual about love.

b. Using pronouns

Coherence can be achieved through the use of pronouns that clearly refer to identifiable antecedents.

| Wrong | The theme of Marvell's "To His Coy Mistress" is that one must make the most of the present, for they may never experience our future age. |
| Improved | The theme of Marvell's "To His Coy Mistress" is that lovers must make the most of the present, for they may never experience the future. |

In the first version, the pronoun "they" has no clear antecedent. The rewritten example makes it clear that "lovers" is the antecedent for "they."

c. Using parallel constructions

Use parallel constructions to achieve sentence balance. Balanced sentences that coordinate the expression of related items are easier to read.

Poor Motor vehicles, jet engines, and the grinding noise emanating from steel refineries--all contribute to the noise pollution in our industrial age.

Improved The noise emanating from motor vehicles, jet engines, and steel refineries--all contribute to the noise pollution of our industrial age.

Poor "Cruel and unusual punishment" includes men assigned to solitary confinement, with no contact with other people, no toilet, food once a day, no light at all, and with poor ventilation and the smells of human waste.

Improved "Cruel and unusual punishment" includes men assigned to solitary confinement where they have no contact with other people, no toilet, no regular meals, no light, and no proper ventilation.

d. Using transitions

Use transitions to identify the logical connections between parts of an argument or to maintain continuity in a discussion.

Poor Three main categories of foods have been recognized as essential for the life processes. Carbohydrates are widely distributed throughout the plant and animal

133

world and help to supply energy for the body. Including such substances as sugars, starch, and cellulose molecules, the carbohydrates can synthesize enzymes in order to obtain the glucose units necessary for essential biochemical processes. Fats represent an even more concentrated source of food energy than do carbohydrates, but they serve as reserve energy rather than quick energy. Proteins are large molecules containing carbon, hydrogen, oxygen, and nitrogen. Protein is not used primarily to provide energy but rather to form the necessary structural material for life.

Improved   Three main categories of foods have been recognized as essential for the life processes. <u>First</u> are the carbohydrates, which are widely distributed throughout the plant and animal world and help to supply energy for the body. Including such substances as sugars, starch, and cellulose molecules, the carbohydrates can synthesize enzymes in order to obtain the glucose units necessary for essential biochemical processes. <u>Next</u> are the fats, which represent an even more concentrated source of food energy than do carbohydrates, but they serve as reserve energy rather than quick energy. <u>Finally</u> there are the proteins, which consist of large molecules containing carbon, hydrogen, oxygen, and nitrogen. Proteins are not used primarily to provide energy but rather to form the necessary structural material for life.

134

7d

The addition of the transitions "First," "Next," and "Finally" divides the discussion into three recognizable parts, thereby making it easier to follow.

Poor   Farm prices fell considerably during the Great Depression. The farmers' liabilities did not fall.

Improved <u>Although</u> farm prices fell considerably during the Great Depression, the farmers' liabilities did not fall.

The transition "Although" establishes a contrast relationship between the ideas in the two sentences.

Poor   Hua Kuo-feng's life is not clearly delineated in the historical records. His parents, his marital status, and his educational background are unknown.

Improved Hua Kuo-feng's life is not clearly delineated in the historical records. For instance, his parents, his marital status, and his educational background are unknown.

The transition phrase "For instance" relates the opening general statement to the more specific facts that follow.

e. *Repeating key terms in a paragraph*

The repetition of key terms is sometimes used to establish an identifiable link between different parts of a paragraph. Here is an example in which "romanticism" and "romantic" are repeated for the sake of added coherence:

During the French revolution, <u>romanticism</u> was the popular mode of thought. In other words, the people trusted their emotions over their reason. Jean-Jacques Rousseau became the outstanding voice of this <u>romanticism</u>. While he spread intellectual ideas, he gave these ideas an emotional base. According to

Rousseau, all people are predominantly <u>romantic</u>; that is, they

act on emotion rather than on reason. Thus, although Rousseau's

ideas were often boldly illogical and self-contradictory, they

still appealed to his followers, who were attuned to <u>romantic</u>

thought and committed to <u>romantic</u> language. Rousseau was able

to move the masses because they were already inclined toward

<u>romanticism</u>.

7d-3 Emphasis

The rhetorical principle of emphasis requires the expression of more important ideas in main or independent clauses, and of less important ideas in dependent or subordinate clauses. In sum, properly emphatic writing will attempt to rank ideas through grammatical structure. Here is an example of an unemphatic piece of writing:

Poor emphasis
The gifted child is a high achiever on a specific
test, either the Otis or Binet I.Q. test. These tests
are usually administered at the end of the second
grade. They determine the placement of the child in
third grade. These tests are characterized by written
as well as verbal questions, so that the child has the
opportunity to express himself creatively.

The grammatical treatment of ideas is altogether too egalitarian. A reader simply cannot distinguish between the important and the unimportant ideas, because they are all expressed in a similar grammatical structure. Here is the same passage made emphatic:

Improved emphasis
A child is considered gifted if he has achieved a high
score on a specific test such as the Otis or Binet
I.Q. test. Characterized by written as well as verbal
questions so that the child has the opportunity to express himself creatively, these tests are administered

```
           at the end of the second grade in order to determine

           the proper placement of the child in third grade.
```

By placing subordinate ideas in subordinate clauses, the writer achieves a purposeful focus missing from the unemphatic version.

Ideas of equal importance of course require equal emphasis, and should be expressed in coordinated grammatical structures. Various coordinating conjunctions can be used to assert different relationships between two ideas.

Use *and* to imply addition.
Use *but* and *yet* to imply qualification, contrast, and contradiction.
Use *for* to imply causation.
Use *or* to imply an alternative relationship.
Use *nor* to imply negation or exclusion.

Beware, however, of excessive coordination, which can make a piece of writing seem childish.

Excessive
coordination

```
It is difficult for the living to talk to the dying

about death.  And embarrassment inevitably causes a

psychological barrier between those in the bloom of

life and those wilting at the edge of death's abyss.

Modern medicine has found miraculous cures for count-

less exotic diseases, and it still has not found a way

to cope with the needs of people who are dying.
```

The passage can be significantly improved by changing its coordination into subordination that indicates causal connection and contrast:

Improved

```
It is difficult for the living to talk to the dying

about death, because embarrassment inevitably causes a

psychological barrier between those in the bloom of

life and those wilting at the edge of death's abyss.

Whereas modern medicine has found miraculous cures for

countless exotic diseases, it still has not found a

way to cope with the needs of people who are dying.
```

137

eight

Punctuation, mechanics, and spelling

8a

Punctuation

Punctuation of the research paper must conform to accepted practices in American English. Though reflecting personal style to some extent, punctuation must nevertheless be clear and consistent. The following sections review the most important rules of punctuation, with emphasis on those rules that especially apply to the research paper.

8a-1 Period (.)

- Use a period at the end of sentences that make a statement or express a command:

```
No one enjoys being ridiculed.
Begin at the top of the page.
The stranger asked whether she could get lodging in the town.
```

- Use a period after most abbreviations:

```
Mr.          B.C.

Dr.          e.g.

Ph.D.        Ave.

A.M.
```

Abbreviations of many international and bureaucratic agencies no longer require periods. When in doubt, check the dictionary.

```
UNESCO, FCC, NATO, HEW, NBC, NAACP
```

A comma or some other punctuation mark may follow the period, if the abbreviation occurs within a sentence; but if the abbreviation occurs at the end of a sentence, only a period is necessary:

```
Long after she earned her B.A., she was still looking for a job.
```

But:

```
The battle of Hastings was fought in 1066 A.D.
```

Exceptions: If the sentence is a question or an exclamation, the period

after the abbreviation will be followed by either a question mark or
an exclamation mark:

```
Was Julius Caesar alive in 55 B.C.?
You mean to say she dropped out after earning her Ph.D.!
```

For the use of ellipsis (. . .), see pp. 121–25. See Chapters 9 and 10
for the use of the period in documentation and bibliography.

8a-2   Comma (,)

■ Use a comma to separate independent clauses joined by a coordinating
conjunction:

```
The interview began with the same questions, but the answers

varied.
```

■ Use a comma between items in a series:

```
Napoleon won the war, the hearts of the people, and the money in

the exchequer.
```

```
Her art broke the harmony of the design, ignored any sense of

rhythm, and lacked all visible balance.
```

■ Use a comma to separate parallel modifiers:

```
He called it a long, lonely journey.
Lancelot gave her a woebegone, ghostly smile.
```

■ Use a comma to set off nonrestrictive elements:

Nonrestrictive   `Fire, which is more symbolic of passion than of`

`anything else, rarely appears in the novel.`

Restrictive   `Fire which burns blue is dangerous.`

Nonrestrictive   `Shakespeare's father, who was a glove tanner by`

`trade, probably belonged to the middle class.`

Restrictive   `Will the student who is wearing a blue blazer`

`please step forward.`

■ Use a comma after an introductory phrase or a subordinate clause:

Phrase   With the entire parliament against him, the king abdicated.

Clause   If King John had listened to his barons, he would have been a more popular king.

Clause   As Fernand Hazan notes, Carpaccio was best known as a painter of cyclical narratives.

■ Use commas to set off interrupting elements:

The Egyptians, on the other hand, often worshiped fantastic creatures.

The French, however, used the rondelet.

Did the Gothic tradition, one might ask, influence his work?

■ Use a comma when necessary for clarity:

After shearing, the sheep were led up Mount Pilatus.

Away beyond, the sunset formed a streaking flame.

Some years before, we had seen Charlie Chaplin in London.

Commas are also used in dates (On January 3, 1943, . . .), in names (William A. Brooks, Esq.), and in addresses (Newhall, California; Paris, France). Do not use a comma and dash together. A comma may be used after parentheses when necessary (as in this case), but not before parentheses. See Chapters 9 and 10 for commas used in documentation and bibliography.

8a-3 Semicolon (;)

■ Use a semicolon between independent clauses not connected by a coordinating conjunction (*and, but, or, nor, for, so, yet*):

Rubens was greatly influenced by Titian; he copied him assiduously.

NOTE: Failure to observe this rule will result in a comma splice or run-on sentence.

- Use a semicolon between independent clauses connected by a conjunctive adverb (*however, nevertheless, then, moreover, consequently*) or a sentence modifier (*in fact, for example, on the other hand, in the first place*):

History is concerned with events as they occurred in a certain order; however, accurate chronology is not the only concern.

Existentialism is chiefly a twentieth-century philosophy; in fact, it received its impetus from the despair following World War II.

- Use a semicolon to separate items in a series already punctuated with commas:

The television interview focused on three guests: a professor at the University of Michigan, well-known for his stand against the neutron bomb; a member of NOW, passionately devoted to passing the ERA; and a clergyman from the Baptist Church in Austin, Texas.

NOTE: Never use a semicolon between items of unequal grammatical rank:

Wrong   Dependent clause   Because Henry VIII was keenly interested in naval affairs;

Independent clause   Queen Elizabeth inherited from him a powerful fleet.

Right   Because Henry VIII was keenly interested in naval affairs, Queen Elizabeth inherited from him a powerful fleet.

143

See Chapters 9 and 10 for the use of the semicolon in documentation and bibliography.

8a-4 Colon (:)

In typing, always skip one space after the colon, except when expressing time.

- Use a colon after a clause that formally introduces a passage:

The architecture consisted of a wide variety of styles: antebel-
lum homes with white colonnades, Italian villas surrounded by
formal gardens, and nondescript California ranch houses.

The Prophet Isaiah, speaking for God, cries out with righteous
indignation:

    Listen! it is the thunder of many peoples,

    they thunder with the thunder of the sea.

    Listen! it is the roar of nations

    roaring with the roar of mighty waters.

                                        (Isaiah xvii.12)

- Use a colon to indicate that what follows is either an example, explanation, or elaboration of what has just been written:

Three kinds of cities underwent extensive urban renewal: Athens
under Pericles, Rome under Augustus, and Paris under Napoleon
III.

Urban Transportation: The Federal Role (book title)

City-county consolidation is more than a term: it means the
process of merging a county government with all municipalities
in the county.

■ Use a colon between the hours and minutes in time:

```
3:13 p.m.
```

■ Use a colon after the greeting in a letter:

```
Dear Mrs. McNully:
```

NOTE: Do not use a colon after a linking verb or preposition:

Wrong   The colors were: red, white, blue, and green.

The noise consisted of: musical instruments, voices, and

machine vibrations.

Right   The colors were red, white, blue, and green.

The noise consisted cf musical instruments, voices, and

machine vibrations.

See Chapters 9 and 10 for the use of the colon in documentation and bibliography.

8a-5   Dash (--)

The dash is typed as two hyphens, with no space before or after.

■ Use a dash to surround parenthetical material that interrupts the flow of writing:

```
The scholar's business is in part constructive--to add to the

general field of knowledge--and in part destructive--to expose

false claims and errors.
```

■ Use a dash for summarizing:

```
Robert Campin, Jan van Eyck, Roger van der Weyden--all were from

the school of ancient Netherlands.
```

- Use a dash to indicate emphasis:

```
All Western thought is a footnote to one author--Plato.
```

8a-6 Parentheses ( )

- Use parentheses to enclose material that explains or amplifies a remark:

```
English is not merely a communication tool (an overused defini-

tion), but also the medium for fine art.

Samuel Gompers (1850-1924) was a British-born American labor

leader.
```

- Use parentheses to enclose the numbers of items in a series or list:

```
It is a Romantic work because (1) it extols nature, (2) it places

feelings above reason, (3) it celebrates democracy.
```

NOTE: A parenthetical sentence within another sentence neither starts with a capital letter nor ends with a period; however, a parenthetical sentence inserted between regular sentences does.

```
John went to the store (he made the trip often) to buy bread.
```

But:

```
John went to the store.  (He made the trip often.)  He went to

buy bread.
```

(See 9m for parenthetical documentation.)

8a-7 Brackets ([ ])

Square brackets may be inserted by hand if they are not on your typewriter.

- Use brackets to enclose a parenthetical remark within a parenthetical statement; however, it is best to avoid such an awkward construction.

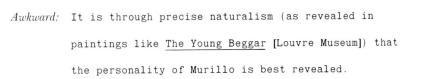

Awkward: It is through precise naturalism (as revealed in paintings like <u>The Young Beggar</u> [Louvre Museum]) that the personality of Murillo is best revealed.

Better <u>The Young Beggar</u>, by Murillo, hangs in the Louvre Museum. It is through the precise naturalism of such paintings that the personality of Murillo is best revealed.

■ Use brackets to enclose an interpolation in a quotation:

Blake is taking a stand against the capitalistic oppression of the poor when he writes: "Is this [the widespread poverty of children] a holy thing to see / In a rich and fruitful land . . . ?"

(See p. 121 for a further example.)

8a-8 Slash (/)

■ Use a slash to separate lines of poetry. (See preceding example.) A slash so used is preceded and followed by a space.
■ Use a slash to separate dates:

19/11/29 (19 November, 1929)

Use the European system, where all dates are written in the order of day, month, and year.

■ Use a slash to separate alternative words:

The athlete must be ill and/or disqualified.

8a-9 Quotation marks (" ")

■ Use quotation marks to enclose the exact words from someone else's work. (See pp. 113–21 for examples.)

- Use quotation marks to indicate dialogue. A change in speaker is indicated by a new paragraph indentation:

Lady Bredmore shook with fear when she heard the knock at the door.

"Who is it?" she called, trembling.

"Danforth," came his voice.

- Enclose in quotation marks any word to which attention is being directed:

The term "Newgate" was used to indicate crime novels.
Over and over again he used the word "veiled."

- Enclose in quotation marks parenthetical English translations of the words or phrases of another language:

Les hommes de ces temps étaient encore chasseurs et pasteurs.

("In those days men were still hunters and shepherds.")

NOTE: Words used in linguistic studies are underlined (see p. 168).

- Enclose in quotation marks any word or words used in a special sense:

Another person who could shed light on Watergate is Charles Colson, a "born again" social worker.

8a-10 Question mark (?)

- Use a question mark after a direct question:

Did Freud really believe that satisfaction of the libido tended toward death?

NOTE: Do not use a question mark in an indirect question:

Wrong   One might well ask if it is not the schizoid personality that will be best able to endure space travel?

(Replace the question mark with a period.)

- Use a question mark to indicate a doubtful date or figure:

John Alden (1599?–1697) was a Mayflower pilgrim.

8a-11 Exclamation mark (!)

- Use an exclamation mark to express a command:

The shark is coming toward us. Hurry!

- Use an exclamation mark to express strong feelings such as surprise, disbelief, or anger:

Leave England? Never!

Oh, how we have been tricked!

Get off my property, you evil omen!

NOTE: Do not use a comma or a period following an exclamation mark:

Wrong "Be off with you!," she screamed.

Right "Be off with you!" she screamed.

NOTE: Do not overuse the exclamation point. Mild expressions of emotions are punctuated with commas or periods:

Oh, don't bother to return the favor.

How placid she looks.

For question marks and exclamation marks used in quotations, see pp. 120–21.

8a-12 Apostrophe (')

The apostrophe is used to form the possessive case of many nouns, to show omissions, and to indicate certain plurals. The use of the apostrophe to indicate contractions, although frequent in informal writing, is rarely acceptable in the research paper.

- Use *'s* to form the possessive of nouns not ending in *s*:

Singular	*Plural*
a dog's life	children's health
his master's voice	men's ideas
hen's teeth	

- Use *'s* or an apostrophe to form the possessive of singular nouns ending in *s*:

  the actress's successes *or* the actress' success

  Ease of pronunciation should guide your decision as to whether or not to add the *s*. The general practice is to add *'s* to monosyllabic names ending in a sibilant sound (Keats's, Marx's), but to add only an apostrophe to multisyllabic names (Dickens', Artixerxes'). The possessive of names ending in a silent *s* is formed by adding an *'s*: Ingres's, Camus's.

- Use only an apostrophe to form the possessive of plural nouns ending in *s*:

  the Smiths' home, the Joneses' car, the districts' high rents

  NOTE: Do not use an apostrophe with personal pronouns in the possessive case:

  its size *not* it's size

  We wanted theirs *not* We wanted their's

  Use *'s* with only the last noun when indicating joint possession:

  Queen Elizabeth and Prince Philip's palace

  (They own a palace jointly.)

  But:

  Queen Elizabeth's and Prince Philip's palace

  (They each own a palace.)

- Use an apostrophe to indicate omissions:

  ten o'clock, roaring '20s, cock o' the walk

- Use an apostrophe to form the plural of numerals, letters, and words used as words:

  All his 8's looked like s's.

  He uses too many but's.

8a-13   Hyphen (–)

■ Use a hyphen to form a compound adjective preceding a noun:

```
a well-deserved honor

heart-warming laughter

a post-dated letter
```

Do not use a hyphen when the first word is an adverb ending in *ly*: superbly flavored soup. No hyphen is needed when the compound adjective follows the noun: The soup is well flavored.

■ Use hyphens to connect prefixes to their capitalized words:

```
post-Victorian

pre-Christian
```

■ Use hyphens to link compound nouns:

```
poet-priest

printer-painter

teacher-scholar
```

Hyphenation practices are not consistent. When in doubt, consult a dictionary. (For hyphenation in documentation and bibliography, see Chapters 9 and 10. For hyphenation in word division, see 8c-2.)

8b

Mechanics

8b-1   Numbers

a. Numerals

The rule of thumb on the use of numerals is this: use a numeral only if the number cannot be spelled out in two words or less. For the Roman numeral "one," use a capital "I"; for the Arabic numeral "one," use either the number "1" on your typewriter keyboard, or the lower case letter "l." Dates and page numbers are usually *not* spelled out: "November 19" or "19 November," and "page 36," are preferred to "the nineteenth of November" and "the thirty-sixth page."

Never begin a sentence with a numeral; instead, rewrite the sentence:

Wrong   25,500 voters hailed the passage of the bill.

Right   The bill was hailed by 25,500 voters.

b. *Percentages and amounts of money*

Figures of percentages or amounts of money are governed by the rule for numerals. Figures or amounts that can be written out in two words or less may be spelled out; otherwise, they must be expressed as numerals.

May be spelled out:	thirteen percent	thirteen Deutsche Mark
	eighty-three percent	fifty British pounds
	ten francs	thirty-six dollars
Should be expressed as numerals:	133%	185 DM
	83.5%	£ 550
	103 fr	$366

c. *Dates*

Consistency is the prime rule governing the inclusion of dates in the paper. Write either "19 November 1929" or "November 19, 1929," but not a mixture of both. Write either "June 1931" or "June, 1931," but not both. (Note: if a comma is placed between the month and the year, a comma must also follow the year, unless some other kind of punctuation mark is necessary.) Centuries are expressed in lower-case letters:

in the thirteenth century

A hyphen must be added when the century is used as an adjective:

twelfth-century literature

seventeenth- and eighteenth-century philosophy

Decades can either be written out:

during the thirties

or expressed in numerals:

during the 1930s

The term "B.C." (meaning before Christ's birth) follows the year; "A.D." (meaning after Christ's birth) precedes the year:

```
in 55 B.C.

in A.D. 1066
```

When using both a Western and a non-Western date, place one or the other in parentheses:

```
1912 (Year One of the Republic)
```

Both "in 1929–30" and "from 1929 to 1930" are correct, as is "from 1929–30 to 1939–40." However, do not write "from 1951–72"; confusion may result from the absence of the preposition "to" after 1951. Rather, write "1951 to 1972."

d. Numbers connected consecutively

When connecting two numbers, give the second number in full for all numbers from one through ninety-nine. For numbers from one hundred on, give only the last two figures of the second number, if it is within the same hundred or thousand:

```
4–5

15–18

106–07

486–523

896–1025

1,860–1,930

1,860–75

1,608–774

13,456–67

13,456–14,007
```

The above examples follow the style of the *MLA Handbook*. However, when a single digit would be dropped from a number in the thousands, that digit may be retained for clarity:

```
1,608–1,774
```

e. Roman numerals

The following require capital Roman numerals:

Major divisions of an outline (see p. 103)

Volumes of a major work
Volume II of Will and Ariel Durant's <u>Story of Civilization</u>

Books as well as parts of a major work
Book I of Milton's <u>Paradise Lost</u>

Part II of Gail Sheehy's <u>Passages</u>

Acts of a play

Act IV of <u>Romeo and Juliet</u>

People in a series, such as monarchs, who share a common name

Henry VIII, King of England

The following require lower-case Roman numerals:

Chapters of a book
Chapter xii of <u>David Copperfield</u>

Scenes of a play
Act I, Scene iii of <u>Romeo and Juliet</u>

Cantos of a poem
Book I, Canto iii of <u>The Faerie Queene</u>

Chapters of books of the Bible
Matthew xxiv

Pages from prefaces, forewords, or introductions to books
Page vii from Preface to George Katkov's <u>Russia 1917: The February Revolution</u>

See also 9d-9 for Roman numerals in documentation.

8b-2 Titles

a. Italicized titles

Certain titles must be italicized and therefore underlined in typewritten work. Underlined titles include the following:

Published books
<u>A Farewell to Arms</u>

Plays
<u>The Devil's Disciple</u>

154

Long poems
    Enoch Arden

Pamphlets
    The Biology of Cancer:A Guide to Twelve College Lectures

Newspapers
    the Los Angeles Times, *but* the Stoneham Gazette

(Underline only those words that appear on the masthead of
the paper.)

Magazines
    U.S. News and World Report

Classical works
    Plutarch's Parallel Lives

Films
    Gone with the Wind

Television programs
    Sixty Minutes (CBS)

Ballets
    The Sleeping Beauty

Operas
    Carmen

Instrumental music listed by name
    Brahms's Rinaldo

But instrumental music listed by form, number, and key is not
underlined
    Brahms's Piano Concerto No. 1, Opus 15 in D minor

Paintings
    Regnault's Three Graces

Sculptures
    Michelangelo's Madonna and Child

Ships
    U.S.S. Charr

Aircraft
    the presidential aircraft Airforce One

NOTE: An initial "a," "an," or "the" is italicized and capitalized when it
is part of the title:

    The Grapes of Wrath

After the use of the possessive case, delete "The," "A," or "An," in a title:

```
Henry James's Portrait of a Lady
```

(The full title is *The Portrait of a Lady.*)

b. *Titles within quotation marks*

The following items should be placed within quotation marks:

Newspaper articles
```
"It's Drag Racing without Parachutes"
```

Magazine or journal articles
```
"How to Cope with Too Little Time and Too Many Meetings"
```

Encyclopedia articles
```
"Ballet"
```

Essays in books
```
"The Solitude of Nathaniel Hawthorne"
```

Unpublished Dissertations
```
"The Local Communications Media and Their Coverage of Local
    Government in California"
```

Lectures
```
"The Epic of King Tutankhamun: Archeological Superstar"
```

Specific school courses
```
"Intermediate French"
```

Television episodes
```
"Turnabout," from the Series The World of Women
```

NOTE: Sacred writings, series, editions, societies, conventional titles, and parts of books use neither underlining nor quotation marks.

Sacred writings
```
the Bible, the Douay Version, the New Testament, Matthew,
    the Gospels, the Talmud, the Koran, the Upanishads
```

Series
```
Masterpiece Theater, the Pacific Union College Lyceum Series
```

Editions
```
the Variorum Edition of Spenser
```

Societies
```
L'Alliance française, the Academy of Abdominal Surgeons
```

Conventional titles
```
Kennedy's First State of the Union Address
```

Parts of books
```
Preface
Introduction
Table of Contents
Appendix
Index
```

c. Titles within titles

If a title enclosed by quotation marks appears within an underlined title, the quotation marks are retained. If an underlined title appears within a title enclosed by quotation marks, the underlining is retained:

Book ```"The Sting" and Other Classical Short Stories```

Article ```"Textual Variants in Sinclair Lewis's Babbit"```

Single quotation marks are used with a title requiring quotation marks appearing within another title also requiring quotation marks:

Article ```"Jonathan's Swift's 'Journal to Stella' "```

A title that would normally be underlined, but that appears as part of another title, is neither underlined nor placed in quotation marks. For example, the title of the book, *The Great Gatsby,* would normally be underlined. But when this title forms part of the title of another book, such as *A Study of* The Great Gatsby, only "A Study of" is underlined:

```
A Study of The Great Gatsby
```

d. Frequent reference to a title

If the research paper refers frequently to the same title, subsequent reference to the title may be abbreviated, once the full title has been initially used. In abbreviating, always use a key word:

```Return``` *for* ```Return of the Native```

```Tempest``` *for* ```Tempest in a Teapot```

```"The Bishop"``` *for* ```"The Bishop Orders His Tomb at Saint Praxis"```

```UNESCO``` *for* ```United Nations Educational, Scientific, and Cultural```

> ```Organization```

For citation of titles in subsequent references in notes, see 9l.

8b-3 Italics

In typewritten work, italics are indicated by underlining. Words making up a phrase or title may be continuously, rather than separately, underlined.

- Underline phrases, words, letters, or numerals cited as linguistic examples:

One cannot assume that the Victorian word <u>trump</u> is an amalgamation of <u>tramp</u> and <u>chump</u>.

- Underline foreign words used in English texts:

It seemed clearly a case of <u>noblesse oblige</u>.

He used the <u>post hoc ergo propter hoc</u> fallacy.

NOTE: Exceptions to the rule include quotations entirely in another language, titles of articles in another language, and words anglicized through frequent use, such as: détente, laissez faire, gestalt, et al. In papers dealing with the arts, foreign expressions commonly used in the field need not be underlined: hubris, mimesis, leitmotif, pas de deux.

See 8b-2 for italics in titles.

8b-4 Capitalization

- Use a capital letter to begin a sentence.

Philosophy is the study of ideas.

- Capitalize proper nouns—the names of particular people, places, or things:

George Washington, Concord Square, the Lincoln Monument

Capitalize the pronoun "I."

- Capitalize the first, last, and all other words in a title except articles, prepositions, conjunctions, and the "to" in infinitives.

"How the Water Wells Will Dry Up"

<u>For Whom the Bell Tolls</u>

158

```
"The Search for Youth in the Turn-of-the-Century Novel"
```

```
"After Apple-Picking"
```

<u>The Rise and Fall of the Third Reich</u>

Prepositions that function as adverbs in a title must also be capitalized.

```
"The Going Up and Down"
```

Note that words in hyphenated compounds are capitalized. See also Chapters 9 and 10 for additional examples of titles.

■ Capitalize titles before a name and before titles of high rank:

```
President Kennedy
```

```
Her Royal Highness the Duchess of Kent
```

NOTE: A title by itself is usually not capitalized, unless it specifically substitutes for a name:

```
He wanted to be a congressman.
```

But:

```
Congressman Smith did not answer the call; the Congressman

knew exactly who was at the other end of the line.
```

■ Capitalize degrees and titles following a name:

```
Veloris Hallberg, Ed.D.
```

```
Bert Beverly Beach, Ph.D.
```

```
Vincenze Modero, Papal Nunzio to Barcelona, Spain
```

```
George T. Harding, M.D.
```

■ Capitalize words that denote family relationships, if the words are used instead of names. Words that denote family relationships are not capitalized when preceded by a possessive pronoun:

```
When Mother died, Father continued to write.
```

But:

```
When her mother died, her father continued to write.
```

■ Capitalize proper nouns and their derivatives:

```
the East, Easterner

Shakespeare, Shakespearean

McCarthy, McCarthyism

Machiavelli, Machiavellian
```

■ Capitalize the names of movements, organizations, and periods of history:

```
the Romantic Movement

the Democratic Party

the Neoclassical Age
```

■ Capitalize months of the year, days of the week, and holidays:

```
Tuesday, February 20

Valentine's Day
```

■ Capitalize names of the Deity, religions, and sacred books:

```
Messiah, Jehovah, our Creator, Allah, Buddha, Jesus,

     the Trinity

Methodist, Catholic, Islamic

the Bible, the Koran, the Talmud
```

NOTE: Some editors insist on capitalizing all pronouns referring to the Deity:

```
Praise God for His bounty.
```

■ Capitalize names of specific school courses, but do not capitalize the general names of courses (unless they contain a proper noun):

```
He had registered for Biology 103.
```

But:

```
He is enrolled in several sociology and French courses.
```

NOTE: The initial definite article in the titles of magazines or newspapers is not usually treated as part of the title:

according to the <u>New York Times</u>

The words "series" and "edition" are capitalized only if part of an exact title:

Norton Critical Edition *but* Washington Square edition

Headings like "Preface" or "Introduction" are capitalized if formally cited; but capitalization is not needed if the reference to them is general.

Many introductions do not mention theme.

The prefaces are brief.

Capitalize a noun followed by a numeral referring to the specific part of a sequence:

Vol. III of 3 vols., Part IV., No. 5, Act VI, Ch. iii,

Version B

Do not capitalize col., l., n., p., or sig. (See 11h-1 for the proper abbreviations.) Never capitalize all the words of a title cited in your text or notes.

Wrong: THE GREAT GATSBY

8b-5 Names of persons

■ In general, omit formal titles (Mr., Mrs., Miss, Ms., Dr., Professor) when referring to persons, living or dead, by their last names. However, convention dictates that certain persons be referred to by title:

Mme de Staël, Mrs. Humphry Ward

■ It is acceptable to use simplified names for famous people:

Dante *for* Dante Alighieri

Vergil *for* Publius Vergilius Maro

Michelangelo *for* Michelangelo Buonarroti

It is also acceptable to use an author's pseudonym rather than the author's real name:

George Sand *for* Amandine-Aurore-Lucie Dupin

Mark Twain *for* Samuel Clemens

Molière *for* Jean-Baptiste Poquelin

- The *von, van, van der,* and *de* of foreign names are usually not included in references to people:

Goethe (Hans Wolfgang von Goethe)

Frontenac (Louis de Frontenac)

Ruysdael (Salman van Ruysdael)

However, certain names are traditionally not used with the last name alone:

Van Dyck *not* Dyck

De Gaulle *not* Gaulle

von Braun *not* Braun

O. Henry *not* Henry

8c

Spelling

8c-1 General principles

Spelling must be consistent throughout the paper. Consult a current dictionary when in doubt about the spelling of a word. Quoted material must be reproduced in the exact spelling of the original.

In spelling words, do not be misled by their pronunciations. For example, words such as *fasten, marine, acknowledge,* or *bargain* are not spelled the way they sound. Further, many words—called homonyms—sound alike but are spelled differently: *blew/blue, bough/bow, knight/night.* Words that are perennially misspelled include the following: *recieve* for *receive, athelete* for *athlete,* or *goverment* for *government.* Moreover, the groups of words listed below are commonly confused with one another. Be sure that you know the correct spelling and meaning of each.

accept, except	passed, past
advice, advise	personal, personnel
affect, effect	pore, pour, poor
allusive, elusive, illusive	precede, proceed
altar, alter	principal, principle
cite, sight, site	prophecy, prophesy
complement, compliment	quiet, quit, quite
conscience, conscious	stationary, stationery
council, counsel	then, than
dominant, dominate	their, there, they're
elicit, illicit	to, too, two
instance, instants	weather, whether
lead, led	who's, whose
loose, lose	your, you're
moral, morale	

8c-2 Word division

- If possible, avoid dividing a word at the end of a typewritten line. But if a word must be divided for the sake of a balanced margin, make the division at the end of a syllable.

de-ter-mined	haz-ard-ous
i-vo-ry	grad-u-al
con-clud-ing	dress-er

Correct syllabification of words is listed in a dictionary. College dictionaries indicate the syllables of words with dots: bru · tal · i · ty; far · ci · cal.

- Never hyphenate a one-syllable word, such as "twelfth," "screamed," or "brought."

- Do not end or begin a line with a single letter:

  ```
  a-mend, bur-y
  ```

- Make no division that might cause confusion in either the meaning or pronunciation of a word:

  ```
  sour-ces, re-creation
  ```

- Divide hyphenated words only at the hyphen:

  ```
  editor-in-chief, semi-retired
  ```

- Do not divide proper names, such as "Lincoln" or "Italy."
- Do not end several consecutive lines with a hyphen.

8c-3 Foreign-language markings

Words or phrases from a foreign language must be reproduced with all their accent marks. If you are doing a lengthy paper on a foreign language or on comparative literature, consider renting a typewriter with an international keyboard. Otherwise, the accent marks of foreign words must be written in by hand. Pay special attention to the following:

- It is not necessary to accent the capital letters of French words.

  ```
  énormément, but Enormément or ENORMEMENT
  ```

- For German words with the umlaut, use two dots rather than an "e," even for initial capitals:

  ```
  Überhaupt not Ueberhaupt

  fröhlich not froehlich
  ```

- Proper names retain their conventional spelling:

  ```
  Boehm not Böhm

  Dürrenmatt not Duerrenmatt
  ```

- Digraphs (two letters that represent only one sound) can be typed without connection (ae, oe), can be written in by hand (æ, œ), or can be connected at the top ($\overline{ae}$, $\overline{oe}$). In American English, the digraph "ae" is being abandoned:

  ```
  archeology not archaeology

  medieval not mediaeval

  esthetic not aesthetic
  ```

nine

Documentation

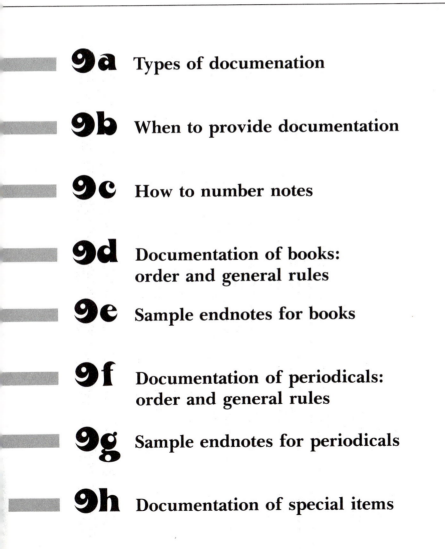

9i Content notes

9j Consolidation of references

9k Repeated or interpretive use of a single source

9l Subsequent references

9m Parenthetical references

9n Documentation in scientific writing

9a

Types of documentation

Documentation is the process by which you give credit to the appropriate sources for every borrowed idea used in the paper. Borrowed ideas may have been incorporated into the paper either as direct quotations, summaries, or paraphrases. But no matter what form you use to incorporate the idea of another into your paper, you must give appropriate credit in a specific and conventional form that allows a reader to trace your sources and, if necessary, to investigate their accuracy.

Two kinds of documentation are used in research papers: (1) footnotes or endnotes that acknowledge specifically where an idea came from, and (2) bibliography entries that give full publication information on the source of a borrowed idea. Each source will therefore be documented at least twice: as a footnote or endnote, and as a bibliography entry. Slight differences exist in the format of each kind of documentation—differences which must nevertheless be observed. Footnotes or endnotes cannot be simply tranferred to the bibliography page of the paper; nor can a bibliography entry be simply moved over to serve as a footnote. In this chapter we will deal specifically with the documentation format used in footnotes or endnotes. In the next chapter we will cover the format for bibliography entries.

9b

When to provide documentation

Neither general knowledge, common sayings, nor self-evident opinions or conclusions need to be documented. The rule of thumb is simply this: if the idea, opinion, or conclusion is of the kind that any well-read person is likely to know, then no documentation is necessary. For instance, the assertion that the Nazi regime under Hitler committed atrocities against the Jews, is common knowledge and therefore requires no documentation. However, if you quoted from eyewitness accounts of these atrocities, acknowledgment must be given in either a footnote or endnote. In sum, any idea, conclusion, information, or data specifically derived from the work of someone else must be acknowledged.

9c

How to number notes

See 7c-3.

9d

Documentation of books: order and general rules

The general order of notes that document books is as follows.

9d-1 Author

The full name of the author (or authors) comes first. List the name in normal order, with the Christian name first, followed by the surname and a comma. Use the name by which the author is customarily known, even if it is an abbreviated name:

```
C. S. Lewis
```

Brackets may be used to expand on an author's initials:

```
C[live] S[taples] Lewis
```

In some cases the name of an editor, translator, or compiler will be cited before the name of an author, especially if the actual editing, translating, or compiling is the subject of discussion (see 9d-4 below).

9d-2 Chapter or part of book

If part of an entire book is being cited, the title of the cited chapter or part of the book is given within quotation marks, followed by a comma inside the final quotation mark. The word "in" should be used to indicate that the cited work is part of a collection:

```
"Parliament in the Air Raids," in Modern English Eloquence
```

The words "Preface" or "Introduction" or other untitled parts of a book are capitalized, but are neither underlined nor placed within quotation marks (see p. 161). If a work originally published separately is being cited as part of a collection, underline the title of the work:

```
Anton Chekhov, The Cherry Orchard. in The Art of Drama
```

9d-3 Title of work

The title of the work is underlined and followed by a comma. No comma is used if the title ends with some other kind of punctuation such as a question mark or an exclamation mark, or if the next item after the title is enclosed in parentheses. Ignore any unusual typographical style, such as ALL CAPITAL LETTERS, or any peculiar arrangement of capitals and lower-case letters, unless the author is specifically known to insist on such a typography. Copy the title exactly as it appears on the title page. Capitalize any subtitle and separate it from the title by a colon:

<u>Aerobics at Home: A Manual for Joggers</u>

Subtitles may be omitted in footnotes or endnotes, but must be included in the bibliography entry.

9d-4 Name of editor, compiler, or translator

The name of the editor(s), compiler(s), or translator(s) is given in normal order, preceded by "ed.," "comp.," or "trans.":

Homer, <u>The Iliad</u>, trans. Richard Lattimore

However, if the actual editing, translating, or compiling is the subject of the paper, the name of the editor, translator, or compiler is listed *before* the name of the author, followed by the abbreviation "ed.," "comp.," or "trans." and a comma. The name of the author is then listed *after* the title, preceded by the word "by":

Richard Lattimore, trans., <u>The Iliad</u>, by Homer

9d-5 Edition

The edition being used is cited, if it is other than first. Cite the edition in Arabic numerals (3rd ed.) followed by a comma, unless the next item is enclosed in parentheses. Always use the latest edition of a work, unless you have some specific reason of scholarship for using another.

[4] John C. Hodges and Mary E. Whitten, <u>Harbrace College Handbook</u>, 8th ed. (New York: Harcourt Brace Jovanovich, Inc., 1977), p. 149.

For reprints of old editions, especially paperback reprints of little-known works, cite the date of the original edition along with the reprint information:

[11] Gilbert Highet, <u>The Art of Teaching</u> (1950; rpt. New York: Vintage Books, 1958), p. 51.

The original copyright date should also be given, or the work may appear to be more recently published than it really is.

9d-6   Series

The name of a series is given, capitalized, without quotation marks and not underlined, followed by a comma and by an Arabic numeral indicating the number of the cited work in the series. The series number is then followed by a comma, unless the next item is enclosed in parentheses:

[6] Jack Ludwig, <u>Recent American Novelists</u>, University of

Minnesota Pamphlets on American Writers, 22 (Minneapolis: Uni—

versity of Minnesota Press, 1962), p. 25.

9d-7   Number of volumes

If more than one volume bears this same title, the number of volumes is given in Arabic numerals. Include this only if referring to the work as a whole, rather than to a specific passage:

[19] Will Durant and Ariel Durant, <u>The Story of Civilization</u>,

10 vols. (New York: Simon and Schuster, 1968).

The page number is omitted, since the citation is to the multivolume work as a whole.

9d-8   Place, publisher, and date of publication

The place, publisher, and date of publication are given within parentheses. A colon follows the place, a comma the publisher, and the closing parenthesis the date:

(New York: Atheneum Publishers, Inc., 1975)

Copy the place of publication from the title or copyright page. If no place or publisher is given, write "n.p." followed by a colon to indicate "no place," and "n.p." followed by the closing parenthesis to indicate "no publisher":

(n.p.: n.p.)

If no date of publication is given, use "n.d." All three abbreviations could conceivably be used in a single citation:

(n.p.: n.p., n.d.)

Names of well-known publishers may be sensibly abbreviated—Alfred A. Knopf, Inc., Harcourt Brace Jovanovich, Inc., and The Bobbs-Merrill Company, Inc., for example, as Knopf, Harcourt, and Bobbs-Merrill. Do not abbreviate the name of a university press; the press may exist independently of the university, and the abbreviation may cause confusion between the two. If no publication date appears on the title page, use the most recent copyright date that appears on the copyright page. For books published before 1900, the name of the publisher may be omitted. If the source contains neither author, title, nor publication information, use brackets to indicate whatever information you were able to obtain:

⁸ Photographs of Historic Castles ([St. Albans, England]:

n.p., n.d.), p. 10.

9d-9 Volume number

If the reference is to one of several volumes, the volume number is cited in capital Roman numerals, preceded and followed by a comma:

³ W. T. Jones, A History of Western Philosophy (New York:

Harcourt, 1952), II, 13.

The "p" or "pp" for page(s) is omitted when the page number follows a volume number.

If the volumes were published in different years, indicate this by placing the volume number *before* the facts of publication.

¹⁰ George Grote, History of Greece, V (New York: Harper &

Brothers, 1860), 155.

For separately titled individual volumes of a multivolume work, use the following form:

² George K. Anderson and Robert Warnock, The Modern World,

Vol. II of The World in Literature (New York: Scott, Foresman

and Company, 1951), pp. 5–10.

9d-10 Page numbers

Page numbers are given in Arabic numerals (unless the original has Roman numerals), preceded by a comma and followed by a period, unless some other notation is necessary:

```
p. 5, col. 3
```

Cite all the pages from which the idea, summary, quotation, or paraphrase was taken.

9e

Sample endnotes for books

The samples, though widely varied, cannot anticipate every conceivable kind of citation. If you need to cite a source for which this book provides no model, use your common sense. Bear in mind, moreover, that the purpose of documentation is to allow a curious reader to reconstruct your research and thinking. You should therefore provide enough information to enable a reader to easily locate any cited source.

All samples are given in the endnote format, with double spacing. A footnote is single-spaced within each note, but separated from another footnote by a double space. See 7c-1 and 7c-2 for a summary of the footnote/endnote formats.

9e-1 Book with a single author

```
    ¹ Fawn M. Brodie, Thomas Jefferson: An Intimate History
```

```
(New York: W. W. Norton & Company, Inc., 1974), p. 181.
```

If an author's name has already been supplied in the text, it may be omitted in the note:

Text

```
    In Thomas Jefferson: An Intimate History Fawn M. Brodie

suggests that Jefferson was our most controlled

president.²
```

Note

```
        ² Thomas Jefferson: An Intimate History (New York:

W. W. Norton & Company, Inc., 1974), p. 21.
```

172

9e-2 Book with two or more authors

Cite all authors (up to three) in order of appearance on the title page. For a book written by more than three authors, use in full the first name listed, followed by "et al." or "and others," with no comma in between:

³ John C. Bollens and Grant B. Geyer, <u>Yorty: Politics of a Constant Candidate</u> (Pacific Palisades, Calif.: Palisades Publishers, 1973), p. 73.

⁴ Gordon W. Allport, Philip E. Vernon, and Gardner Lindzey, <u>Study of Values</u> (New York: Houghton Mifflin Co., 1951), p. 12.

⁵ Ruth Brown et al., <u>Agricultural Education in a Technical Society: An Annotated Bibliography of Resources</u> (Chicago: American Library Association, 1973), p. 220.

9e-3 Book with a corporate author

Organizations that author books may either be treated like an author or may follow the title of the books, preceded with "by":

⁶ American Institute of Physics, <u>Handbook</u>, 3rd ed. (New York: McGraw-Hill Book Company, 1972), p. 10.

⁶ <u>Handbook</u>, by the American Institute of Physics, 3rd ed. (New York: McGraw-Hill Book Company, 1972), p. 10.

If the name of the corporate author is specified in the title of the work, no other listing of the corporate author is necessary:

⁷ <u>Report of the Special Commission to Investigate the Assassination of John F. Kennedy</u> (Washington, D.C.: Office of Government Publications, 1964), p. 888.

9e-4 Book with an anonymous or pseudonymous author

When the author of a book is anonymous, merely list the title. Neither "anonymous" nor "anon." needs to be added:

⁸ <u>Current Biography</u> (New York: H. W. Wilson, 1976),

pp. 20–22.

If you are able to research an author's name, supply it in brackets:

⁹ [Adlai Stauffer], <u>Cloudburst</u> (Knoxville, Tenn.: Review and

Courier Publishing Assoc., 1950), p. 18.

The name of an author who writes under a pseudonym (or *nom de plume*) may also be given in brackets:

¹⁰ Mary Ann Evans [George Eliot], <u>Daniel Deronda</u> (London,

1876), p. 58.

NOTE: Since the book was published before 1900, no publisher has to be named.

9e-5 Work in several volumes or parts

In a reference to a multivolume work in its entirety, state the number of volumes after the title:

¹¹ T. Walter Wallbank and Alastair M. Taylor, <u>Civilization</u>

<u>Past and Present</u>, 2 vols. (New York: Scott, Foresman and Com-

pany, 1949).

Since the reference is to the entire work, no page is cited.

But if the reference is to a specific volume, the volume number must be listed in Roman numerals after the facts of publication (unless the volumes were published in separate years, in which case the Roman numeral appears *before* the facts of publication [see also 9d-9]):

¹¹ T. Walter Wallbank and Alastair M. Taylor, <u>Civilization</u>

<u>Past and Present</u> (New York: Scott, Foresman and Company, 1949),

II, 217.

¹² J. F. C. Fuller, <u>A Military History of the Western World</u>,

III (New York: Funk & Wagnalls Company, 1956), 271–83.

For individual volumes of a multivolume work with separate titles, use the following form:

¹³ Paul Jacobs, Saul Landen, and Eve Pell, <u>Colonials and So-</u><u>journers</u>, Vol. II of <u>To Serve the Devil</u> (New York: Random House, 1971), pp. 37–39.

9e-6 Work within a collection of pieces, all by the same author

For anthologies or collections of a single author's work, place the cited title in quotation marks; underline the title of the collection and precede it with the word "in":

¹⁴ Edgar Johnson, "The Keel of the New Lugger," in <u>The Great</u> <u>Unknown</u>, Vol. II of <u>Sir Walter Scott</u> (New York: The Macmillan Company, 1970), p. 775.

¹⁵ Richard Selzer, "Liver," in <u>Mortal Lessons</u> (New York: Si-mon & Schuster, 1976), p. 37.

9e-7 Chapter or titled section in a book

In this sense, "book" means a work that deals with a single or unified subject, as distinguished from a collection of unrelated essays or pieces. For citations to a specific chapter or section of such a work, rather than to the entire book itself, use the following form:

¹⁶ Norma Lorre Goodrich, "Gilgamesh the Wrestler," <u>Myths of</u> <u>the Hero</u> (New York: The Orion Press, 1960), pp. 4–5.

Notice that in this case the "in" is omitted.

9e-8 Collections: anthologies, casebooks, and readers

For a work included in a casebook, anthology, essay collection, and the like—that is, a collection of different pieces by different authors—use the following form:

¹⁷ Eudora Welty, "The Wide Net," in <u>Story: An Introduction</u> <u>to Prose Fiction</u>, ed. Arthur Foff and Daniel Knapp (Belmont, Calif.: Wadsworth Publishing Company, 1966), p. 166.

If possible, specify the original date and publication source of the cited piece. (This information can usually be found either in a footnote or in the copyright acknowledgments of the collection.)

[18] Malcolm Cowley, "Sociological Habit Patterns in Linguistic Transmogrification," The Reporter, 20 Sept. 1956, pp. 257–61; rpt. in Readings for Writers, ed. Jo Ray McCuen and Anthony C. Winkler, 2nd ed. (New York: Harcourt Brace Jovanovich, Inc., 1977), pp. 489–93.

Notice that "rpt. in" for "reprinted in" precedes the title of the collection.

9e-9 Double reference—a quotation within a cited work

Use the following form for referring to a quotation within a cited work:

[19] Lin Piao as quoted in Jean Daubier, A History of the Chinese Cultural Revolution, trans. Richard Seaver (New York: Random House, 1974), p. 83.

9e-10 Reference works

a. Encyclopedias

For signed articles in well-known encyclopedias, supply name of author, title of entry, name of encyclopedia, and year of edition:

[20] Albert George Ballert, "Saint Lawrence River," Encyclopaedia Britannica, 1963 ed.

The authors of articles in reference works are usually identified by initials that are decoded in a special index volume. If the article is unsigned, begin with the title entry:

[21] "House of David," Encyclopedia Americana, 1974 ed.

Generally, for works alphabetically arranged, volume and page number are not supplied. However, if a citation refers to a single page of a multipage article, volume and page must be given:

[22] Morroe Berger and Dorothy Willner, "Near Eastern

Society," International Encyclopedia of the Social Sciences,

1968 ed., II, 97.

b. Dictionaries and annuals

Use the same form as for encyclopedias:

[23] "Barsabbas, Joseph," Who's Who in the New Testament

(1971).

Since only one edition of this work has been published, "ed." after the publication date is not necessary.

[24] "Telegony," Dictionary of Philosophy and Psychology

(1902).

Items in a little-known reference work are treated the same as items in a collection (see 9e-8).

9e-11 Work in a series

a. A numbered series

[25] Louis Auchincloss, Edith Wharton, University of Minnesota

Pamphlets on American Writers, No. 12 (Minneapolis: University

of Minnesota Press, 1961), p. 17.

b. An unnumbered series

[26] Sally Miller, The Radical Immigrant, The Immigrant Heri-

tage of America Series (New York: Twayne Publishers, 1974), pp.

20-22.

9e-12 Reprint

A citation to a reprint should include the date of the original version. If the work was first published in a foreign country, supply the original place of publication:

²⁷ John J. Babson, <u>History of the Town of Gloucester, Cape Ann, Including the Town of Rockport</u> (1860; rpt. New York: Peter Smith Publisher, Inc., 1972), p. 300.

Without a listing of the original publication date, this work appears to be deceivingly recent.

²⁸ William Makepeace Thackeray, <u>Vanity Fair</u> (London, 1847–48; rpt. New York: Harper & Brothers, Publishers, 1968), pp. 103–06.

The original publication date is usually not supplied for popular paperback reprints.

9e-13 Edition

The word "edition" can be understood in three different ways: it can mean (1) a revised printing of a work; (2) a collection of items edited by one or several authors; (3) the edited version of one or more works by an editor or editors. The proper forms to use in each of these cases are as follows:

- For a revised edition:

²⁹ Porter G. Perrin and Jim W. Corder, <u>Handbook of Current English</u>, 4th ed. (Glenview, Ill.: Scott Foresman and Company, 1975), pp. 304–05.

- For an edited collection:

³⁰ Charles Clerc, "Goodbye to All That: Theme, Character and Symbol in <u>Goodbye, Columbus</u>," in <u>Seven Contemporary Short Novels</u>, ed. Charles Clerc and Louis Leiter (Glenview, Ill.: Scott, Foresman and Company, 1969), p. 107.

The reference here is to an editorial critique on one of the novels in the collection.

- For the work of an editor:

³¹ Hardin Craig and David Bevington, eds., <u>The Complete Works of Shakespeare</u>, rev. ed. (Glenview, Ill.: Scott, Foresman and Company, 1973), pp. 31–38.

Because the reference is to the editorial work of Craig and Bevington, the names of these editors are listed in place of the author's. But when the paper deals with the work of the original author, rather than with the work of an editor or translator, the author's name must then be listed first:

³² Sylvia Plath, <u>Letters Home</u>, ed. Aurelia Schober Plath

(New York: Harper & Row Publishers, 1975), pp. 153–54.

9e-14   Book published in a foreign country

³³ Louis Vialleton, <u>L'Origine des êtres vivants</u> (Paris: Librairie Plon, 1929), p. 25.

³⁴ Oliver Ransford, <u>Livingston's Lake: The Drama of Nyasa</u>

(London: Camelot Press, 1966), p. 83.

Only proper nouns in French titles are capitalized. However, it is customary to capitalize the first word of a title, and also the second word if the first word is an article:

Les Citadins de Paris

The adjective that precedes the first noun in a title is also capitalized:

La Belle Epoque

9e-15   Introduction, preface, foreword, or afterword

Introductions, prefaces, forewords, or afterwords, when written by someone other than the editor or author, are treated as follows:

³⁵ Marshall B. Davidson, Introd., <u>The Age of Napoleon</u>, by J.

Christopher Herold (New York: The American Heritage Publishing

Co., Inc., 1963), p. 8.

Notice that the words "Introd.," "Pref.," etc., are not placed within quotation marks. "Introd." and "Pref." are abbreviated; "Foreword" and "Afterword" are spelled out.

9e-16 Translation

When the translation itself is under discussion, the name of the translator should appear first.

³⁶ John Addington Symons, trans., <u>Autobiography of Benvenuto</u>

<u>Cellini</u>, by Benvenuto Cellini (New York: Washington Square

Press, Inc., 1963), pp. 76–82.

But when the work of the original author is under discussion, the order of names is reversed:

³⁷ Benvenuto Cellini, <u>Autobiography of Benvenuto Cellini</u>,

trans. John Addington Symons (New York: Washington Square Press,

Inc., 1963), pp. 75–79.

9e-17 Dissertation

Unpublished: The title is placed within quotation marks and the work identified by "Diss.":

³⁸ Joyce Raymonde Cotton, "<u>Evan Harrington</u>: An Analysis of

George Meredith's Revisions," Diss. University of Southern Cali-

fornia 1968, p. 48.

Published: It is treated as a book, except for including the label "Diss." and stating where and when the dissertation was originally written:

³⁹ Teresa Cortey, <u>Le Rêve dans les contes de Charles Nodier</u>,

Diss. University of California, Berkeley 1975 (Washington, D.C.:

University Press of America, 1977), p. 46.

9e-18 Pamphlet

Citations of pamphlets should conform as nearly as possible to the format used for citations of books. Give as much information on the pamphlet as is necessary to help a reader find it:

⁴⁰ Calplans Agricultural Fund, <u>An Investment in California</u>

<u>Agricultural Real Estate</u> (Oakland, Calif.: Calplans Securities,

Inc., n.d.), p. 3.

⁴¹ Charles W. Cooper and Edmund J. Robins, <u>The Term Paper: A Manual and Model</u>, 3rd ed. (Stanford, Calif.: Stanford University Press, 1934), p. 21.

9e-19 Government publication or legal reference

Because of their complicated origins, government publications can be difficult to document. Generally, the citation of a government publication should list first the author or agency, then the title of the publication (underlined), followed by the publication facts (place, name, date) and the page reference. Although no standard format exists for all such publications, we have tried to supply samples for the kinds of government sources most often cited in undergraduate papers.

a. The Congressional Record

A citation to the *Congressional Record* requires only title, date, and page(s):

⁴² <u>Cong. Rec.</u>, 15 Dec. 1977, p. 19740.

b. Congressional publications

The authors are listed either as "U.S. Cong., Senate," "U.S. Cong., House," or "U.S. Cong., Joint":

⁴³ U.S. Cong., Senate, Permanent Subcommittee on Investigations of the Committee on Government Operations, <u>Organized Crime—Stolen Securities</u>, 93rd Cong., 1st sess. (Washington, D.C.: GPO, 1973), pp. 1–4.

"GPO" is the accepted abbreviation for "U.S. Government Printing Office."

⁴⁴ U.S. Cong., House, Committee on Foreign Relations, <u>Hearings on S. 2793, Supplemental Foreign Assistance Fiscal Year 1966—Vietnam</u>, 89th Cong., 2nd sess. (Washington, D.C.: GPO, 1966), p. 9.

The titles of government publications, although long and cumbersome, must nevertheless be accurately cited.

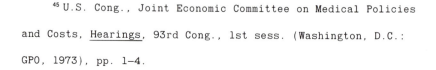

[45] U.S. Cong., Joint Economic Committee on Medical Policies and Costs, _Hearings_, 93rd Cong., 1st sess. (Washington, D.C.: GPO, 1973), pp. 1-4.

c. Executive Branch publications

[46] Ernest L. Boyer, U.S. Commissioner of Education, "Emergency Adult Education Program for Indochina Refugees," _Federal Register_, 27 June 1977, p. 32589, cols. 1-3.

[47] Department of State, _United States Treaties and Other International Agreements_ (Washington, D.C.: GPO, 1975), XXVI, 1448-49.

[48] Bureau of the Census, U.S. Department of Commerce, _Statistical Abstracts of the United States_ (Washington, D.C.: GPO, 1963), p. 567.

d. Legal publications

[49] Office of the Federal Register, "The Supreme Court of the United States," _United States Government Manual_ (Washington, D.C.: GPO, 1976), p. 67.

Names of laws, acts, and the like are generally neither underlined nor placed within quotation marks: Constitution of the United States, Declaration of Independence, Bill of Rights, Humphrey-Hawkins Bill, Sherman Anti-Trust Act. Citations of legal sources usually refer to sections rather than to pages. Certain conventional abbreviations are also used in such citations:

[50] U.S. Const., art. I, sec. 2.

[51] 15 U.S. Code, sec. 78j(b) (1964).

[52] U.C.C., art. IX, pt. 2, par. 9-28.

Names of law cases are abbreviated, and the first important word of each party is spelled out: Brown v. Board of Ed. stands for Brown versus the Board of Education of Topeka, Kansas. Cases, unlike laws, are italicized in the text but not in the notes. Text: Miranda v. Arizona. Note: Miranda v. Arizona. The following information must be supplied in a citation of law cases: (1) name of the first plaintiff and the first defendant; (2) the volume, name, and page (in that order) of the law report cited; (3) the name of the court that decided the case; (4) the year in which the case was decided:

    [53] Richardson v. J. C. Flood Co., 190 A.2d 259 (D.C. App.

    1963).

Interpreted, the above means that the Richardson v. J. C. Flood Co. case can be found on page 259 of volume 190 of the Second Series of the Atlantic Reporter. The case was settled in the District of Columbia Court of Appeals during the year 1963. For further information on the form for legal references, consult *A Uniform System of Citation,* 12th ed. (Cambridge: Harvard Law Review Association, 1976).

9e-20   Citations to footnotes or endnotes

A citation to a footnote or endnote in a source takes the following form:

    [54] M. D. Faber, The Design Within: Psychoanalytic Approaches

    to Shakespeare (New York: Science House, 1970), p. 205, n. 9.

The accepted abbreviation for "note" is "n." The citation here is to footnote 9, which occurs on page 205 of the book.

9e-21   Manuscript or typescript

The citation to a manuscript or typescript from a library collection should provide the following information: (1) location of script; (2) whether a manuscript (MS) or typescript (TS); (3) library number of the script; (4) page or foliation number (fol.). (Scripts are usually foliated— counted by leaf—rather than paginated.)

    [55] Huntington Library MS. Ellesmere Chaucer, E126C9, fol. 25.

    [56] Exeter Cathedral MS. The Wanderer, fol. 10.

    [57] British Museum MS. Cotton Vitellius, A. SV, fols. 129a–

    198b.

(The last is a reference to the famous *Beowulf* manuscript.)

9e-22 Play

a. Classical play

> [58] William Shakespeare, <u>Antony and Cleopatra</u>, in <u>The Complete Works of Shakespeare</u>, ed. Hardin Craig and David Bevington, rev. ed. (Glenview, Ill.: Scott, Foresman and Company, 1973), p. 1105 (V.ii.120–30).

In citations of classical plays, give the act, scene, and lines in parentheses at the end of the note. Such information makes it easier for a reader using a different edition to find the source.

b. Modern play

If published as a single work, the play is treated like a book:

> [50] Arthur Miller, <u>The Crucible</u> (New York: Bantam Books, Inc., 1952), p. 13.

If published as part of a collection, the play is cited in this form:

> [60] Anton Chekhov, <u>The Cherry Orchard</u>, in <u>The Art of Drama</u>, ed. R. F. Dietrich, William E. Carpenter, and Kevin Kerrane, 2nd ed. (New York: Holt, Rinehart and Winston, 1976), p. 325.

9e-23 Poem

a. Long classical poem

> [61] Lucretius [Titus Lucretius Carus], <u>Of the Nature of Things</u>, trans. William Ellery Leonard, in <u>Backgrounds of the Modern World</u>, Vol. I of <u>The World in Literature</u>, ed. Robert Warnock and George K. Anderson (New York: Scott, Foresman and Company, 1950), p. 345 (Bk. II. 11. 270–75).

In the above note, "ll" stands for "lines."

b. Short classical poem

⁶² Horace [Quintus Horatius Flaccus], "To Licinius," trans. William Cowper, in <u>Backgrounds of the Modern World</u>, Vol. I of <u>The World in Literature</u>, ed. Robert Warnock and George K. Anderson (New York: Scott, Foresman and Company, 1950), p. 406.

c. Long modern poem

Such a poem is usually published in a book:

⁶³ Lord Byron, <u>Don Juan</u>, ed. Leslie A. Marchand (Boston: Houghton Mifflin Company, 1958), p. 13.

For a long poem in a collection, see 9e-23a.

d. Short modern poem

⁶⁴ Marianne Moore, "Poetry," in <u>Fine Frenzy</u>, ed. Robert Baylor and Brenda Stokes (New York: McGraw-Hill Book Company, 1972), pp. 372-73.

9e-24 Classical works in general

In citing a classical work that is subdivided into books, parts, cantos, verses, and lines, specify the appropriate subdivisions so that a reader using a different edition of the work can easily locate the reference:

⁶⁵ Homer, <u>The Iliad</u>, trans. Richmond Lattimore (Chicago: University of Chicago Press, 1937), p. 101 (III.15-20).

⁶⁶ Dante Alighieri, <u>The Inferno</u>, trans. John Ciardi (New York: New American Library, 1954), p. 37 (ii.75-90).

Books or parts are usually indicated by large Roman numerals, cantos or verses by small Roman numerals, and lines by Arabic numerals.

9e-25 The Bible

Because the King James Bible is such a familiar document, only the appropriate book and verse need be cited. Translations other than the King James must be indicated within parentheses:

    [67] Isaiah XII.15.

    [68] II Ephesians II.10 (Revised Standard Version).

Or:

    [67] Isaiah 12:15.

    [68] II Ephesians 2:10 (Revised Standard Version).

9f

Documentation of periodicals: order and general rules

Citations of periodicals should be made in the following general order. Skip any item that does not apply and go on to the next.

9f-1 Author

Give the author's full name in normal order, followed by a comma. If more than one author is involved, observe the form for multiple authors of books given in 9e-2. If only the initials of an author are given, type out each initial with a period, leaving one space after each period: H. A. W. Often you will find the author(s) listed at the end of the article:

    Ron Reid, "Black and Gold Soul with Italian Legs," Sports

    Illustrated, 11 Dec. 1972, pp. 36–37.

9f-2 Title of article

The title of the article, copied as listed, appears next within quotation marks, and is followed by a comma, unless the title itself ends with another punctuation mark such as an exclamation mark. (See preceding example.)

186

9f-3 Name of periodical

The name of the periodical, as it appears on the front cover of the magazine, is underlined and followed by a comma. (See preceding example.) List the name of a newspaper as it appears on its masthead. If not part of the masthead, the city of publication may be given in square brackets following the name of the newspaper:

> The Christian Science Monitor [Boston]

If the periodical is little known or if another periodical by the same name exists, add in brackets the name of the city or institution issuing the periodical:

> Pacific Union Recorder [Angwin, Calif.]

9f-4 Volume number

The volume number (not preceded by "Vol.") is written in Arabic numerals, and is followed by a comma unless the next item is within parentheses:

> Sewanee Review, 84 (1976), 474.

Omit the volume number for weekly or monthly periodicals paged anew in each issue (that is, when each new issue begins with page 1). Instead, give the complete date of each issue, set off by commas and not within parentheses, or supply the month or season of the issue, with the year, within parentheses:

> Time, 2 Feb. 1978, p. 31.

> Harper's (May 1970), p. 20.

For citations of a newspaper, it may be helpful to supply the edition:

> New York Times, Late City Ed., 15 April 1977, p. 2, col. 1.

9f-5 Issue number

Give the issue number when pagination of the issue is separate for each volume, and the month or season of publication is not supplied:

> Oklahoma English Bulletin, 2, No. 2 (1965), 15.

Without the issue number, the article could be found only by a search of page 15 of every 1965 issue.

9f-6 Month and year

Supply the month (if needed) and the year, within parentheses, followed by a comma. If all issues of a journal fall within a calendar year, use only the year. However, if each issue of a periodical is separately paginated, always list the month before the year (Nov. 1976) or the season before the year (Fall 1977). When in doubt about the pagination, give the month or season of publication:

> Change (March 1978), pp. 38–39.

Here no volume or issue number is supplied, since each issue is paged anew and the periodical comes out monthly.

   If all of the year's issues are bound together in one continuously paged volume, it is unnecessary to cite the month: the volume number, however, is given:

> Studies in Short Fiction, 12 (1975), 91.

If the volume number of a journal does not coincide with the calendar year, citing the month of publication makes the reference easier to find:

> College English, 39 (Dec. 1977), 427.

(The first issue of this periodical is published in October.)

9f-7 Page numbers

The page number or numbers are given in Arabic numerals, followed by a period unless more information follows. Use the abbreviations "p." or "pp." only when a volume number is *not* part of the reference.

> The Chronicle of Higher Education, 6 March 1972, p. 9.

Here, since a volume number is not supplied, "p." is used. But if a volume number is supplied, "p." is left out:

> PMLA, 93 (1978), 67.

If, however, the reference is to a footnote or endnote in an article, additional information must be supplied:

> George W. Carey, "Separation of Powers and the Madisonian
>
> Model: A Reply to the Critics," The American Political Science
>
> Review, 72 (March 1978), 153, note 17.

In newspaper references it is helpful to supply the edition or section or part, and the column(s) and page(s):

> <u>Los Angeles Times</u>, 12 March 1978, Part IV, p. 3, cols. 2-4.

9g

Sample endnotes for periodicals

9g-1 Anonymous author

> [1] "Elegance Is Out," <u>Fortune</u>, 13 March 1978, p. 18.

Most periodical articles are written by unidentified correspondents.

9g-2 Single author

> [2] Hugh Sidey, "In Defense of the Martini," <u>Time</u>, 24 Oct. 1977, p. 38.

9g-3 More than one author

> [3] Clyde Ferguson and William R. Cotter, "South Africa--What Is To Be Done," <u>Foreign Affairs</u>, 56 (1978), 254.

The format of a citation to a multiple authored magazine article is the same as for a multiple authored book. For three authors, list the names of the authors exactly as they appear in the article. Separate the first and second name by a comma, and the second and third by a comma followed by the word "and." For more than three authors, list the name of the first author followed by "et al." or "and others" with no comma in between. See 9e-2.

9g-4 Journal with continuous pagination throughout the annual volume

> [4] Anne Paolucci, "Comedy and Paradox in Pirandello's Plays," <u>Modern Drama</u>, 20 (1977), 322.

Since there is only one page 322 throughout volume 20 of 1977, it is unnecessary to add the month.

9g-5 Journal with separate pagination for each issue

⁵ Claude T. Mangrum, "Toward More Effective Justice," <u>Crime</u> <u>Prevention Review</u>, 5 (Jan. 1978), 7.

Since each issue of this journal is paged anew, page 7 will occur in all issues of volume 5; therefore the addition of the month is necessary.

⁶ Robert Brown, "Physical Illness and Mental Health," <u>Phi-</u> <u>losophy and Public Affairs</u>, 7 (Fall 1977), 18–19.

Since this journal is published quarterly and in volumes that do not coincide with the year, adding the season of publication makes the source easier to locate.

⁷ Walter H. Cappe, "Humanities at Large," <u>The Center Maga-</u> <u>zine</u>, 11, No. 2 (1978), 2.

Since this issue covers both March and April, it is simpler to supply the issue number than the months.

9g-6 Monthly magazine

⁸ Mark Crispin Miller, "The New Wave in Rock," <u>Horizon</u>, March 1978, pp. 76–77.

⁹ Flora Davis and Julia Orange, "The Strange Case of the Children Who Invented Their Own Language," <u>Redbook</u>, March 1978, pp. 113, 165.

Note the split page reference to the *Redbook* article, which began on one page and was continued at the back of the magazine.

9g-7 Weekly magazine

¹⁰ Suzy Eban, "Our Far-Flung Correspondents," <u>The New</u> <u>Yorker</u>, 6 March 1978, pp. 70–72.

¹¹ "Philadelphia's Way of Stopping the Shoplifter," <u>Business Week</u>, 6 March 1972, pp. 57–59.

Since the author is not listed, the citation begins with the title of the article.

9g-8 Newspaper

¹² James Tanner, "Disenchantment Grows in OPEC Group with Use of U.S. Dollar for Oil Pricing," <u>The Wall Street Journal</u>, 9 March 1978, p. 3, cols. 3–4.

The listing of the columns as well as the page makes this article easier to locate.

¹³ Daniel Southerland, "Carter Plans Firm Stand with Begin," <u>The Christian Science Monitor</u>, Western Ed., 9 March 1978, p. 1, col. 4.

Listing the edition makes it easier for a reader to locate this article.

¹⁴ Emily Malino, "A Matter of Placement," <u>Washington Post</u>, 5 March 1978, Section L, p. 5, cols. 3–5.

When citing crowded (e.g. Sunday) editions of newspapers, always supply the section or part.

9g-9 Editorial
Signed:

¹⁵ William Futrell, "The Inner City Frontier," Editorial, <u>Sierra</u>, 63, No. 2 (1978), 5.

Unsigned:

¹⁶ "Criminals in Uniform," Editorial, <u>Los Angeles Times</u>, 7 April 1978, Part II, p. 6, cols. 1–2.

9g-10 Letter to the editor

[17] Donna Korczyk, Letter, <u>Time</u>, 20 March 1978, p. 4.

9g-11 Critical review

[18] Peter Andrews, rev. of <u>The Strange Ride of Rudyard Kip-</u><u>ling: His Life and Works</u>, by Angus Wilson, <u>Saturday Review</u>, 4 March 1978, p. 24.

Supply also any readily available publication facts of the books being reviewed:

[19] Robert V. Daniels, rev. of <u>Stalinism: Essays in Histori-</u><u>cal Interpretations</u>, ed. Robert C. Tucker (New York: W. W. Nor-ton, 1977), <u>The Russian Review</u>, 37 (1978), 102.

For unsigned reviews with a title, use the following format:

[20] "Soyer Sees Soyer," rev. of <u>Diary of an Artist</u>, by Ralph Soyer, <u>American Artist</u>, March 1978, pp. 18–19.

For a review with neither title nor author, use the following format:

[21] Rev. of <u>Charmed Life</u>, by Diana Wynne Jones, <u>Booklist</u>, 74 (Feb. 1978), 1009.

9g-12 Published interview

[22] "Why the Tide of Illegal Aliens Keeps Rising," Interview with Leonel J. Castillo, Commissioner, Immigration and Naturali-zation Service, <u>U.S. News and World Report</u>, 20 Feb. 1978, p. 33.

If the interviewee's position is listed, mention it in the citation.

9h
Documentation of special items

Citation samples of other sources commonly used in research papers are given below. For citation forms on sources not covered here, consult with your instructor. Bear in mind that the prime rule of documentation is to provide the information necessary for a reader to trace any cited source.

9h-1 Lecture

As minimum information cite the speaker's name, the title of the lecture in quotation marks, and the sponsoring organization, location, and date:

[1] Gene L. Schwilck, "The Core and the Community," Danforth Foundation, St. Louis, Missouri, 16 March 1978.

9h-2 Film

Film citations should include the director's name, the title of the film (underlined), the name of the leading actor or actors, the distributor, and the date of showing. Information on the producer, writer, and size or length of film may also be supplied, if necessary to your study:

[2] Herbert Ross, dir., The Turning Point, with Anne Bancroft, Shirley MacLaine, Mikhail Baryshnikov, and Leslie Brown, Twentieth Century-Fox, 1978.

9h-3 Radio or television program

Citations should include the title of the program (underlined), the network or local station, and the city and date of broadcast. If appropriate, the title of the episode is listed in quotation marks before the title of the program, while the title of the series, neither underlined nor in quotation marks, comes after the title of the program. The name of the writer, director, narrator, or producer may also be supplied, if significant to your paper:

[3] "Diving for Roman Plunder," narr. and dir. Jacques Cousteau, The Cousteau Odyssey, KCET, Los Angeles, 14 March 1978.

[4] "Chapter 2," writ. Wolf Mankowitz, <u>Dickens of London</u>, dir. and prod. Marc Miller, Masterpiece Theater, introd. Alistair Cooke, PBS, Los Angeles, 28 Aug. 1977.

[5] <u>World of Survival</u>, narr. John Forsythe, CBS Special, Los Angeles, 29 Oct. 1972.

9h-4 Theatrical performance

Theatrical performances are cited in the form used for films, with added information on the theater, city, and date of performance. In opera, concert, or dance productions you may also wish to cite the conductor (cond.) or choreographer (chor.). Place the name of either the author, composer, or director first, depending on the desired emphasis. This citation emphasizes the director:

[6] Gordon Davidson, dir., <u>Getting Out</u>, by Marsha Norman, with Susan Clark, Mark Taper Forum, Los Angeles, 2 April 1978.

This citation emphasizes the playwright:

[7] Simon Gray, <u>Otherwise Engaged</u>, dir. Harold Pinter, with Dick Cavett, Plymouth Theater, New York, 30 Oct. 1977.

These citations emphasize the conductor:

[8] James Conlon, cond., "<u>La Bohème</u>," with Renata Scotto, Metropolitan Opera, Metropolitan Opera House, New York, 29 Oct. 1977.

[9] Lorin Maazel, cond., New York Philharmonic Orchestra, Avery Fisher Hall, New York, 10 Nov. 1977.

This citation emphasizes the conductor and the guest performer:

[10] Sergiu Commissiona, cond., Baltimore Symphony Orchestra, with Albert Markov, violin, Brooklyn College, New York, 8 Nov. 1977.

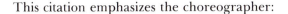

This citation emphasizes the choreographer:

¹¹ George Balanchine, chor. <u>Pas de Deux</u>, New York City Bal-

let, New York State Theater, New York, 19 Nov. 1977.

9h-5 Musical composition

Whenever possible cite the title in your text, as for instance:

Bach's <u>Well-Tempered Clavier</u>

However, when opus numbers would clutter the text, then cite the composition in a footnote or endnote following the rules on p. 155:

¹² Edvard Grieg, Menuet in E minor, Op. 7, No. 3.

9h-6 Work of art

Cite the title of a work of art in your text whenever possible:

Antonio Pollaiolo's <u>Portrait of a Woman</u>

If, however, a work of art must be cited in a footnote or endnote, underline the title and state the name of the city and institution housing the work:

¹³ Beato Angelico, <u>Madonna dei Linaioli</u>, Museum of San

Marco, Florence, Italy.

If you are citing an illustration from some published work, supply the source preceded by "illus. in":

¹⁴ G. P. A. Healy, <u>The Meeting on the River Queen</u>, White

House, Washington, D.C., illus. in <u>Lincoln: A Picture Story of</u>

<u>His Life</u>, by Stefan Lorent, rev. and enl. ed. (New York: Harper

& Brothers, 1957), p. 235.

9h-7 Recording (disc or tape)

For commercially available recordings, cite the following: composer or performer, title of recording or of work(s) on the recording, artist(s), manufacturer, catalog number, and date of issue (if not known, state "n.d."):

¹⁵ The Beatles, "I Should Have Known Better," The Beatles

Again, Apple Records, Inc., SO-385, n.d.

(This is a reference to one of several songs on a disc.) A citation to a recording of classical music may omit the title of the recording and instead list the works recorded. Musical compositions identified by form, key, and number are neither underlined nor placed within quotation marks:

¹⁶ Johann Sebastian Bach, Toccata and Fugue in D minor, Toc-

cata, Adagio, and Fugue in C major, Passacaglia and Fugue in C

minor; Johann Christian Bach, Sinfonia for Double Orchestra, Op.

18, No. 1, cond. Eugene Ormandy, The Philadelphia Orchestra,

Columbia, MS 6180, n.d.

(When two or more composers and their works are involved, a semicolon separates each grouping.) Citations to recordings of the spoken word list the speaker first:

¹⁷ Swift Eagle, The Pueblo Indians, Caedmon TC 1327, n.d.

For a recording of a play, use the following form (the participating actors are listed):

¹⁸ Shakespeare's Othello, with Paul Robeson, Jose Ferrer,

Uta Hagen, and Edith King, Columbia, SL-153, n.d.

In addition to the speaker and title, a citation to a noncommercial recording should state when the recording was made, for whom, and where. The title of the recording is not underlined:

¹⁹ Michael Dwyer, Readings from Mark Twain, recorded 15

April 1968, Humorist Society, San Bernardino, California.

For citations of private or archival recordings, use the following form (listing the inches per second [ips] is optional):

²⁰ Irish Folksongs, recorded by D. K. Wilgus, 9 March 1969,

University of California, Los Angeles Folklore Archives, T7-69-

22 (7½ ips).

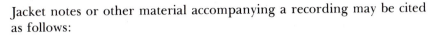
Jacket notes or other material accompanying a recording may be cited as follows:

²¹ Charles Burr, Jacket Notes, <u>Grofe: Grand Canyon Suite</u>,

Columbia, MS 6003, n.d.

9h-8 Personal letter

Published letters are treated as titles within a book (see 9e-7). Add the date of the letter, if available:

²² "To Mrs. Alfred Hunt," 25 Aug. 1880, <u>The Letters of Oscar</u>

<u>Wilde</u>, ed. Rupert Hart-Davis (New York: Harcourt, Brace & World,

Inc., 1962), pp. 67-68.

Unpublished letters in a library collection are treated similarly to a manuscript or typescript (see 9e-21):

²³ Dylan Thomas, Letter to Trevor Hughes, 12 Jan. 1934, Dy-

lan Thomas Papers, Lockwood Memorial Library, Buffalo, New York.

For letters personally received, use the following form:

²⁴ Letter received from Gilbert Highet, 15 March 1972.

9h-9 Interview

Citations of interviews should specify the kind of interview, the name (and, if pertinent, the title) of the interviewed person, and the date of the interview:

²⁵ Personal interview with Dr. Charles Witt, 23 March 1976.

²⁶ Telephone interview with Edward Carpenter, librarian at

Huntington Library, 2 March 1978.

9i

Content notes

In addition to identifying the sources of borrowed material, footnotes or endnotes may be used to explain a term, to expand on an idea, or to refer the reader to an additional source.

9i-1   Note explaining a term

¹ The "Rebellion of 1837" refers to December of 1837, when William Lyon Mackenzie, a newspaper editor and former mayor of Toronto, led a rebellion intended to establish government by elected officials rather than appointees of the British Crown.

9i-2   Note expanding on an idea

² This pattern of development was also reflected in their system of allocation, where only a small percentage of tax money was used for agriculture, whereas great chunks were apportioned to industry.

9i-3   Note referring the reader to another source

³ For further information on this point, see Gilbert W. King and Hsien-Wu Chang, "Machine Translation of Chinese," Scientific American, 208 (June 1963), 124–35.

9j
Consolidation of references

If a substantial part of your paper is based on several sources that deal with the same idea, consolidating the references into a single note may save space and prevent repetition. Simply separate the individual citations with semicolons:

¹ For this idea I am indebted to Laurence Bedwell Holland, The Expense of Wisdom (Princeton, N.J.: Princeton University Press, 1964), p. 32; James K. Folsom, "Archimago's Well: An Interpretation of The Sacred Fount," Modern Fiction Studies, 7 (Summer 1961), 136–44; and Pelham Edgar, Henry James: Man and

Author (Toronto, 1927; rpt. New York: Russell & Russell,

1964), pp. 15–17.

9k

Repeated or interpretive use of a single source

If a major section of the paper is derived from a single source, say so in the initial, full citation:

¹ Earl Warren, The Memoirs of Chief Justice Earl Warren

(Garden City, N.Y.: Doubleday & Company, Inc., 1977), p. 149.

Throughout I follow Earl Warren's account of the interning of

the Japanese-Americans during World War II.

9l

Subsequent references

Subsequent citations to an already identified source are given in abbreviated form. The rule is to make subsequent citations brief but not cryptic. Ordinarily the author's last name, or a key word from the title followed by a page number, will do. Latin terms such as "op. cit." ("in the work cited"), "loc. cit." ("in the place cited"), and "ibid." ("in the same place") are no longer used.

■ First reference:

¹ John W. Gardner, Excellence (New York: Harper & Brothers,

1961), p. 47.

■ Subsequent reference:

² Gardner, p. 52.

If two or more subsequent references cite the same work, simply repeat the name of the author and supply the appropriate page numbers. Do not use "ibid."

³ Gardner, p. 83.

⁴ Gardner, p. 198.

If, however, your paper also contains references to Gardner's other book, *Self-Renewal,* the two books should be distinguished by title in subsequent references:

⁵ Gardner, Excellence, p. 61.

⁶ Gardner, Self-Renewal, p. 62.

If two of the cited authors share the same last name, subsequent references should supply the full name of each author:

⁷ Henry James, p. 10.

⁸ William James, pp. 23–24.

For a long, cumbersome citation that will appear repeatedly throughout the paper, use an abbreviated form in subsequent references, after warning the reader in the first note:

⁹ Edwin G. Boring, A History of Experimental Psychology,

2nd ed. (New York: Appleton–Century–Crofts, Inc., 1950), p. 461;

hereafter cited as HEP.

Such shortened references can then easily be incorporated into your text (see 9m below).

For a subsequent reference to an anonymous article in a periodical, use a shortened version of the title.

■ First reference:

¹⁰ "The Wooing of Senator Zorinsky," Time, 27 March 1978,

p. 12.

■ Subsequent reference:

¹¹ "Zorinsky," p. 13.

For subsequent references to unconventional or special sources, you may need to improvise.

■ First reference:

¹² U.S. Statutes at large 1972, Vol. 86, 1973, Public Law

92–347.

■ Subsequent reference:

    ¹³ Public Law 92-347.

9m

Parenthetical references (see also 9l, n. 9.)

Parenthetical documentation—that is, notes placed within a text—should be used only for papers requiring few notes or for bibliographical studies. Parenthetical references should include all the information normally found in a note:

    In The Birth of the German Republic (New York: Russell & Rus-

    sell, Inc., 1962), p. 21, Arthur Rosenberg states that . . .

or:

    Max I. Dimont—The Indestructible Jews (New York: New American

    Library, 1971), p.154—concludes that . . .

or:

    C. S. Lewis (Perelandra, New York: Macmillan, 1944, pp. 72-85)

    suggests . . .

For extensive references to a single author or a single work such as a novel, play, or classic in some field, supply complete publication information in your first note, then abbreviate subsequent references and place them parenthetically within the text.

■ First note:

    ¹ Thomas Carlyle, Sartor Resartus, ed. by Charles Frederick

    Harrold (New York: Odyssey Press, 1937), Bk. I, Ch. ii (p. 12).

    All further references to this work appear in the text.

■ Subsequent reference within the text:

    As Teufelsdröckh continues to get drawn into a deep depression,

    he begins even to doubt the Devil and says: "To me the Universe

```
was all void of Life, of Purpose, of Volition, even of Hostil-

ity; it was one huge, dead, immeasurable Steam-engine, rolling

on, in its dead indifference, to grind me limb from limb" (Bk.

II, Ch. vii; p. 164).
```

For plays and long poems, the first note should state the edition being used. Subsequent notes should cite a short title followed by a main division (e.g., the act of a play or the book of a poem) and the line numbers, the division and line numbers being separated by periods without spacing. This brief subsequent reference should appear within parentheses immediately after a quotation:

```
Achilles is described as "brandishing from his right shoulder

the Pelian ash, his terrible spear" (Iliad, XXII.86-88).
```

The reference is to Book 22, lines 86 to 88, of Homer's *Iliad*.

Some samples of widely used abbreviations are:

```
FQ I.iii.7.60
```

(A reference to Spenser's *Faerie Queene*, Book I, Canto 3, stanza 7, line 60.)

```
II Kings xii.6    or    II Kings 12:6
```

(A reference to the King James Bible, second book of Kings, Chapter 12, verse 6.)

```
PL V.722-30
```

(A reference to Milton's *Paradise Lost*, Book 5, lines 722 to 730.)

```
Ham. II.ii.554-58
```

(A reference to Shakespeare's *Hamlet*, Act 2, Scene 2, lines 554 to 558.) A recent tendency is to use Arabic numerals throughout:

```
2 Kings 12.6; FQ 1.3.7.60
```

Check your instructor's preference.

9n

Documentation in scientific writing

Practice varies from one branch of science to another; most disciplines summarize in a style manual the format that writers are expected to observe. Endnotes and footnotes are generally omitted in favor of a system of parenthetical citations within the text. Such citations vary with each field, but usually include the author and a page reference:

```
This effect was observed and documented by at least one re-

searcher (Stempel, 9-22).
```

Some citations of this kind parenthetically list the year of publication along with the name of the author, and the page reference:

```
This effect was observed and documented by at least one re-

searcher (Stempel, 1968, 10-15).
```

Another system of citations parenthetically lists the name of the author, along with the title of the work being cited and a page reference:

```
This effect was observed and documented by at least one re-

searcher (Stempel, Experiments, 9-22).
```

In all such systems, the literature parenthetically cited is indexed in a bibliography at the end of the work. This bibliography is frequently headed as "List of References" or "Literature Cited," and contains entries alphabetized by authors' surnames.

Finally, some disciplines prefer writers to assign each citation a number by which it is identified and listed in a bibliography, and to make parenthetical reference within the text to the appropriate number and page:

```
This effect was observed and documented by at least one re-

searcher (25, 9-22).
```

Bibliography entry number 25 would list the work by Stempel.

For further information, consult the style manual of the appropriate discipline. Generally, such manuals are available from the professional association of the discipline. Thus the American Psychological Association publishes a style manual for Psychology: *Publication Manual of the American Psychological Association.*

ten

Bibliography

10a

Differences between endnotes and bibliography entries

Endnotes and bibliography entries contain the same information, but differ considerably in form, as the following examples make clear:

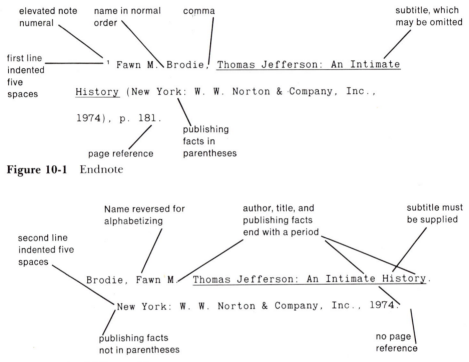

Figure 10-1 Endnote

Figure 10-2 Bibliographic entry

10b

Bibliographic references to books: order and general rules

Bibliographic references to books list items in the following order:

10b-1 Author

The name of the author comes first, alphabetized by surname. If more than one author is involved, reverse the name of only the first and follow it by a comma: Brown, Jim, and John Smith.

For more than three authors, use the name of the first followed by "et al." or "and others," as in notes (see 9e-2).

10b-2 Title

Cite the title in its entirety, including any subtitle. A period follows the title. The use of quotation marks and underlining is the same as for notes (see 8b-2).

10b-3 Publication information

The publication information is provided as in the notes (see 9d-8), but not in parentheses. Publication facts are followed by a period.

10b-4 Volume numbers

An entry for all the volumes of a multivolume work cites the number of volumes before the publication facts:

```
Durant, Will, and Ariel Durant.  The Story of Civilization.  10

    vols.  New York: Simon and Schuster, 1968.
```

An entry for only selected volumes cites the number of the volumes *after* the publication facts:

```
Durant, Will, and Ariel Durant.  The Story of Civilization.  New

    York: Simon and Schuster, 1968.  Vols. II and III.
```

For volumes published in separate years, volume numbers appear *before* the publication information:

```
Grote, George.  History of Greece.  Vol. V.  New York: Harper &

    Brothers, 1860.
```

(See sample cases in 10e-5.)

10b-5 Page numbers

Bibliographical entries for books rarely include a page number; however, entries for shorter pieces appearing within a longer work—articles, poems, short stories, etc., in a collection—should include a page reference. In such a case, supply page numbers for the *entire* piece, not just for the specific page or pages cited in the endnote. Example: for an essay appearing on pages 15 to 27 of an anthology, the listing in the bibliography entry would be "pp. 15–27." Page numbers are preceded by a comma. (See 10e-8 for samples.)

10b-6   Two or more works by the same author

In this case, list the full name of the author (or authors) in only the first entry. For subsequent entries, type ten hyphens followed by a period, skip two spaces, and list the title of the work. The hyphens replace the name of the author in the preceding entry. The names of additional authors or "et al." may follow the ten hyphens. Titles by the same author may be listed either chronologically by date of publication or alphabetically by title:

```
Gardner, John W.  Excellence.  New York: Harper & Brothers,

    1961.



----------. Self-Renewal. New York: Harper & Row, 1964.
```

10c
Spacing and indentation

In bibliographic entries, the second and subsequent lines are indented five spaces; in an endnote the first line is indented five spaces, while subsequent lines are aligned with the left margin (see Figures 10-1 and 10-2, p. 206).

10d
Punctuation

An endnote or footnote is punctuated as a simple sentence, but a bibliographical entry is not; rather, it simply provides blocks of information separated by periods.

10e
Sample bibliographic references to books

The examples of the bibliographic references that follow correspond exactly to the endnote examples listed in 9e.

208

10e-1 Book with a single author (cf. 9e-1)

Brodie, Fawn M. <u>Thomas Jefferson: An Intimate History</u>. New York:
W. W. Norton & Company, Inc., 1974.

10e-2 Book with two or more authors (cf. 9e-2)

Bollens, John C., and Grant B. Geyer. <u>Yorty: Politics of a Constant Candidate</u>. Pacific Palisades, Calif.: Palisades Publishers, 1973.

Allport, Gordon W., Philip E. Vernon, and Gardner Lindzey.
<u>Study of Values</u>. New York: Houghton Mifflin Co., 1951.

Brown, Ruth, et al. <u>Agricultural Education in a Technical Society: An Annotated Bibliography of Resources</u>. Chicago:
American Library Association, 1973.

10e-3 Book with a corporate author (cf. 9e-3)

American Institute of Physics. <u>Handbook</u>. 3rd ed. New York:
McGraw-Hill Book Company, 1972.

<u>Handbook</u>. By the American Institute of Physics. 3rd ed. New
York: McGraw-Hill Book Company, 1972.

<u>Report of the Special Commission to Investigate the Assassina-
tion of John F. Kennedy</u>. Washington, D.C.: Office of Government Publications, 1964.

10e-4 Book with an anonymous or pseudonymous author (cf. 9e-4)

<u>Current Biography</u>. New York: H. W. Wilson, 1976.

[Stauffer, Adlai]. Cloudburst. Knoxville, Tenn.: Review and

Courier Publishing Assoc., 1950.

Evans, Mary Ann [George Eliot]. Daniel Deronda. London, 1876.

10e-5 Work in several volumes or parts (cf. 9e-5)

Wallbank, T. Walter, and Alastair M. Taylor. Civilization Past

and Present. 2 vols. New York: Scott, Foresman and Com-

pany, 1949.

Wallbank, T. Walter, and Alastair M. Taylor. Civilization Past

and Present. New York: Scott, Foresman and Company, 1949.

Vol. II.

Fuller, J. F. C. A Military History of the Western World. Vol.

III. New York: Funk & Wagnalls Company, 1956.

Jacobs, Paul, Saul Landen, and Eve Pell. Colonials and Sojour-

ners. Vol. II of To Serve the Devil. New York: Random

House, 1971.

10e-6 Work within a collection of pieces, all by the same author (cf. 9e-6)

Johnson, Edgar. "The Keel of the New Lugger." In The Great Un-

known. Vol. II of Sir Walter Scott. New York: The Macmil-

lan Company, 1970, pp. 763–76.

Selzer, Richard. "Liver." In Mortal Lessons. New York: Simon

& Schuster, 1976.

10e-7 Chapter or titled section in a book (cf. 9e-7)

Goodrich, Norma Lorre. "Gilgamesh the Wrestler." Myths of the
Hero. New York: The Orion Press, 1960.

10e-8 Collections: anthologies, casebooks, and readers (cf. 9e-8)

Welty, Eudora. "The Wide Net." In Story: An Introduction to
Prose Fiction. Ed. Arthur Foff and Daniel Knapp. Belmont,
Calif.: Wadsworth Publishing Company, 1966, pp. 159–77.

Cowley, Malcolm. "Sociological Habit Patterns in Linguistic
Transmogrification." The Reporter, 20 Sept. 1956, pp. 257–
61. Rpt. in Readings for Writers. Ed. Jo Ray McCuen and
Anthony C. Winkler. 2nd ed. New York: Harcourt Brace Jovanovich, Inc., 1977, pp. 489–93.

10e-9 Double reference—a quotation within a cited work (cf. 9e-9)

Daubier, Jean. A History of the Chinese Cultural Revolution.
Trans. Richard Seaver. New York: Random House, 1974.

Only the secondary source is listed in the bibliography.

10e-10 Reference works (cf. 9e-10)

a. Encyclopedias

Ballert, Albert George. "Saint Lawrence River." Encyclopaedia
Britannica. 1963 ed.

"House of David." Encyclopedia Americana. 1974 ed.

Berger, Morroe, and Dorothy Willner. "Near Eastern Society."
International Encyclopedia of the Social Sciences. 1968 ed.

b. Dictionaries and annuals

"Barsabbas, Joseph." Who's Who in the New Testament (1971).

"Telegony." Dictionary of Philosophy and Psychology (1902).

10e-11 Work in a series (cf. 9e-11)

a. A numbered series

Auchincloss, Louis. Edith Wharton. University of Minnesota
   Pamphlets on American Writers, No. 12. Minneapolis: University of Minnesota Press, 1961.

b. An unnumbered series

Miller, Sally. The Radical Immigrant. The Immigrant Heritage
   of America Series. New York: Twayne Publishers, 1974.

10e-12 Reprint (cf. 9e-12)

Babson, John J. History of the Town of Gloucester, Cape Ann,
   Including the Town of Rockport. 1860; rpt. New York: Peter
   Smith Publisher, Inc., 1972.

Thackeray, William Makepeace. Vanity Fair. London, 1847–48;
   rpt. New York: Harper & Brothers, Publishers, 1968.

10e-13 Edition (cf. 9e-13)

Perrin, Porter G., and Jim W. Corder. Handbook of Current English. 4th ed. Glenview, Ill.: Scott, Foresman and Company,
   1975.

Clerc, Charles. "Goodbye to All That: Theme, Character and Symbol in Goodbye, Columbus." In Seven Contemporary Short

<u>Novels</u>. Ed. Charles Clerc and Louis Leiter. Glenview,

Ill.: Scott, Foresman and Company, 1969, pp. 106–33.

Craig, Hardin, and David Bevington, eds. <u>The Complete Works of</u>

<u>Shakespeare</u>. Rev. ed. Glenview, Ill.: Scott, Foresman and

Company, 1973.

Plath, Sylvia. <u>Letters Home</u>. Ed. Aurelia Schober Plath. New

York: Harper & Row Publishers, 1975.

10e-14 Book published in a foreign country (cf. 9e-14)

Vialleton, Louis. <u>L'Origine des êtres vivants</u>. Paris: Li–

brairie Plon, 1929.

Ransford, Oliver. <u>Livingston's Lake: The Drama of Nyasa</u>. Lon–

don: Camelot Press, 1966.

10e-15 Introduction, preface, foreword, or afterword (cf. 9e-15)

Davidson, Marshall B., Introd. <u>The Age of Napoleon</u>. By J.

Christopher Herold. New York: The American Heritage Pub–

lishing Co., Inc., 1963.

10e-16 Translation (cf. 9e-16)

Symons, John Addington, trans. <u>Autobiography of Benvenuto Cel–</u>

<u>lini</u>. By Benvenuto Cellini. New York: Washington Square

Press, Inc., 1963.

Cellini, Benvenuto. <u>Autobiography of Benvenuto Cellini</u>. Trans.

John Addington Symons. New York: Washington Square Press,

Inc., 1963.

10e-17 Dissertation (cf. 9e-17)

Unpublished:

Cotton, Joyce Raymonde. "Evan Harrington: An Analysis of George
Meredith's Revisions." Diss. University of Southern California 1968.

Published:

Cortey, Teresa. Le Rêve dans les contes de Charles Nodier.
Diss. University of California, Berkeley 1975. Washington,
D.C.: University Press of America, 1977.

10e-18 Pamphlet (cf. 9e-18)

Calplans Agricultural Fund. An Investment in California Agricultural Real Estate. Oakland, Calif.: Calplans Securities, Inc., n.d.

Cooper, Charles W., and Edmund J. Robins. The Term Paper: A
Manual and Model. 3rd ed. Stanford, Calif.: Stanford University Press, 1934.

10e-19 Government publication or legal reference (cf. 9e-19)

a. The Congressional Record

Cong. Rec. 15 Dec. 1977, p. 19740.

b. Congressional publications

U.S. Cong. Senate. Permanent Subcommittee on Investigations of
the Committee on Government Operations. Organized Crime--
Stolen Securities. 93rd. Cong., 1st sess. Washington,
D.C.: GPO, 1973.

U.S. Cong. House. Committee on Foreign Relations. Hearings on

    S. 2793, Supplemental Foreign Assistance Fiscal Year 1966--

    Vietnam. 89th Cong., 2nd sess. Washington, D.C.: GPO,

    1966.

U.S. Cong. Joint Economic Committee on Medical Policies and

    Costs. Hearings. 93rd Cong., 1st sess. Washington, D.C.:

    GPO, 1973.

c. Executive Branch publications

Boyer, Ernest L., U.S. Commissioner of Education. "Emergency

    Adult Education Program for Indochina Refugees." Federal

    Register, 27 June 1977, p. 32589, cols. 1-3.

Department of State. United States Treaties and Other Interna-

    tional Agreements. Washington, D.C.: GPO, 1975. XXVI,

    1448-49.

Bureau of the Census, U.S. Department of Commerce. Statistical

    Abstracts of the United States. Washington, D.C.: GPO,

    1963.

d. Legal publications

Office of the Federal Register. "The Supreme Court of the

    United States." United States Government Manual. Washing-

    ton, D.C.: GPO, 1976.

U.S. Const. Art. I, sec. 2.

15 U.S. Code. Sec. 78j(b) (1964).

U.C.C. Art. IX, pt. 2, par. 9–28.

Richardson v. J. C. Flood Co. 190 A.2d 259. D.C. App. 1963.

10e-20 Citations to footnotes or endnotes (cf. 9e-20)

Faber, M. D. <u>The Design Within: Psychoanalytic Approaches to Shakespeare</u>. New York: Science House, 1970.

No mention is made of the note.

10e-21 Manuscript or typescript (cf. 9e-21)

Huntington Library MS. Ellesmere Chaucer, E126C9.

Exeter Cathedral MS. The Wanderer.

British Museum MS. Cotton Vitellius, A. SV.

10e-22 Play (cf. 9e-22)

a. Classical play

Shakespeare, William. <u>Antony and Cleopatra</u>. In <u>The Complete Works of Shakespeare</u>. Ed. Hardin Craig and David Bevington. Rev. ed. Glenview, Ill.: Scott, Foresman and Company, 1973, pp. 1073–1108.

b. Modern play

Miller, Arthur. <u>The Crucible</u>. New York: Bantam Books, Inc., 1952.

Chekhov, Anton. <u>The Cherry Orchard</u>. In <u>The Art of Drama</u>. Ed. R. F. Dietrich, William E. Carpenter, and Kevin Kerrane. 2nd ed. New York: Holt, Rinehart and Winston, 1976, pp. 314–56.

10e-23 Poem (cf. 9e-23)

a. Long classical poem

Lucretius [Titus Lucretius Carus]. Of the Nature of Things.
Trans. William Ellery Leonard. In Backgrounds of the Modern World. Vol. I of The World in Literature. Ed. Robert
Warnock and George K. Anderson. New York: Scott, Foresman
and Company, 1950, pp. 343–53.

b. Short classical poem

Horace [Quintus Horatius Flaccus]. "To Licinius." Trans. William Cowper. In Backgrounds of the Modern World. Vol. I
of The World in Literature. Ed. Robert Warnock and George
K. Anderson. New York: Scott, Foresman and Company, 1950,
p. 406.

c. Long modern poem

Byron, Lord. Don Juan. Ed. Leslie A. Marchand. Boston: Houghton Mifflin Company, 1958.

d. Short modern poem

Moore, Marianne. "Poetry." In Fine Frenzy. Ed. Robert Baylor
and Brenda Stokes. New York: McGraw-Hill Book Company,
1972, pp. 372–73.

10e-24 Classical works in general (cf. 9e-24)

Homer. The Iliad. Trans. Richmond Lattimore. Chicago: University of Chicago Press, 1937.

Alighieri, Dante. The Inferno. Trans. John Ciardi. New York:
New American Library, 1954.

10e-25 The Bible (cf. 9e-25)

```
The Bible


The Bible.  Revised Standard Version.
```

10f

Bibliographic references to periodicals: order and general rules

In general, use the same order required for periodical note citations (see 9f), observing the same rules that govern journals paginated anew in each issue or numbered consecutively throughout the volume (see 9f-4 and 9f-5). Key differences between endnotes and bibliographic references to periodicals are:

- Authors are alphabetized by surnames

```
Smith, John not John Smith
```

  If there is more than one author involved, reverse the name of only the first and follow it by a comma

```
Brown, Jim, and John Smith
```

- The bibliographic entry consists of blocks of information punctuated by periods rather than commas.
- The page reference must cover the entire article, not just the page referred to in the text.
- The second and subsequent lines of a bibliographic entry are indented five spaces; the first line is aligned with the left margin:

```
Reid, Ron.  "Black and Gold Soul with Italian Legs."  Sports Il-

    lustrated, 11 Dec. 1972, pp. 36-37.
```

10g

Sample bibliographic references to periodicals

The bibliographic references that follow correspond exactly to the note samples listed in 9g.

218

10g-1 Anonymous author (cf. 9g-1)

"Elegance Is Out." Fortune, 13 March 1978, p. 18.

10g-2 Single author (cf. 9g-2)

Sidey, Hugh. "In Defense of the Martini." Time, 24 Oct. 1977,

    p. 38.

10g-3 More than one author (cf. 9g-3)

Ferguson, Clyde, and William R. Cotter. "South Africa––What Is

    To Be Done." Foreign Affairs, 56 (1978), 254–74.

If three authors have written the article, place a comma after the second author, followed by "and" and the name of the third author. If more than three authors have collaborated, list the first author, followed by "et al." or "and others" with a comma in between:

Enright, Frank, et al.

10g-4 Journal with continuous pagination throughout the annual volume (cf. 9g-4)

Paolucci, Anne. "Comedy and Paradox in Pirandello's Plays."

    Modern Drama, 20 (1977), 321–39.

10g-5 Journal with separate pagination for each issue (cf. 9g-5)

Mangrum, Claude T. "Toward More Effective Justice." Crime Pre-

    vention Review, 5 (Jan. 1978), 1–9.

Brown, Robert. "Physical Illness and Mental Health." Philoso-

    phy and Public Affairs, 7 (Fall 1977), 18–19.

Cappe, Walter H. "Humanities at Large." The Center Magazine,

    11, No. 2 (1978), 2–6.

10g-6 Monthly magazine (cf. 9g-6)

Miller, Mark Crispin. "The New Wave in Rock." Horizon, March

    1978, p. 76–77.

Davis, Flora, and Julia Orange. "The Strange Case of the Children Who Invented Their Own Language." Redbook, March
1978, pp. 113, 165–67.

10g-7 Weekly magazine (cf. 9g-7)

Eban, Suzy. "Our Far-Flung Correspondents." The New Yorker,
6 March 1978, pp. 70–81.

"Philadelphia's Way of Stopping the Shoplifter." Business Week,
6 March 1972, pp. 57–59.

10g-8 Newspaper (cf. 9g-8)

Tanner, James. "Disenchantment Grows in OPEC Group with Use of
U.S. Dollar for Oil Pricing." The Wall Street Journal,
9 March 1978, p. 3, cols. 3–4.

Southerland, Daniel. "Carter Plans Firm Stand with Begin." The
Christian Science Monitor, Western Ed., 9 March 1978,
p. 1, col. 4, p. 9, cols. 1–3.

Malino, Emily. "A Matter of Placement." Washington Post,
5 March 1978, Section L, p. 5, cols. 3–5.

10g-9 Editorial (cf. 9g-9)
Signed:

Futrell, William. "The Inner City Frontier." Editorial.
Sierra, 63, No. 2 (1978), 5.

Unsigned:

"Criminals in Uniform." Editorial. Los Angeles Times, 7 April
1978, Part II, p. 6, cols. 1–2.

10g-10 Letter to the editor (cf. 9g-10)

Korczyk, Donna. Letter. <u>Time</u>, 20 March 1978, p. 4.

10g-11 Critical review (cf. 9g-11)

Andrews, Peter. Rev. of <u>The Strange Ride of Rudyard Kipling:</u>
    <u>His Life and Works</u>, by Angus Wilson. <u>Saturday Review</u>, 4
    March 1978, pp. 24–25.

Daniels, Robert V. Rev. of <u>Stalinism: Essays in Historical In-</u>
    <u>terpretations</u>. Ed. Robert C. Tucker. New York: W. W. Nor-
    ton, 1977. <u>The Russian Review</u>, 37 (1978), 102–03.

"Soyer Sees Soyer." Rev. of <u>Diary of an Artist</u>, by Ralph Soyer.
    <u>American Artist</u>, March 1978, pp. 18–19.

Rev. of <u>Charmed Life</u>, by Diana Wynne Jones. <u>Booklist</u>, 74 (Feb.
    1978), 1009.

10g-12 Published interview (cf. 9g-12)

"Why the Tide of Illegal Aliens Keeps Rising." Interview with
    Leonel J. Castillo, Commissioner, Immigration and Naturali-
    zation Service. <u>U.S. News and World Report</u>, 20 Feb. 1978,
    pp. 33–35.

10h

Sample bibliographic references to special items

The bibliographic references that follow correspond exactly to the note samples listed in 9h.

10h-1 Lecture (cf. 9h-1)

Schwilck, Gene L. "The Core and the Community." Danforth Foundation, St. Louis, Missouri. 16 March 1978.

10h-2 Film (cf. 9h-2)

Ross, Herbert, dir. The Turning Point. With Anne Bancroft,
Shirley MacLaine, Mikhail Baryshnikov, and Leslie Brown.
Twentieth Century-Fox, 1978.

10h-3 Radio or television program (cf. 9h-3)

"Diving for Roman Plunder." Narr. and dir. Jacques Cousteau.
KCET, 14 March 1978.

"Chapter 2." Writ. Wolf Mankowitz. Dickens of London. Dir. and
prod. Marc Miller. Masterpiece Theater. Introd. Alistair
Cooke. PBS, 28 Aug. 1977.

World of Survival. Narr. John Forsythe. CBS Special, 29 Oct.
1972.

10h-4 Theatrical performance (cf. 9h-4)

Davidson, Gordon, dir. Getting Out. By Marsha Norman. With
Susan Clark. Mark Taper Forum, Los Angeles. 2 April 1978.

Gray, Simon. Otherwise Engaged. Dir. Harold Pinter. With Dick
Cavett. Plymouth Theater, New York. 30 Oct. 1977.

Conlon, James, cond. La Bohème. With Renata Scotto. Metropolitan Opera. Metropolitan Opera House, New York. 29 Oct.
1977.

Maazel, Lorin, cond. New York Philharmonic Orchestra. Avery

Fisher Hall, New York. 10 Nov. 1977.

Commissiona, Sergiu, cond. Baltimore Symphony Orchestra. With

Albert Markov, violin. Brooklyn College, New York. 8 Nov.

1977.

Balanchine, George, chor. Pas de Deux. New York City Ballet.

New York State Theater, New York. 19 Nov. 1977.

10h-5   Musical composition (cf. 9h-5)

Grieg, Edvard. Menuet in E minor, Op. 7, No. 3.

10h-6   Work of art (cf. 9h-6)

Angelico, Beato. Madonna dei Linaioli. Museum of San Marco.

Florence, Italy.

Healy, G. P. A. The Meeting on the River Queen. White House,

Washington, D.C. Illus. in Lincoln: A Picture Story of His

Life. By Stefan Lorent. Rev. and enl. ed. New York: Har-

per & Brothers, 1957.

10h-7   Recording (disc or tape) (cf. 9h-7)

Beatles, The. "I Should Have Known Better." The Beatles Again.

Apple Records, Inc., SO—385, n.d.

Bach, Johann Sebastian. Toccata and Fugue in D minor, Toccata,

Adagio, and Fugue in C major, Passacaglia and Fugue in C

minor; Johann Christian Bach. Sinfonia for Double Orches-

tra, Op. 18, No. 1. Cond. Eugene Ormandy. The Philadel-

phia Orchestra, Columbia, MS 6180, n.d.

Eagle, Swift. <u>The Pueblo Indians</u>. Caedmon, TC 1327, n.d.

<u>Shakespeare's Othello</u>. With Paul Robeson, Jose Ferrer, Uta
Hagen, and Edith King. Columbia, SL–153, n.d.

Dwyer, Michael. Readings from Mark Twain. Recorded 15 April
1968. Humorist Society. San Bernardino, California.

Irish Folksongs. Recorded by D. K. Wilgus. 9 March 1969. University of California, Los Angeles Folklore Archives, T7–
69–22 (7½ ips).

Burr, Charles. Jacket Notes. <u>Grofe: Grand Canyon Suite</u>. Columbia, MS 6003, n.d.

10h-8 Personal letter (cf. 9h-8)
Published:

Hart–Davis, Rupert, ed. <u>The Letters of Oscar Wilde</u>. New York:
Harcourt, Brace & World, Inc., 1962.

Unpublished:

Thomas, Dylan. Letter to Trevor Hughes. 12 Jan. 1934. Dylan
Thomas Papers. Lockwood Memorial Library, Buffalo, New
York.

Personally received:

Highet, Gilbert. Letter to author. 15 March 1972.

10h-9 Interview (cf. 9h-9)

Witt, Dr. Charles. Personal interview. 23 March 1976.

Carpenter, Edward. Telephone interview. 2 March 1978.

eleven

Preparing the final typescript

11a
Finished form of the paper

In its finished form the paper consists of the following parts:

> Outline (if required)
> Title page
> Text of the paper
> Endnotes (or footnotes, if required)
> Bibliography

The paper should be neatly typed on one side only of each page with a fresh black ribbon. Papers typed in script characters are frequently more difficult to read and therefore unacceptable. Use heavy (20 pound) 8 ½″×11″ white bond paper. Erasable bond smudges too easily for a teacher to pencil in corrections; therefore it should not be used. If you must use erasable bond, have the paper photocopied on uncoated paper and submit the photocopy. Do not staple the pages or submit the paper inside a folder. Simply clip the pages together with a paper clip and submit the paper as a loose-leaf manuscript. Give the paper a ruthless proofreading before submitting it to the teacher for evaluation.

11b
Outline

The outline that precedes the text of the paper should look uncluttered and balanced. Pages of an outline need not be numbered. For the exact outline format, see pp. 102–08, and sample student-paper outlines on pp. 241 and 265.

11c
Title page

A separate title page is not required. Instead, the first page should contain the full title of the paper, your name, the instructor's name, the course for which the paper was written, the date, and the opening text of your paper. The following facsimile of a typical opening page includes marginal measurements and line spacing. (See also the first page of the sample papers, pp. 243 and 266.)

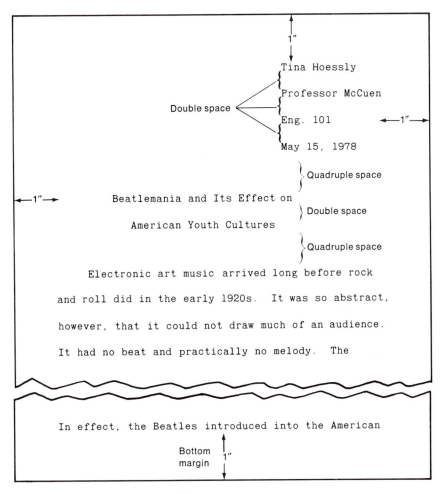

Figure 11-1 Sample student title page

This first page, and all subsequent pages, must contain one-inch margins on all sides. The first page need not be numbered, but is counted as part of the page total; numbering begins with page 2. Except for titles of published works appearing within it, the title of the paper is neither underlined nor entirely placed in capitals. If the title takes up two or more lines, position the extra lines so as to form a double-spaced inverted pyramid, with each line centered on the page:

```
Study of Values: A Scale of Measuring

        the Dominant Interests

           in Personality
```

Do not use a period at the end of the title.

11d
Text

- Normal paragraphing must be used throughout the paper. If your paper contains subdivisions (only lengthy papers should), use subtitles either centered on the page or aligned with the left margin. Underline but do not capitalize subtitles. Separate subtitles from the last line of the previous section by quadruple spacing.
- Double-space the text, quotations, and endnotes. Footnotes are double-spaced between notes but single-spaced within. (See 7c-2 and student sample papers on pp. 241–58 and pp. 265–72.)
- Number pages consecutively in the upper right-hand corner of the paper. Numbers are not followed by hyphens, parentheses, periods, or other characters. Neither the first page of the text, nor the first page of endnotes, nor the first page of the bibliography is numbered. Such pages, however, are included in the total page count.
- Footnote/endnote numerals are placed one half space above the line within the text of the paper. Each superscript numeral should be placed immediately after the material to which it refers (see 7c-4).
- Unless otherwise indicated by your teacher, a footnote must appear on the bottom of the same page on which its numeral occurs. The first line of each footnote is indented five spaces; second and subsequent lines are aligned with the left margin. For both footnotes and endnotes use elevated numerals (a half space above the line) and follow the numerals with one space. (See sample notes in 9e.)
- If possible, use pica type, which is easier to read than elite. Script type or other artistic typefaces are often difficult to read and therefore unacceptable. If in doubt, consult your teacher.
- Avoid multiple corrections. If a correction is unavoidable, type it, or write it in legibly with black ink.

11e
Tables, charts, graphs, and other illustrative materials

Papers in many fields frequently require tables, graphs, charts, maps, drawings, and other illustrations. For example, a paper on the decline of basic skills among high school students may include a graph that plots this decline over the past five years. An economics paper may require charts that explain certain economic growths or changes. An

228

anthropology paper may include drawings of primitive artifacts. A history paper may illustrate some historic battle with a map. A biology paper may include drawings of enlarged cells. The possibilities are nearly endless. The general rule, however, is for all illustrative materials to appear as close as possible to the part of the text that they illustrate.

11e-1 Tables

Tables are usually labeled, numbered with Arabic numerals, and captioned. Both labels and captions are in capital letters. The source of the table and accompanying notes should be placed at the bottom of the table. If no source is listed, a reader will assume that the table is your original work. Indicate notes to tables with asterisks, crosses, or lowercase letters to avoid confusion with endnotes, footnotes, or other textual notes.

TABLE 2

SIGNIFICANCE OF DIFFERENCES BETWEEN
MEAN GRADE POINT AVERAGES
OF MALE ACHIEVERS AND UNDERACHIEVERS
FROM GRADE ONE THROUGH ELEVEN

| Grade | Mean grade point average | | F | P | t | P |
	Achievers	Under-achievers				
1	2.81	2.56	1.97	n.s.†	1.44	n.s.
2	2.94	2.64	1.94	n.s.	1.77	n.s.
3	3.03	2.58	1.49	n.s.	2.83	.01*
4	3.19	2.72	1.03	n.s.	2.96	.01*
5	3.28	2.75	1.02	n.s.	3.71	.01*
6	3.33	2.67	1.33	n.s.	4.46	.01*
7	3.25	2.56	1.02	n.s.	5.80	.01*
8	3.36	2.50	1.59	n.s.	6.23	.01*
9	3.25	2.14	1.32	n.s.	10.57	.01*
10	3.13	1.87	1.30	n.s.	10.24	.01*
11	2.81	1.85	4.05	.02**	5.46	.01*

* Yields significance beyond the .01 level.

** Yields significance beyond the .02 level but below the .01 level.

† No significance.

Figure 11-2 Sample table

11e-2 Other illustrative materials

Other illustrative materials should be labeled "Fig." or "Figure" and numbered with Arabic numerals: Fig. 3. Each figure should be captioned and capitalized like a title:

Fig. 12.   Chart Tracing the Development of the Alphabet

Again, the source of the illustration and any notes should be placed immediately below the illustration. If no source is cited, a reader will assume that the illustration is your original work. Indicate notes to illustrations with asterisks, crosses, or lower-case letters, so as to avoid confusion with other footnote or endnote numbers in the text. A few sample illustrations follow.

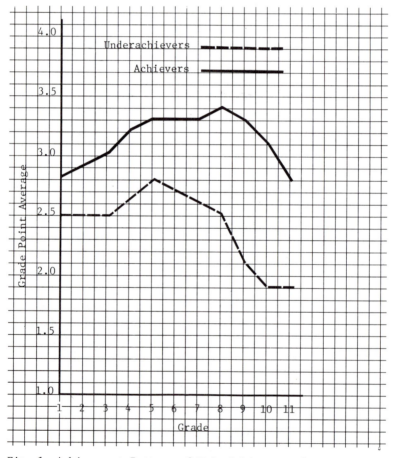

Fig. 1. Achievement Pattern of Male Achievers and
Underachievers from Grades One Through Eleven

Figure 11-3 Sample line graph

Figure 11-4 Sample illustration

Fig. 2. African Doll (Akua'ba)
Source: American Museum
of Natural History

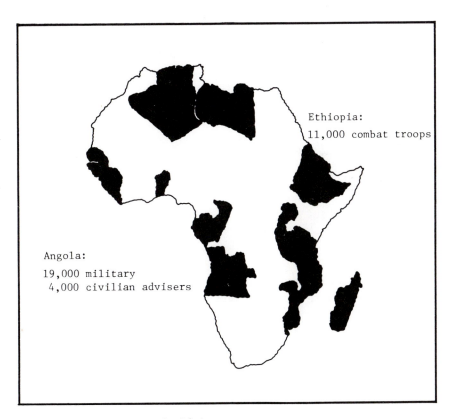

Fig. 3. Cuban Presence in Africa
Source: U.S. Government Estimates, 1978

Figure 11-5 Sample map

231

155   **Figure 11-6** Sample bar graph

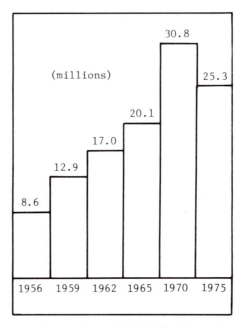

Fig. 4. Number of individuals owning
shares in public corporations
Source: New York Stock Exchange

11f
Endnotes

Endnotes appear on a separate page at the end of the paper, preceded by the centered heading "Notes." (See 7c-1 and sample student paper on pp. 256–57.)

11g
Bibliography

The bibliography appears on a separate page at the end of your paper, marked by the centered heading "Bibliography."

Figure 11-7   Sample bibliography page

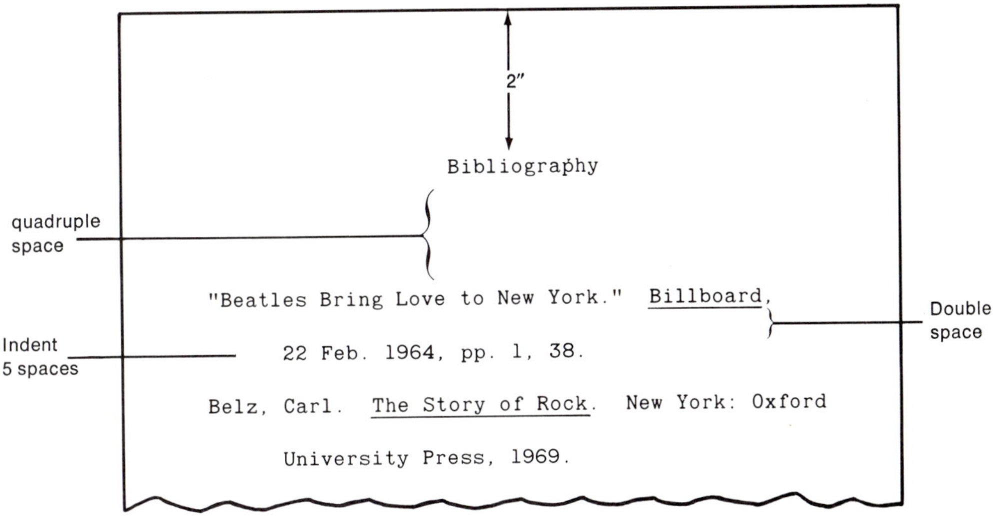

(See also the sample student papers, pp. 258 and 272.) For details on the form for various bibliographic entries, see 10e, 10g, and 10h.

11h

Abbreviations in the text

11h-1 Abbreviations and reference words commonly used

A.D.	*anno Domini* 'in the year of the Lord.' No space between; precedes numerals (A.D. 12).
anon.	anonymous
app.	appendix
art., arts.	article(s)
assn.	association
b.	born
B.C.	before Christ. No space between; follows numerals (23 B.C.).
bibliog.	bibliography, bibliographer, bibliographical
biog.	biography, biographer, biographical
bk., bks.	book(s)
©	copyright (© 1975)
c., ca.	*circa* 'about.' Used with approximate dates (c. 1851).
cf.	*confer* 'compare.' Do not use "cf." if "see" is intended.

233

ch., chs. (or chap., chaps.)	chapter(s)
chor., chors.	choreographed by, choreographer(s)
col., cols.	column(s)
comp., comps.	compiled by, compiler(s)
cond.	conducted by, conductor
Cong.	Congress
Cong. Rec.	*Congressional Record*
d.	died
DAB	*Dictionary of American Biography*
dir., dirs.	directed by, director(s)
diss.	dissertation
DNB	*Dictionary of National Biography*
E, Eng.	English
ed., eds.	edited by, editor(s), editions(s)
e.g.	*exempli gratia* 'for example.' Preceded and followed by a comma.
enl.	enlarged (as in "rev. and enl. ed.")
esp.	especially (as in "pp. 124–29, esp. p. 125)
et al.	*et alii* 'and others'
et seq.	*et sequens, sequentia* 'and the following.' "Page 10 et seq." means page 10 and the following page(s).
etc.	*et cetera* 'and so forth.' Do not use in text.
ex., exs.	example(s)
f., ff.	and the following (with a space after a numeral) page(s) or line(s). Exact references are preferable: pp. 89–90 instead of pp. 89f.; pp. 72–79 instead of pp. 72ff.
facsim. (or facs.)	facsimile
fig., figs.	figure(s)
fol., fols.	folio(s)
Fr.	French
front.	frontispiece
Ger.	German
Gk.	Greek
GPO	Government Printing Office, Washington, D.C.
hist.	history, historian, historical
ibid.	*ibidem* 'in the same place,' i.e., in the cited title. Avoid using. Cite instead the author's last name and the page number.
i.e.	*id est* 'that is'
illus.	illustrated (by), illustrator, illustration(s)

introd.	(author of) introduction, introduced by, introduction
ips	inches per second (used on labels of recording tapes)
It.	Italian
jour.	journal
L., Lat.	Latin
l., ll.	line(s)
lang., langs.	language(s)
L. C.	Library of Congress. Typed with a space between.
loc. cit. (not l.c.)	*loco citato* 'in the place (passage) cited.' Avoid using. Repeat the citation in shortened form.
M.A.	Master of Arts. No space between.
mag.	magazine
ME	Middle English
ms, mss	manuscript(s) (the many mss of Chaucer). Capitalized and followed by a period when referring to a specific manuscript.
M.S.	Master of Science. No space between.
n., nn.	note(s)
narr., narrs.	narrated by, narrator(s)
N.B.	*nota bene* 'take notice, mark well.' Not spaced.
n.d.	no date (in a book's imprint). No space between.
N.E.D.	*New English Dictionary.* No spaces between. Cf. *OED.*
no., nos.	number(s)
n.p.	no place (of publication); no publisher. Not spaced.
n. pag.	no pagination. Space between.
OE	Old English
OED	*Oxford English Dictionary.* Formerly the *New English Dictionary (N.E.D.)*
op.	opus (work)
op. cit.	*opere citato* 'in the work cited.' Avoid using. Repeat citation in shortened form.
p., pp.	page(s). Omit if volume number precedes.
par., pars.	paragraph(s)
passim	'throughout the work, here and there' (as "pp. 84, 97, et passim")
Ph.D.	Doctor of Philosophy. No space between.
philos.	philosophical
pl., pls.	plate(s)
pref.	preface
prod., prods.	produced by, producer(s)
pseud.	pseudonym
pt., pts.	part(s)
pub. (or publ.), pubs.	published by, publication(s)

rept., repts.	reported by, report(s)
resp.	respectively (pp. 61, 84, 7, resp.)
rev.	revised (by), revision; review, reviewed (by). Spell out "review," if there is any possibility of ambiguity.
rpm	revolutions per minute (used on recordings)
rpt.	reprinted (by), reprint
sc.	scene
sec., secs. (or sect., sects.)	section(s)
ser.	series
sic	'thus, so.' Put between square brackets when used to signal an editorial interpolation.
soc.	society
Sp.	Spanish
st., sts.	stanza(s)
St., Sts.	Saint(s)
supp., supps.	supplement(s)
TLS	typed letter signed
trans. (or tr.)	translated by, translator, translation
TS	typescript. Cf. "ms."
v., vs.	versus 'against.' Cf. "v., vv."
v., vv. (or vs., vss.)	verse(s)
vol., vols.	volume(s) (Vol. II of 3 vols.). Omit "Vol." and "p." when both items are given.

11h-2 The Bible and Shakespeare

Use the following abbreviations in notes and parenthetical references; do not use them in the text (except parenthetically).

a. The Bible

OLD TESTAMENT (OT)

Gen.	Genesis	Ruth	Ruth
Exod.	Exodus	1 Sam.	1 Samuel
Lev.	Leviticus	2 Sam.	2 Samuel
Num.	Numbers	1 Kings	1 Kings
Deut.	Deuteronomy	2 Kings	2 Kings
Josh.	Joshua	1 Chron.	1 Chronicles
Judg.	Judges	2 Chron.	2 Chronicles
Ezra	Ezra	Dan.	Daniel
Neh.	Nehemiah	Hos.	Hosea
Esther	Esther	Joel	Joel

Job	Job	Amos	Amos
Ps.	Psalms	Obad.	Obadiah
Prov.	Proverbs	Jonah	Jonah
Eccl.	Ecclesiastes	Micah	Micah
Song. Sol.	Song of Solomon	Nahum	Nahum
(also Cant.)	(also Canticles)	Hab.	Habakkuk
Isa.	Isaiah	Zeph.	Zephaniah
Jer.	Jeremiah	Haggai	Haggai
Lam.	Lamentations	Zech.	Zechariah
Ezek.	Ezekiel	Mal.	Malachi

SELECTED APOCRYPHAL AND DEUTEROCANONICAL WORKS

1 Esdras	1 Esdras	Baruch	Baruch
2 Esdras	2 Esdras	Song 3	Song of the
Tobit	Tobit	Childr.	Three
Judith	Judith		Children
Esther	Esther	Susanna	Susanna
		Bel and Dr.	Bel and the
(Apocr.)	(Apocrypha)		Dragon
Wisd. of Sol.	Wisdom of	Prayer	Prayer of
(also Wisd.)	Solomon	Manasseh	Manasseh
	(also Wisdom)	1 Macc.	1 Maccabees
Ecclus.	Ecclesiasticus	2 Macc.	2 Maccabees
(also Sir.)	(also Sirach)		

NEW TESTAMENT (NT)

Matt.	Matthew	1 Thess.	1 Thessalonians
Mark	Mark	2 Thess.	2 Thessalonians
Luke	Luke	1 Tim.	1 Timothy
John	John	2 Tim.	2 Timothy
Acts	Acts	Tit.	Titus
Rom.	Romans	Philem.	Philemon
1 Cor.	1 Corinthians	Heb.	Hebrews
2 Cor.	2 Corinthians	Jas.	James
Gal.	Galatians	1 Pet.	1 Peter
Eph.	Ephesians	2 Pet.	2 Peter
Phil.	Philippians	1 John	1 John
Col.	Colossians	2 John	2 John
3 John	3 John	Rev. (also	Revelation (also
Jude	Jude	Apoc.)	Apocalypse)

SELECTED APOCRYPHAL WORKS

G. Thom.	Gospel of Thomas	G. Pet.	Gospel of Peter
G. Heb.	Gospel of the Hebrews		

b. *Shakespeare*

Ado	*Much Ado about Nothing*	*MND*	*A Midsummer Night's Dream*
Ant	*Antony and Cleopatra*		
AWW	*All's Well That Ends Well*	*MV*	*The Merchant of Venice*
AYL	*As You Like It*	*Oth.*	*Othello*
Cor.	*Coriolanus*	*Per.*	*Pericles*
Cym.	*Cymbeline*	*PhT*	*The Phoenix and the Turtle*
Err.	*The Comedy of Errors*	*PP*	*The Passionate Pilgrim*
F1	First Folio ed. (1623)	Q	Quarto ed
F2	Second Folio ed. (1632)	*R2*	*Richard II*
Ham.	*Hamlet*	*R3*	*Richard III*
1H4	*Henry IV, Part I*	*Rom.*	*Romeo and Juliet*
2H4	*Henry IV, Part II*	*Shr.*	*The Taming of the Shrew*
H5	*Henry V*	*Son.*	*Sonnets*
1H6	*Henry VI, Part I*	*TGV*	*The Two Gentlemen of Verona*
2H6	*Henry VI, Part II*		
3H6	*Henry VI, Part III*	*Tim.*	*Timon of Athens*
H8	*Henry VIII*	*Tit.*	*Titus Andronicus*
JC	*Julius Caesar*	*Tmp.*	*The Tempest*
Jn.	*King John*	*TN*	*Twelfth Night*
LC	*A Lover's Complaint*	*TNK*	*The Two Noble Kinsmen*
LLL	*Love's Labour's Lost*	*Tro.*	*Troilus and Cressida*
Lr.	*King Lear*	*Ven.*	*Venus and Adonis*
Luc.	*The Rape of Lucrece*	*Wiv.*	*The Merry Wives of Windsor*
Mac.	*Macbeth*		
MM	*Measure for Measure*	*WT*	*The Winter's Tale*

twelve

A sample student paper

■ The following is a sample paper, researched and written by a college freshman. The paper, except for a few minor corrections, is reproduced as it was submitted. The accompanying outline and note cards illustrate the paper in various stages of preparation.

Rasputin's Other Side

Thesis: After six decades of being judged a demoniacal
        libertine, Rasputin now deserves to be viewed
        from another point of view--as a man who was
        intensely religious, who passionately desired peace,
        and who was deeply devoted to his family and friends.

  I.   The real Rasputin is difficult to discover.

       A.   The birth of Rasputin coincided with a "shooting star."
       B.   The popular historical view of Rasputin portrays him as
            primarily evil.
            1.   Supporters called him a spiritual leader.
            2.   Detractors called him a satyr and charged that his depraved
                 faithful were merely in awe of his sexual endowments.

 II.   Rasputin had intense religious feelings.

       A.   He had a rich nature and an exuberant vitality.
       B.   He had a simple peasant faith in God.

III.   Rasputin's passionate desire for peace in Russia revealed itself in
       several ways.

       A.   He was concerned for the Russian underdog.
            1.   He wanted a Tsar who would stand mainly for the peasantry.
            2.   He spoke out boldly against anti-Semitism.
       B.   Because of his humanitarian spirit, he was opposed to all wars.

 IV.   Rasputin had a gentle, compassionate side.

       A.   He showed great kindness to the Romanovs.
       B.   Maria Rasputin tells of her father's love for his family.

Smith, p.1, col.4.   Introduction

An enormous influence on the popular
view of Rasputin was the character
played on stage by the famous
Lionel Barrymore — a devilish, mysterious
starets.

Smith, p.1, col.4.   Introduction

A 1977 article in L.A. Times admits
that in 1965 the U.P.I. "omitted one
of the most elementary journalistic
restraints" by calling Rasputin mad,
filthy, licentious, semiliterate, fiendish,
lecherous.

My own comment   Historical opinion

Several sources mention the fact
that when he was born (Jan. 23, 1871),
a great meteor burned its way
across the skies of Western Siberia.

Elaine Spray

Professor McCuen

English 101

June 21, 1978

Rasputin's Other Side

The name "Rasputin" commonly evokes an image of unbridled, mystical evil. Few figures have fared as badly in the popular memory. In the 1930s, Lionel Barrymore transfixed thousands of movie goers by portraying him as a devilish, licentious, mysteriously hypnotic fiend. Hundreds of books published since his murder in 1916 unanimously agree on his sub-humanity. Reporting a libel trial involving one of his murderers, the United Press International in 1965 casually labeled Rasputin as mad, filthy, licentious, semiliterate, fiendish, and lecherous.[1] After six decades of being judged a demoniacal libertine, Rasputin now deserves to be viewed from another point of view—as a man who was intensely religious, who passionately desired peace, and who was deeply devoted to his family and friends.

Who was this so-called horror incarnate, this man named Rasputin? It is said that on the night of January 23, 1871, a great meteor seared a flaming path across the skies of Western Siberia, hurtled in an arc over the little village of Pokrovskoye and, at the very moment that the meteor burned out, a seven-pound boy was born to Anna Egorovina, the wife of Efim Akovlevich, a Russian farmer. The couple named the boy, their second son, Grigori Efimovich Rasputin.

243

Smith, p. 10, col. 1.   Historical opinion

"Supporters called him a spiritual leader
and claimed he had healing powers;
detractors called him a satyr and
said his depraved faithful were
merely in awe of his sexual endowments."

Halliday, p. 83.   Historical opinion

By the time he was lured to his death
in a St. Petersburg palace in 1916, Rasputin
had aroused such intensities of hatred and
loyalty that fact and fantasy were difficult
to separate among all partisan views.
Questions:
    At sixteen an insatiable lecher?
    Gifts of second sight and prophecy?
    Disappeared from home to wander
        about Russia and the Holy Land?
    Drunkard?
    Member of the secret "Khlysts"?

Maria Rasputin, p. 15.   Intense religious feelings

"Entering his 14th year, my father passed into
a new phase, his interest, which soon
blossomed into a preoccupation with religion.
Although he had not learned to read or
write, skills he did not acquire until his
later years in St. Petersburg, he possessed
a remarkable memory and could quote
whole passages of the Bible from having
heard them read but once."

What was this second son, this Rasputin, really like? "Supporters called him a spiritual leader and claimed he had healing powers; detractors called him a satyr and said his depraved faithful were merely in awe of his sexual endowments."[2] By the time he was lured to his death in the basement of a St. Petersburg palace in 1916, he had aroused such intensities of hatred and loyalty that the facts of his early life had already become blurred and sensationalized. Was it true that at sixteen he was already known in his part of Siberia as an insatiable lecher whom peasant girls found irresistible? Did he really have gifts of second sight and prophecy that cast a glow of religious mysticism around him? Did he disappear from his home for long intervals, wandering about Russia and even to the Holy Land as a starets, a pilgrim of God, who was simultaneously a drunkard and an insatiable womanizer? Was he really a member of the secret group known as the Khlysts, outlawed fanatics who held frenzied rites in torch-lit forest glades that ended with wild, naked dancing and savage sexual orgies?[3] In these suppositions—all part of the legend before Rasputin died—there is probably a kernel of truth. Nevertheless, this remarkable man also had another side, which has been entirely overlooked.

To begin with, Rasputin was a man of intense religious feelings. His love for Christianity bordered on an exuberant devotion. Maria Rasputin writes of her father's simple peasant faith:

> Entering his fourteenth year, my father passed into a new
> phase, his interest, which soon blossomed into a preoccupation,
> with religion. Although he had not learned to read or write,

Maria Rasputin, pp. 130-31.   Intense religious feelings

Rasputin had the remarkable ability to translate abstruse theology into simple terms that even the common plowman could understand. Thus it was that he was sought out more and more by the common man in the street as orthodoxy waned among the aristocrats. However, many aristocrats, too, turned to him rather than to the clergy. Even the Tsar consulted him on religious matters.

Fülöp-Miller, p. 26.   Intense religious feelings

Rasputin tended to observe his home (peasant) customs while in the capital – even while sitting among wealthy women in elegant drawing rooms at breakfast, holding forth with animation on the "Mysterious resurrection."

Soft humming
Voices join in
Loud chorus
Leaping, dancing
} All accepted as sincere rite of primitive peasant religion – assuming the character of prayer.

Halliday, p. 85.   Desire for peace in Russia

Rasputin was a sort of Robin Hood. He often took large sums of money from the wealthy (bribes) and handed them to the poor. He had ideas about turning over landowners' property to the peasants and their mansions to the educational system.

skills he did not acquire until his later years in St. Petersburg, he possessed a remarkable memory and could quote whole
passages of the Bible from having heard them read but once.[4]

Rasputin, moreover, taught a lofty, sublime sort of Christianity at
a time when numerous Russian politicians were becoming suspicious of the
Christian religion. Yet his teaching, made all the more simple by his
innate ability to explain abstruse theological concepts in plain, comprehensible terms, was understood by even the most common plowman. Consequently, as Christian Orthodoxy waned among those in power, Rasputin was
sought out more and more by the ordinary man in the street.[5]

When Rasputin moved to St. Petersburg, he could often be found
breakfasting with women followers and talking about God and the "Mysterious resurrection." Suddenly, he would begin to hum softly to himself.
Soon the voices around him would join in, swelling to a loud chorus.
Then he would leap from his seat and dance around the room.[6] This religious demonstration was accepted as sincere by the Russian peasants, with
whom dance had remained a rite of primitive religious activity, assuming
the character of prayer.[7]

But a vital religion was not the only positive force in the life of
Rasputin. He also expressed a passionate desire for peace and political
harmony in Russia. For instance, he was deeply concerned about the
Russian underdog. He had vague notions of turning over the landowners'
land to the peasants, and the landowners' mansions to the educational
system. He was genuinely concerned about the treatment of Jews and other
minorities. His concern about the poor people caused many to liken him

Pares, p. 388.   Desire for peace in Russia

"He wanted a Tsar who would stand primarily for the peasantry and would have liked him to receive frequent visits, from representatives of this class."

Pares, p. 388.   Desire for peace in Russia

Rasputin seemed to have an instinctual sense of protecting the underdog. For example, at a court where Jew-baiting was popular, he took definite action to protect the Jews. He always believed in "tolerance for all religions and insisted to the Emperor that all his subjects, of whatever race, claimed the same care."

Maria Rasputin, p. 206.   Desire for peace in Russia

One of Rasputin's contributions was a bill, passed in the Duma, to protect the rights of the Jews, even the right to a public education. This was the first such bill to pass in history.

to Robin Hood, for he often took large sums of money from the wealthy—bribes for favors—which he distributed among the poor.[8] His political position, as the noted Russian historian, Bernard Pares, points out, shows a democratic impulse: "He wanted a Tsar who would stand primarily for the peasantry and would have liked him to receive frequent visits from representatives of this class."[9]

Rasputin was sure that all races and religions were equal in the sight of God. He spoke out against anti—Semitism. In a Court where Jew-baiting had always been popular, he took definite protective action on behalf of the Jews.[10] After some struggle and a good deal of maneuvering, he managed to have a bill presented in the Duma that protected the rights of the Jews, including their right to receive an education in the state schools. The first of its kind in the history of Russia, the bill was passed.[11] Rasputin believed in "tolerance for all religions and insisted to the Emperor that all his subjects, of whatever race, claimed the same care."[12]

But perhaps his finest characteristics were revealed in his fierce loyalty to friends and family. He was unselfishly devoted to the Russian imperial family and to the regime that was then in power. Foreseeing what a holocaust World War I would bring to Russia, Rasputin tried desperately to make Nicholas understand the disastrous implications of the conflict, sending the Tsar telegrams and notes that conveyed his vision of the impending calamity.[13] In a letter to the Tsar, in late July of 1914, Rasputin pleaded prophetically against Russia's imminent entry into war:

Halliday, p. 85.   Desire for peace in Russia

Foreseeing what World War I would do
to Russia, he tried desperately to
force Tsar Nicholas to see the impending
doom and to avert it. (Sent him
telegrams and notes.)

Maria Rasputin, p. 198.   Desire for peace in Russia
    Letter written to Tsar in July of 1914:
"My Friend:
    Once again I repeat; a terrible storm menaces Russia.
Woe ... suffering without end. It is night. There is not one star ...
a sea of tears. And how much blood!
    I find no words to tell you more. The terror is
infinite. I know that all desire war of you, even the most
faithful. They do not see that they rush toward the abyss.
You are the Tsar, the father of the people.
    Do not let fools triumph, do not let them throw
themselves and us into the abyss. Do not let them
do this thing ... Perhaps we will conquer Germany,
but what will become of Russia? When I think
of that, I understand that never has there been
so atrocious a martyrdom. Russia drowned in
her own blood, suffering the infinite desolation."

Pares, 132.   gentle, compassionate side
    Birth of prince:
    "The birth was a peculiarly easy one, but it was
almost at once discovered that the boy suffered
from a terrible hereditary disease which the
mother herself had for the first time brought
into the Russian reigning family." It was
hemophilia.
Pares, 139.
    The emperor admits being influenced by
Rasputin:
    "He is just a good, religious, simple-minded
Russian. When in trouble or assailed by doubts
I like to have a talk with him and
invariably feel at peace with myself
afterwards."

My Friend:

Once again I repeat; a terrible storm menaces Russia. Woe
. . . suffering without end. It is night. There is not one
star . . . a sea of tears. And how much blood!

I find no words to tell you more. The terror is infinite.
I know that all desire war of you, even the most faithful.
They do not see that they rush toward the abyss. You are the
Tsar, the father of the people.

Do not let fools triumph, do not let them throw themselves
and us into the abyss. Do not let them do this thing. . . .
Perhaps we will conquer Germany, but what will become of
Russia? When I think of that, I understand that never has
there been so atrocious a martyrdom. Russia drowned in her own
blood, suffering, and infinite desolation.[14]

On August 12, 1904, an heir to the Russian throne was born. Pares
wrote that the "birth was a particularly easy one, but it was almost at
once discovered that the boy suffered from a terrible hereditary disease
which the mother herself had for the first time brought into the Russian
reigning family."[15] It was hemophilia, a condition where the clotting
time of the blood is severely prolonged. The most important measure of
treatment is to stop the bleeding. "Rasputin was somehow able--call it
hypnotism, autosuggestion, faith healing or divine intervention--to stop
the hemorrhaging."[16] He accomplished the miracle which the doctors had
declared to be impossible, and thereby endeared himself to the Empress.
He was like a holy man to her, an answer to her prayers. Even the
Emperor admitted to being influenced by him:

Smith, p. 10, col. 1.   gentle, compassionate side

"Rasputin was somehow able — call it
hypnotism, autosuggestion, faith healing
or divine intervention — to stop the
hemorrhaging."

Massie, p. 189.   gentle, compassionate side

Rasputin felt at home with the Romanovs
calling them "Batiushka" and "Matushka."
He felt free to laugh loudly and
criticize freely although he always
showed respect. He liked to lard
his language with Biblical quotations
and old Russian proverbs.

Maria Rasputin, p. 242.   gentle, compassionate side

Maria Rasputin about her father, after
learning of his death:

"He had been the central point in my
life. He had stood like a giant monolith,
in the shadow of which one might play
without concern, yet all the while knowing
that he was there protecting me with
his love and kindness."

He is just a good, religious, simple-minded Russian. When in

trouble or assailed by doubts I like to have a talk with him

and invariably feel at peace with myself afterwards.[17]

"Batiushka and Matushka"--Russian peasant words meaning "Father" and

"Mother"--were the names by which Rasputin knew the Romanovs. He was re-

spectful but never fawning; he felt free to laugh loudly and to criticize

honestly, larding his criticisms heavily with Biblical quotations and old

Russian proverbs.[18]

Rasputin was, moreover, a devoted father to his three children,

often playing with them on their farm, taking them fishing in the Tura,

and insisting that they observe all the rituals of the Church--the cate-

chisms, school studies, prayers before bedtime, and grace before meals.

The family unfailingly attended church on Sundays and holy days. Maria

Rasputin, upon learning that her father had been killed, summarized her

feelings about him this way:

He had always been the central point in my life. He had stood

like a giant monolith, in the shadow of which one might play

without concern, yet all the while knowing that he was there

protecting me with his love and kindness.[19]

Until her death in 1977, Maria Rasputin staunchly maintained that her

father had been a kind, spiritual man and that his name had been vilified

by old enemies "who retained their influential voices even out of the

wreckage of Imperial Russia."[20] Said she:

Maria Rasputin, p. 63.   gentle, compassionate side

" All of those who came to know my father, all, that is, except his political enemies, were in agreement on at least one count: He was a kindly and humane man with great love in his heart for people."

Smith, p. 1, col. 4.   gentle, compassionate side

Maria Rasputin went to her death in 1977 maintaining that her father was a kind, spiritual man whose name was maligned by old enemies" who retained their influential voices even out of the wreckage of Imperial Russia."

All of those who came to know my father, all, that is, except

his political enemies, were in agreement on at least one count:

He was a kindly and humane man with great love in his heart for

people.[21]

Years from now the world may come to see that Maria's view of her father

was the truest--that he was neither madman, nor lecher, nor conniving

monk, but simply a devoutly religious peasant who loved his family, his

Emperor, and his country, and who has been luridly misrepresented to pos-

terity and history.

Notes

[1] Dave Smith, "Casting a Light on Rasputin's Shadow," <u>Los Angeles Times</u>, 9 June 1977, Part IV, p. 1, col. 4.

[2] Smith, p. 10, col. 1.

[3] E. M. Halliday, "Rasputin Reconsidered," <u>Horizon</u>, 8 (Autumn 1967), 83.

[4] Maria Rasputin and Patte Barham, <u>Rasputin: The Man Behind the Myth</u> (Englewood Cliffs, N.J.: Prentice—Hall, Inc., 1977), p. 15.

[5] M. Rasputin, p. 130.

[6] René Fülöp—Miller, <u>Rasputin, the Holy Devil</u> (New York: Garden City Publishing Co., Inc., 1927), p. 268.

[7] Fülöp—Miller, p. 267.

[8] Halliday, p. 85.

[9] Bernard Pares, <u>The Fall of the Russian Monarchy</u> (New York: Alfred A. Knopf, 1939), p. 388.

[10] Pares, p. 388.

[11] M. Rasputin, p. 206.

[12] Pares, p. 388.

[13] Halliday, p. 85.

[14] M. Rasputin, p. 198.

[15] Pares, p. 132.

[16] Smith, p. 10, col. 1.

[17] Pares, p. 139.

[18] Robert K. Massie, <u>Nicholas and Alexandra</u> (New York: Atheneum, 1972), p. 189.

[19] M. Rasputin, p. 242.

[20] Smith, p. 1, col. 4.

[21] M. Rasputin, p. 63.

Bibliography

Fülöp—Miller, René. Rasputin, the Holy Devil. New York: Garden City
     Publishing Co., Inc., 1927.

Halliday, E. M. "Rasputin Reconsidered." Horizon, 8 (Autumn 1967), 81–
     87.

Massie, Robert K. Nicholas and Alexandra. New York: Atheneum, 1972.

Pares, Bernard. The Fall of the Russian Monarchy. New York: Alfred A.
     Knopf, 1939.

Rasputin, Maria, and Patte Barham. Rasputin: The Man Behind the Myth.
     Englewood Cliffs, N.J.: Prentice—Hall, Inc., 1977.

Smith, Dave. "Casting a Light on Rasputin's Shadow." Los Angeles Times,
     9 June 1977, Part IV, p. 1, cols. 1–3, p. 10, cols, 1–4, and p. 11,
     col. 1.

thirteen

A brief guide to writing about literature

13a

Adapting the research paper to the literary topic

Literary research topics require particular caution and skill. Students who set out to write a full-blown interpretation of a novel, play, short story, or poem had therefore better know their subject and have a good idea about what they intend to do. The problem with any sort of literary analysis conducted in the format of a research paper is that few teachers will accept an undocumented, purely interpretive paper as fulfillment of the research paper assignment. As we said at the beginning of this book, a research paper is exactly what its name implies—a paper assembled after painstaking research. It is not merely a vehicle for a single writer's unsupported assertions, no matter how original or clever. Teachers expect research papers to have bibliographies, footnotes or endnotes, and note cards—in short, to reflect every inch of the research process that went into the paper's writing. Consequently, if you have a splendid new slant on interpreting a literary work, the research paper is probably not the place to express it. An informal or personal essay would probably be a better medium for such a purely interpretive paper.

The problem with doing the research paper on a literary topic is basically this: literary works, and the interpretations that have accumulated around them over the years, are deceptively like icebergs: more lies hidden beneath the surface than is visible to the casual glance. With many literary works, vast bibliographies lurk beneath the surface—especially if the work is a classic. The student, for instance, who innocently decides to do a literary paper on a play such as Shakespeare's *Hamlet*, has already bitten off more than perhaps he or she would wish to chew. There are literally hundreds—perhaps thousands—of papers, books, and essays about *Hamlet*. Almost every inch of the play has been studiously pored over and copiously written about. And in the hundreds of years since Shakespeare wrote *Hamlet*, the play has gathered generations of opinions and interpretations. In short, the job of sorting through the thousands of opinions on *Hamlet* would stagger even the most experienced researcher.

The very opposite case, however, is true of modern and contemporary literature. Many such works have never been formally interpreted at all, or at the moment are no more than grist in the dissertation mill. Students who decide to shun the classics and concentrate instead on contemporary literature, will often find that no critical opinions exist that can be used for documentation in a research paper. Or, if interpretive opinions exist, they will often be either eccentric or farfetched.

The novice researcher therefore has good reason to be leery of the literary topic. Often what seems a perfectly straightforward and reasonable literary topic, will turn out to be impossibly difficult to research, and simply too trying for a beginner to write about. We recommend that you clear any literary topic with your teacher in advance of attempting to write a paper on it. Or at the very least, that you do a preliminary search of the available bibliography before committing yourself to any literary topic.

13b
Literary criticism

Criticism, used in a literary sense, does not mean the same as it does in the ordinary usage of the word. First of all, to criticize a literary work isn't necessarily to say bad or cutting things about it. The word "criticism," as literary critics use and understand it, is synonymous with "evaluation and interpretation," for this dual task is generally what the literary critic means to do in any criticism of literature. A critic may set out to interpret some facet of a work without making any decisive evaluation of it. Or a critic may set out to evaluate a work, without attempting to systematically interpret it. Or a critic may simultaneously do both—interpret and evaluate.

In short, it does not follow that because a critic is criticizing a work, that there is something either deficient, murky, or incomprehensible about it. The interpretation of literature is the business of each generation. Every age sees the world differently than the one before, holds different theories about behavior, places different values on life. For this reason, succeeding generations are scarcely content with their forebears' interpretations of literature. Criticism is consequently a never-ending process of constantly rereading, reseeing, and reinterpreting literature.

One small example will illustrate. When Shakespeare wrote *Hamlet*, it is highly likely that he believed in the reality of the ghost of Hamlet's father, since Renaissance men and women generally believed in ghosts. But in our time ghosts are suspect phenomena; we are not nearly as certain that they actually exist. Some critics nowadays interpret the whole business of the ghost as an elaborate hallucination suffered by Hamlet. Clinical labels are used to describe Hamlet and what he thought he saw. Viewed in this way, the play has an entirely different meaning to us than it would have had to an Elizabethan audience.

Criticism, in sum, is a matter of perspective. What a critic sees in a work will often depend on what the critic is looking for. Few critics can boast of having entirely plumbed the depths of any literary work. Such a thing is rarely, if ever, done. Good literature is susceptible to an almost endless number of interpretations; bad literature is not. And one way to tell the difference between the two, is by the complexity and richness of meaning that the work can yield under analysis.

The various perspectives of criticism have become established in so-called critical schools. Among the most important schools of criticism are moral, psychological, sociological, formalist, and archetypal. Moral criticism is concerned with the portrayal of people in literature as ethical beings. For instance, a paper written from the perspective of moral criticism might analyze the right and wrong of Ahab's actions in *Moby Dick*. Psychological criticism is concerned not with ethics, but with the unconscious motivations and personality dynamics of literary characters. Thus a psychological critic might do a paper analyzing the revenge motive of Iago in Shakespeare's *Othello*. Sociological criticism, on the other hand, focuses on the literary work as a reflection of a social milieu. A paper written from this perspective might therefore treat Loraine Hansberry's play *Raisin in the Sun* as a reflection of the black ghetto experience. Formalist criticism takes an entirely different tack, focusing on the explication of imagery and style and on textual analysis. A paper written from this perspective might analyze Milton's use of color imagery in *Paradise Lost*. Finally, archetypal criticism, which derives from the work of Carl Jung, the noted Swiss psychoanalyst, is interested in literature as a source of human myth. Archetypal critics analyze literature for such universal themes as the search for immortality, the urge for baptismal cleansing, or the cyclical nature of life.

It follows from this discussion that the student who wishes to do a paper from the perspective of one of these critical schools, needs to know the vocabulary of the critical school and its ways of interpreting. Writing a critical paper, in short, involves more than simply saying what one thinks a literary work means. The student must make a convincing case for the interpretation by showing how it was derived, by citing supportive evidence in the text, and by referring to substantiating opinions in the works of other critics.

13c
Literary scholarship

Focused primarily on older literature, literary scholarship is concerned principally with the reconstruction of meaning. Once an era has passed and a generation died away, the literature remaining tends to become progressively more puzzling to future generations. Words that had definite meanings at the time the literary work was written, may take on entirely different meanings later. Customs, manners, and conventions carefully observed by the dead generation may have entirely changed, or somehow become lost from memory. The characters of ancient literature therefore soon become incomprehensible to later readers, who live by an entirely different set of values and ways. It is with this sort of reconstruction that scholarship is primarily concerned—with the restoration of meanings that a literary work may have had for its own generation.

The literary paper reproduced at the end of this chapter exemplifies a student attempt at literary scholarship. In the example the student documents her thesis, namely that the cosmological beliefs of the Renaissance are inseparably part of Shakespeare's ideas about the earth, the universe, and human emotions. She draws her documentation from primary sources—Shakespeare's works, and from secondary sources—books and essays written about Shakespeare.

The paper at the end of this chapter is a thesis paper, but a report paper can also be written about a literary topic. For example, a student could do a paper on the major interpretations of O'Neill's *The Iceman Cometh*. The paper would simply catalog and explain the major interpretations of the play. A scholarly paper on literature, in short, may be either a thesis paper or a report paper.

Such scholarly papers, however, are never easy to write. The student must sift through mountains of contradictory opinions in order to evaluate the quality of scholarship. Access to a first-rate library is a prerequisite for any decent attempt at literary scholarship. Moreover, the student has to have a thorough knowledge of the literary work in order to fathom the scholarly works written about it.

13d
Format of the literary paper .

The literary paper has basically the same format as any research paper, but with this difference: multiple citations to a literary work are usually made within the text of the paper, rather than in a footnote or endnote. (See the sample literary paper that follows.) Further, if the paper is about a well-known work, a standard abbreviation of its title may be used. For instance, the student paper that follows abbreviates *Julius Caesar* as *JC*, *King Richard II* as *R2*, and *Venus and Adonis* as *Ven*. (For a list of accepted abbreviations of the titles of the Bible and Shakespeare, see 11h-2.) It is also customary to identify the source from which the literary text was taken, and in the case of a classic work, to give parenthetical citations to part, canto, act, scene, and line. (For more information, see Chapter 9 on documentation.) For instance, in an initial footnote the student cites the text from which she took the plays of Shakespeare:

> ¹ Hardin Craig and David Bevington, eds. <u>The Complete Works of Shakespeare</u>, rev. ed. (Glenview, Ill.: Scott, Foresman and Company, 1973), <u>JC</u> I.i.36. All further references to Shakespeare's works are from this edition and appear in the text.

With these exceptions, the paper on a literary topic uses exactly the same format as any other kind of research paper.

13e
A sample student literary paper

The following student paper illustrates a literary topic set in the standard research paper format.

Shakespeare's Cosmology

Thesis: The cosmological beliefs of the Renaissance are
        inseparably part of Shakespeare's ideas about the
        earth, the universe, and human emotions.

  I. Shakespeare's ideas about the earth were derived from the
      Renaissance belief that everything has its appointed place in the
      universe.

      A. The order of life descends from God to vegetation.
      B. Atmospheric disturbances are prophetic and revealing.
      C. The earth is symbolic of the mother.

 II. Shakespeare's ideas about the universe were derived from some
      common Renaissance beliefs.

      A. The sun and stars revolve around the earth.
      B. Heaven is peaceful while hell is loud.
      C. The stars represent good and evil influences.
      D. The moon is a benevolent influence.

III. Shakespeare's ideas about human emotions were derived from the
      belief that love is a unifying force in the cosmos.

      A. Love creates harmony out of chaos.
      B. The opposite of love is fear, which is the greatest evil
          intrinsic to man.

Mary Kubalik

Professor McCuen

Eng. 101

June, 1978

Shakespeare's Cosmology

Every distinctive era in history subscribes to its own cosmology--to

a constellation of beliefs about the form and ways of the physical uni-

verse. Thinking people of the Renaissance held cosmological beliefs

uniquely their own, which are clearly reflected in the works of Shakespeare.

Indeed, the cosmological beliefs of the Renaissance are inseparably

part of Shakespeare's ideas about the earth, the universe, and human

emotions.

The belief that every creature has a place in the order of the uni-

verse--a view widely held in the Renaissance--is implicit in

Shakespeare's ideas about the earth. The order of life, as stated in

Julius Caesar, descends from God and the angels to man, to woman, to the

lowest animals, to the most inferior "stones" or "senseless things."[1]

Unified in an endless flow emanating from God, creation is therefore

infused with a "law of nature" that enables humans to determine the

---

[1] Hardin Craig and David Bevington, eds., The Complete Works of
Shakespeare, rev. ed. (Glenview, Ill.: Scott, Foresman and Company,
1973), JC I.i.36. All further references to Shakespeare's works are
from this edition and appear in the text.

266

difference between right and wrong.[2] From this perspective, the nature of

man becomes "the life force of the universe."[3]

Because of his belief in this infusion of all life by the force of

God, the Renaissance thinker saw atmospheric disturbances as prophetic

and revealing, as signs of the cosmic war between good and evil. Foul

weather signified ominous happenings. King Lear, quite appropriately,

goes mad during a violent tempest. Sir Richard Croop sees "tidings of

calamity" as equal to "an unseasonable stormy day" in King Richard II (R2

III.ii.5,6). A red sunset forecasts "wrack to the seaman, tempest to the

field, sorrow to the shepherds, woe unto the birds" in Venus and Adonis

(Ven. 455–56). Violent storms, lightning, thunder, and rain often pre-

cede evil supernatural occurrences, such as the appearance of ghosts or

witches.[4] Atmospheric disturbances were never random, never separate from

human conduct.

In Shakespeare's world view, the earth is symbolic of the mother.

Her womb is the place of birth and of death. This dichotomy is made

clear in the descriptions of the earth given throughout Shakespeare's

works: the earth is variously called a place of renewal, a final shelter

for the dead, a place where birth and death meet, the moment of concep-

---

[2] Kenneth Muir and S. Schoenbaum, eds., A New Companion to Shakespeare (New York: Cambridge University Press, 1971), pp. 181–85.

[3] Caroline F. E. Spurgeon, Shakespeare's Imagery (New York: Cambridge
University Press, 1968), p. 14.

[4] T. F. Thiselton Dyer, Folk–Lore of Shakespeare (New York: Dover
Publications, Inc., 1966), pp. 60–61.

tion, the return of the son to his mother.[5] To many of the main characters in Richard II, for instance, the earth is a mother and a nurse.
Richard himself describes the earth as "a long-parted mother with her
child" (R2 III.ii.8). On the other hand, Scotland is referred to as a
grave under Macbeth's tyrannical rule (Mac. IV.iii.165).

Shakespeare's ideas about the universe were also derived from a Renaissance belief—that the sun was a planet which, propelled by the
motion of a sphere, revolved around a fixed earth. If this sphere were
destroyed, the sun would be lost in space, and the earth enveloped in
darkness. Cleopatra expresses this idea when, in despair over Antony's
death, she cries out, "O sun, burn the great sphere thou movst in!" (Ant.
IV.xv.9). And in human society, as Shakespeare portrayed it, the king is
the equivalent of the sun. Henry VIII of England and Francis I of France
are referred to as "two lights of men," and as "suns of glory" (H8
I.i.6). The rising sun is a source of delight and inspiration in Shakespeare, signifying youth, strength, splendor, and the renewal of life.
Conversely, the setting sun is a source of depression, signifying old
age, storms, and sorrow.[6]

The cosmological notions of the Renaissance influenced even Shakespeare's views of heaven, described as a state in which there "are no
storms, no noise, but silence and eternal sleep" (Tit. I.i.155). Hell,
on the other hand, is a place of physical discomfort, of torment and

---

[5] Alex Aronson, Psyche and Symbol in Shakespeare (Bloomington: Indiana University Press, 1971), pp. 191-204.

[6] Spurgeon, pp. 63, 238, et passim.

4

noise.[7] Mortals on earth, condemned to what Shakespeare calls "this muddy vesture of decay," occasionally sense heaven as a "concord of sweet sounds," and then know "the touches of sweet harmony" (<u>MV</u> V.i.50–64). In sum, people sometimes hear and see signs of heaven, but must choose whether to heed or to ignore them.[8]

In the cosmology of the Renaissance, the stars represent both good and evil influences. Everyone was thought to be born under a certain star and subject to its appropriate quality.[9] Beatrice in <u>Much Ado About Nothing</u> therefore blames her sanguine personality on having been born under a sanguine star (<u>Ado</u> II.i.349). Edmund in <u>King Lear</u> ridicules the popular belief that since he was born under Ursa Major and begat by his father under the Dragon's Tail, he should therefore be "rough and lecherous" (<u>Lr</u>. I.ii.142).

A similar superstition existed in the Renaissance towards the moon, although its influence was thought to be benevolent. Enobarbus says, in <u>Antony and Cleopatra</u>, "Be witness to me, O thou blessed moon!" (<u>Ant</u>. IV.ix.5). Equated with love in Renaissance thought, the moon was believed to influence the weather and to symbolize stability. There is moonlight wooing in <u>Romeo and Juliet</u>; there are moonlit lovers' gardens in <u>Merchant of Venice</u>.

Shakespeare's ideas about human emotions are derived from the belief

[7] Spurgeon, p. 78.

[8] Donald A. Stauffer, <u>Shakespeare's World of Images</u> (New York: W. W. Norton and Company, Inc., 1949), p. 371.

[9] Spurgeon, p. 274.

that love is the unifying force of the cosmos--the force that creates harmony out of chaos. The love theme dominates many of Shakespeare's plays. Equated with loyalty and faith, love becomes the teacher of society in Romeo and Juliet. In King Lear, love destroys hate and renders even power helpless. The harmony of love in Antony and Cleopatra makes the discord of world empires seem trivial by comparison. Love is so giving in Merchant of Venice that it transcends selfish interests. Harmony is also achieved in As You Like It and in Twelfth Night through unselfish love.

The opposite of love and therefore the disrupter of human relations is, according to Shakespeare, fear. Because fear drives out love and leads to every other kind of evil, Shakespeare regarded fear as the worst kind of evil.[10] Indeed, Shakespeare repeatedly stresses the Renaissance notion that this evil is intrinsic to man. The evil man is interested in satisfying selfish desires and will kill his brother to feed these desires. Richard III feared everyone who might compete with him for power, and this fear drove him to foulest murder. In his final moments he formulates his own epitaph: "There's no creature loves me; / And if I die, no soul shall pity me" (R3 V.iii.200-01). In Measure for Measure there is also an allusion to the evil within: "Our natures do pursue . . . a thirsty evil, and when we drink, we die" (MM I.ii.132-34). In sum, men learn by experience to live side by side with the evil intrinsic in their nature.[11]

---

[10] Spurgeon, p. 155.
[11] Stauffer, pp. 26-27.

The wonder is not that Shakespeare's works reflected the cosmological notions prevalent among the thinkers of his time. The work of all
artists in any era will be a summative source of the ideas of their day.
But what is unsurpassable in Shakespeare is the vividness, the clarity,
the force of language that he used to give expression to these cosmological ideas. As George Gottfried Gervinus says of Shakespeare, "He is master of human nature."[12]

---

[12] As quoted in Arthur M. Eastman, A Short History of Shakespearean
Criticism (New York: Random House, Inc., 1968), p. 177.

Bibliography

Aronson, Alex. Psyche and Symbol in Shakespeare. Bloomington: Indiana
    University Press, 1972.

Craig, Hardin, and David Bevington, eds. The Complete Works of Shake-
    speare. Rev. ed. Glenview, Ill.: Scott, Foresman and Company,
    1973.

Dyer, T. F. Thiselton. Folk-Lore of Shakespeare. New York: Dover Publi-
    cations, Inc., 1966.

Eastman, Arthur M. A Short History of Shakespearean Criticism. New
    York: Random House, Inc., 1968.

Muir, Kenneth, and S. Schoenbaum, eds. A New Companion to Shakespeare.
    New York: Cambridge University Press, 1971.

Nicoll, Allardyce. Shakespeare: An Introduction. New York: Oxford Uni-
    versity Press, 1968.

Spurgeon, Caroline F. E. Shakespeare's Imagery. New York: Cambridge
    University Press, 1968.

Stauffer, Donald A. Shakespeare's World of Imagery. New York: W. W.
    Norton and Company, Inc., 1949.

Index

A 9
B 0
C 1
D 2
E 3
F 4
G 5
H 6
I 7
J 8